W9-BFY-950

THE ESSENTIAL GUIDE TO

ENGLISH USAGE

THE ESSENTIAL GUIDE TO

ENGLISH USAGE

John Bailie & Moyna Kitchin

First published in Great Britain in 1979 by
The Hamlyn Publishing Group Limited
under the title *Guide to English Usage*

This edition published in 1988 by
Chancellor Press
Michelin House
81 Fulham Road
London SW3 6RB

ISBN 1 85152 083 X

Printed in Yugoslavia

Introduction

Anyone who sets out to write *A Guide to English Usage* is faced with a formidable task. One dictionary defines 'usage' as 'the customary manner of using a language or any of its forms, especially standard practice in a given language.' This will serve very nicely as a definition, but it can be of only limited assistance to the compilers of a book on the subject. One of the chief difficulties confronting them is that usage is constantly changing. What may have been unacceptable twenty years ago is now standard English. There is nothing particularly surprising in this: the English language, like everything else in this world, is constantly evolving and twenty years is quite long enough for some slang terms and colloquialisms to achieve the status of respectability, and for others to alter their meaning or to fade away altogether.

However, there is a real problem in dealing with words or phrases which are in some sense 'borderline cases' and have not yet become universally acceptable either because they are new or are being used in a new way. Thus the authors are constantly faced with a choice. Do they accept or reject? Is it their function to tell people what they *ought* to say or to describe what they *do* say? How is the written language to be distinguished from the spoken language?

In the *Guide to English Usage* the authors have faced these dilemmas to the best of their ability. They have pointed out instances where what may be acceptable in speech is not yet so in more formal language. They have indicated where words or meanings have become so entrenched in the language that they must be tolerated, however regrettable this may be. They have fought rearguard actions to try and preserve useful distinctions of meaning where these were in danger of being lost and have provided a sturdy defence against slipshod expressions and the vague and woolly thinking behind the use of so many vogue words and clichés.

The chief aim of the *Guide to English Usage* is to help people to express themselves clearly and to communicate more easily in both speech and writing through a better understanding of the English language. Set out in alphabetical order for ease of reference, the *Guide* deals with a variety of topics. There are articles on punctuation showing the correct use of commas, quotation marks, semicolons, the apostrophe and others. Although it is in no sense a grammar book, it does deal with specific points of grammar where these may prove a source of difficulty and of course the aid of grammar is enlisted where necessary to point out the misuse of words – a frequent source of error. English spelling bristles with difficulties and a number of entries have been devoted to this particular problem. Special attention has also been paid to American spelling where this differs from British English. Words whose meanings are confused (and there are, unfortunately, a large number of these) are dealt with together so that the distinction between them can be clearly pointed out.

This book is intended to be a concise but comprehensive guide to good English, and every effort has been made to present the information it contains in the simplest possible terms and to illustrate it with examples wherever practicable. The authors hope that, with the *Guide*, they have made a useful contribution to the understanding of English, in which everybody will find something of value.

A

a, an Use *a* before all words beginning with a consonant except silent *h* and before all words beginning with vowels which are sounded like consonants:

A good boy, a harvest, a historical event, a hotel, a unifying factor, a European.

Use *an* before words beginning with a vowel or a silent *h*:

An apple, an energetic man, an hour, an honour.

The use of *a* or *an* before initial letters pronounced as letters depends on whether these have a consonant or vowel sound at the beginning:

A B.A., a D.F.C., an F.A. cup match, an SOS signal.

It was formerly quite common to use *an* before an unstressed syllable in certain words beginning with an *h*:

An hereditary peer, an habitual response.

Some speakers and writers still do so but it is no longer considered current usage.

A and *an* are sometimes wrongly introduced in certain comparative expressions preceded by *no*:

No easier a task, no more formidable an opponent.

In the above phrases both *a* and *an* should be omitted.

a-, an- This is a Greek prefix meaning 'not' or 'without' which should normally be attached only to words of Greek origin, e.g. *anarchy*. It has, however, occasionally been prefixed to Latin words, e.g. *amoral* and *asexual*.

abbreviations and contractions Abbreviations are usually followed by a full stop:

mi. (mile, miles), Jan. (January), Lat. (Latin).

But there is an increasing tendency to omit the full stop in contractions – shortened forms of words in which the first and last letters of the full word are shown:

Dr, Mr, St, ft (foot, feet).

The full stop is usually omitted after points of the compass:

N, E, S, W, SW, NNE.

But note that in most cases it is better to spell these out. It is usually omitted after the shortened forms used in metric units of measurement:

km, m, cm, mm, kg.

It is usually omitted after symbols used in chemistry and physics:

H (hydrogen), Mg (magnesium), F (Fahrenheit).

The full stop is left out in words which have become fully accepted as independent although they are abbreviations of other words:

bra(ssiere), disco(theque), pop(ular), pub(lic house).

The full stop is also frequently omitted from the abbreviated titles of organizations which are usually known by their initials, especially when the initials are commonly pronounced as a word:

BBC, NATO, UNESCO, GATT.

abetter, abettor The generally accepted spelling is *abetter*, although *abettor* is preferred in the legal sense of one who encourages the commission of a crime.

abide This has the past tense *abode* when used in its archaic sense of 'dwell' or 'stay'. However, *abide by* has *abided* in the past tense:

He abided by his decision.

ability, capacity Although there is generally some overlapping in the way these words are used, the following distinction should be made. *Ability* is the power to accomplish things, whether physical or mental, and the skill displayed in so doing:

He showed great ability as a chess player.

Capacity means the power to absorb and hold things, such as ideas, impressions or knowledge:

She was not very talented but had a great capacity for hard work.

abjure, adjure These two verbs can cause some confusion. *Abjure* means to renounce or repudiate:

He abjured his errors.

Adjure is to request earnestly and solemnly, often under oath:

The priest adjured him to consider carefully before abandoning his religious beliefs.

-able Adjectives ending in *-able* may be formed from any transitive verb and from some nouns. If the verb ends in a silent *-e* this is usually dropped in the adjective:

desirable, pleasurable, insurable, debatable.

However, if the mute or silent *-e* is preceded by a soft *c* or *g* it is retained:

serviceable, replaceable, changeable, manageable.

There are a number of exceptions to the rule that the *-e* should be dropped, especially when the verb has only one syllable, and the following are a sample of those about which no agreement has yet been reached:

blamable or blameable, ratable or rateable, salable or saleable.

Final consonants are usually doubled before *-able* when they are also doubled in the present participle of the verb:

deferrable (deferring), forgettable (forgetting), regrettable (regretting).

The following are some exceptions:

inferable (inferring), preferable (preferring), transferable (transferring).

When the verb ends in a *y* preceded by a consonant, the *y* becomes an *i*:

deniable, justifiable, reliable.

If there is a vowel before the *y*, the *y* is retained:

payable, enjoyable.

[See also *spelling*]

ablutions Most authorities still deplore the use of this word except in the context of specific religious ceremonial. Condemned as pompous or pedantic, it is best avoided unless being deliberately used facetiously.

abnormal, subnormal Anything which does not conform to the rule or standard or to what is accepted is *abnormal*:

Everyone noticed his abnormal behaviour.

Subnormal means below or inferior to the normal or average:

Temperatures in the Arctic are usually subnormal.

aboriginal This adjective is also used as the singular of the noun *aborigines*. The form *aborigine* is generally little employed.

about When giving distances, measurements, etc. *about* should be used only with round numbers:

about 30 feet long *not* about 30.25 feet long.

above As an adjective in *the above statement*, as a noun in *the above* or as an adverb in *the statement above*, this word has attracted some criticism from modern writers as being both pedantic and not altogether clear. However, provided it is not overworked it can still serve a useful function.

abrasive This is a vogue word which has become very popular in the past few years in the sense of 'irritating' or 'tending to annoy'. It is already less fashionable and the reader is advised not to use it.

abridgement, abridgment The first spelling is now the preferred one.

abrogate, arrogate Similarity in spelling occasionally causes these two verbs to be confused. To *abrogate* is to repeal or abolish:

The new king abrogated many of his predecessor's laws.

To *arrogate* (to oneself) is to claim or assume unjustly or unreasonably:

The president arrogated to himself the final decision in everything.

absolute terms There are certain adjectives, such as *infinite*, *unique*, *maximum*, *ultimate*, which express an absolute idea – there are no degrees of infiniteness. Consequently these adjectives must not be preceded by *more*, *most*, *very* or *less*, because they cannot have a comparative form.

abstract words The primary aim of the speaker or writer should be to make himself understood. Accordingly, the advice given by reputable grammarians over the years to avoid the abstract and use concrete words and expressions wherever possible remains as sound as ever it was.

abysmal, abyssal Both these words were formerly employed in much the same way, but their meanings are now quite distinct. *Abysmal* means 'measureless' or 'bottomless' and is generally used figuratively:

He showed abysmal ignorance of the subject.

Abyssal means 'belonging to the ocean depths below a certain level' and is used as a technical term:

The abyssal zone of the ocean.

academic This is a word whose original meaning of having to do with learning and scholarship or a place of learning has been overshadowed by its current and rather less agreeable connotation, i.e. of purely theoretical interest, impractical, or remote from everyday life.

accent marks In words reprinted from foreign languages which use the Roman alphabet any accent marks should be retained:

Liège, Malmö, San Sebastián, Košice.

It is better to avoid using accents in words from languages such as Russian, Arabic and Chinese which have to be transliterated into the Roman alphabet.

accept, except *Accept* means to take, receive or agree to:

He accepted their offer.

Except means to leave out or exclude:

Present company excepted.

acceptance, acceptation These words were formerly interchangeable in several of their meanings but are now quite distinct. *Acceptance* means the act of acceptance or a favourable reception:

His ready acceptance of the new position pleased everybody.

Acceptation means the usual or generally agreed sense:

The acceptation of this word is quite clear.

access, accession The most important distinction between these two words is that *access* means the possibility or opportunity of approaching or gaining admittance, whereas *accession* means actually arriving at or reaching. *Accession* is generally restricted to the meanings of 'coming into possession of a dignity or office', 'an increase' or 'something added'. *Access* has the additional sense of a sudden attack of illness or anger.

accessary, accessory Both as an adjective and as a noun *accessary* formerly carried the notion of complicity in a crime. *Accessory*, a more general word meaning, as a noun, 'an accompaniment', and, as an adjective, 'subsidiary', 'subordinate', has also largely taken over the meaning of *accessary*, thus blurring a useful distinction.

accommodation This word, beloved of local authorities, is much too frequently used in official communications to mean 'house' or 'flat', which are almost invariably preferable in all contexts.

accompanist, accompanyist *Accompanist* has now more or less completely replaced *accompanyist* in the sense of a musician who accompanies another player, although it is an unusual way of forming a noun from a verb. [See also *-ist*]

accord, account The prepositions used with the two phrases embodying these words are sometimes confused. The correct forms are *of one's own accord* and *on one's own account.*

achieve This means 'to bring to a successful end' and should not be used as a synonym for *get*, *reach* or *arrive at.*

acknowledgement, acknowledgment The first spelling is the preferred one.

acquaint This is always followed by *with*:

To acquaint someone with the facts.

It is, however, generally considered a rather stilted substitute for *inform* or *tell.*

acronym This is a word formed from the initial letters of other words such as *NATO*, *radar* and *UNESCO*. Such formations have become increasingly popular in recent years.

act as This means to take someone's place or to perform specific duties or functions on a particular occasion and should not be used as a more elaborate alternative to *is* or *are*:

He acted as spokesman for the company,

Not:

He acted as his company's representative for the northeastern region.

activate, actuate *Activate*, for long a rarely used word, has recently acquired fresh currency in scientific language and may be confused with *actuate. Activate* means to make active or to render radioactive:

To activate a catalyst.

Actuate means to cause to act, to prompt or motivate:

He was actuated by his own selfish desires.

adapt, adopt *Adapt* means to change or make suitable for a purpose:

The car has been adapted to carry heavy loads.

Adopt means to take and use as one's own:

They adopted the committee's recommendations entirely.

adaptation, adaption *Adaptation* is now the form in general use and *adaption* occurs only rarely.

addict, devotee An *addict* is a person who is physically dependent upon something:

A drug addict needs careful treatment.

A *devotee* is one who is strongly attracted to something and generally carries a favourable connotation:

He is a devotee of classical music.

adduce, deduce Confusion sometimes arises between these two words. *Adduce* means to bring forward in argument or to quote as conclusive evidence:

He adduced reasons to support his point of view.

Deduce means to draw as a conclusion from something known or assumed:

From the available evidence he deduced that the boy had been lying.

adhere, cohere *Adhere* means to stick fast to or to be strongly attached to a cause or belief:

To adhere to a political party.

Cohere means to hold or stick together or be united:

The particles of wet sand cohered to form a solid mass.

adherence, adhesion The chief distinction between these two words is that *adherence* is generally used figuratively. Its primary meaning is attachment to a cause or belief:

He was well known for his adherence to free speech.

Adhesion usually means the sticking of one thing to another:

The adhesion of newspaper to a wall.

It can, however, be used in the sense of *adherence* above.

adjacent, contiguous *Adjacent* means lying near or close, or adjoining:

A small field lay adjacent to the main road.

Contiguous has the more restricted sense of touching or being in close proximity to:

France is contiguous to Spain.

In practice the two words are virtually interchangeable in most of their meanings, but *adjacent* is much more commonly used.

adjective An adjective is a word which in some way modifies the meaning of a noun or pronoun, by describing, limiting or defining them. Adjectives may be used attributively, that is, they precede the noun they qualify:

a blue hat, every girl, my book.

Alternatively, they may be used predicatively, that is, after the verb *to be* and some other verbs:

She is angry, the dog is lively, he seems lonely.

adjectives, comparison of Adjectives of one syllable usually add *-er* and *-est* to make the comparative and superlative forms:

hard, harder, hardest; great, greater, greatest; nice, nicer, nicest.

Adjectives of two syllables which either have the stress on the second syllable or end in *-er*, *-le*, *-ow*, or *-y* take *-er* and *-est* to make the comparative and superlative forms:

polite, politer, politest; narrow, narrower, narrowest; able, abler, ablest; happy, happier, happiest.

Some other adjectives with two syllables which cannot readily be classified also take *-er* and *-est*. These include:

cruel, pleasant, quiet, stupid.

All other adjectives generally use *more* and *most* to form the comparative and superlative forms, although there are many exceptions.

adjectives, position of It is important to ensure that adjectives are placed immediately before the nouns they qualify in order to avoid any possibility of ambiguity. *Men's fashionable clothing* is preferable to *fashionable men's clothing*, since *fashionable* presumably applies to *clothing* and not to *men*.

adjectives, unnecessary It is better not to use adjectives which add nothing to the meaning of the noun they accompany. Phrases such as *grave crisis*, *serious emergency*, *definite decision* and *real danger* are to be avoided.

adjure see **abjure**

admission, admittance The use of *admittance* is now largely restricted to 'permission to enter', *admission* being employed in all senses.

admit *Admit of* meaning 'to leave room for', unlike *admit*, usually takes an impersonal noun as subject:

The problem admits of no other solution.

Admit to is now frequently used in answer to a charge:

He admitted to having stolen the watch.

However, correct usage still prefers *admit* without the addition of *to*.

adopt see **adapt**

adopted, adoptive The distinction between these two words is as follows. A child is described as being *adopted* by its new parents. They are referred to as the *adoptive* not *adopted* parents.

advance, advancement *Advance* means progress or moving forwards:

The advance of science.

Advancement means promotion, preferment or helping to move forwards:

The advancement of a cause dear to his heart.

advantage, vantage Both words mean a superior or favourable position, but *advantage* is generally used in a non-physical sense:

His good education gave him an advantage over all the other candidates.

Vantage may be used figuratively, but is more often employed in a purely literal sense:

He watched the battle from the vantage point of the hill top.

adventure, venture Both *adventure* and *venture* can be used to mean a hazardous or daring undertaking with an uncertain outcome. But whereas *adventure* is usually associated with danger and excitement in a physical sense, *venture* more often refers to a business enterprise or to commercial or financial speculation.

adventurous, venturesome These two words have supplanted *adventuresome* and *venturous* in current usage, but because of the similarity in spelling of all four of them the possibility of confusion remains.

adverb An *adverb* is a word which modifies a verb, an adjective or another adverb, altering in some way their meaning:

He spoke sharply. The weather was very hot. The water level rose extremely quickly.

The characteristic ending of the adverb is *-ly*, although a few common adverbs, such as *fast* and *hard*, have the same form as the adjective. There are, however, a number of adjectives which end in *-ly*, such as *lonely*, *holy* and *slovenly*. The addition of *-ly* to produce a form like *holily* is generally avoided by using a phrase such as *in a holy manner* or *in a slovenly fashion*.

adverbs, comparison of Most adverbs form their comparative and superlative forms by the addition of *more* and *most*, so as to avoid endings like *-lier*, *-liest*:

bravely, more bravely, most bravely; pleasantly, more pleasantly, most pleasantly.

Adverbs of only one syllable usually form their comparative and superlative forms by adding *-er* and *-est*.

late, later, latest; hard, harder, hardest; soon, sooner, soonest.

adverbs, unnecessary Just as superfluous adjectives are all too readily added to nouns, adjectives themselves are frequently adorned with unwanted adverbs. These include *absolutely*, *comparatively*, *relatively* and *vitally* and appear in such phrases as *absolutely essential* and *vitally important*.

adverse, averse These two words are quite similar in meaning. *Adverse* is 'antagonistic', 'hostile' or 'contrary', and, when used after a verb, can be followed only by *to*:

He was the victim of an adverse fate.
I am not adverse to your suggestion.

Averse means 'disinclined', 'opposed' or 'reluctant' and is usually followed by *to*, although some purists insist on using *from*:

He was by inclination averse to any kind of flattery.

-ae, -as see **Latin and French plurals**

aero-, air- The prefix *aero-* has been losing ground for some time to *air-* and is found only in *aeroplane* and *aerodrome*. *Air-* is now far more common, for example, *aircraft*, *airfield*, *airport*.

affect, effect Despite the similarity in their appearance these two words are completely different in meaning. *Affect* means to produce a change in or have an influence upon:

The loss of his children affected his health.

Effect means to bring about or accomplish:

His financial troubles did not prevent him from effecting his plans for sweeping changes.

Affect is all too frequently used instead of a more precise verb:

Work on the new building has been affected by bad weather.

It would have been better to use *hindered* or *delayed* in this context.

affinity There is some disagreement about what prepositions may be used after this word. Normally it is followed by *between* or *with*, but in modern usage *to* and *for* are becoming acceptable, *for* especially in scientific language.

afflict, inflict These two words are occasionally confused. *Afflict* means to distress with physical or mental pain:

She was afflicted with gout.

Inflict means to impose or lay on, invariably something which has to be endured or suffered:

A severe punishment was inflicted on the prisoner.

affront, effrontery An *affront* is an offensive act or a show of disrespect:

His conduct was an affront to the prime minister.

Effrontery means 'impudent boldness' or 'barefaced audacity'.

He had the effrontery to ask for a free ticket.

afraid This perfectly respectable word meaning 'feeling fear or apprehension or filled with concern or regret' has undergone an unwarranted extension of its original sense in such phrases as:

I am afraid that I can't come

or

I am afraid there are no oranges left.

It is best used only when there is real cause for concern or regret.

afterwards, afterward *Afterwards* is the only form of the adverb now found in British English. *Afterward* is the usual American form.

agenda This is a Latin word, the plural form of *agendum*, but in English it is always treated as a singular noun followed by a singular verb:

The agenda for the meeting has been drawn up.

aggravate Attempts by some grammarians to restrict the meaning of this word to 'make worse' or 'intensify' have been unsuccessful. Its popular sense of 'annoy' or 'irritate' is now firmly entrenched in the language.

agnostic, atheist Confusion sometimes arises between these two terms. An *agnostic* believes that nothing can be known about the existence of God and accordingly it cannot be proved or disproved. An *atheist* is one who denies or disbelieves the existence of God.

ago, since These two words are frequently but wrongly used together in sentences such as:

It is ten years ago since I last saw him.

Ago can be followed only by *that*, so the sentence must be recast in one of two following ways:

It was ten years ago that I last saw him.
It is ten years since I last saw him.

Alternatively it can be shortened to the following:

I last saw him ten years ago.

agree This is normally used as an intransitive verb followed by the prepositions *to*, *on*, or *with*. However, it has shown a tendency in recent years to discard its prepositions and appear as a transitive verb meaning 'to reach agreement about':

The board has agreed the price increase.

Despite protests from some quarters there seems every likelihood that this change will eventually win complete acceptance.

agreement of verbs Verbs must agree with their subject in number and person. Difficulties over whether verbs should be singular or plural sometimes arise in the following instances.

Collective nouns: These may be used with either a singular or a plural verb. The singular is more appropriate when the emphasis is on the body as a whole or a unit and the plural when the emphasis is on a collection of individuals:

The committee has agreed upon its programme.

The committee were divided about the merits of the scheme.

Words joined by and: These are almost invariably followed by a plural verb unless the linked words are very closely associated:

A boy and a girl were approaching the house,

but:

Bread and butter is his staple diet.

Words joined by with: If the subject is singular the verb must also be singular:

The chairman, together with the managing director, is coming.

Alternative subjects: *Either* and *neither* are always followed by a singular verb when there are two singular subjects:

Either the front door or the back door is sure to be open.

Neither business expertise nor a knowledge of printing techniques is essential.

If both alternatives are in the plural then the verb is plural:

Neither the soldiers nor their officers were fit for combat.

However, if one of the alternatives referred to is in the singular and the other in the plural, the verb may agree with the nearest subject, though it might be found preferable to rephrase the sentence:

Either the boy or his parents are supposed to attend.

Use of each: When *each* is the subject of a sentence it is followed by a singular verb:

Each of the boys was given a room for the night.

When it refers to a plural antecedent, however, it takes a plural verb:

They arrived early and were each given a ticket.

Use of none: This is usually followed by a singular verb when it means *no amount*, *no quantity*, *not one* or *no one*:

None of the jewellery is missing.

None of his friends was able to come.

When *none* means *no people* or *no things* the verb is generally in the plural:

Some of the lorries arrive late but none reach the depot after 8 pm.

agriculturalist, agriculturist Both forms are still perfectly acceptable English but *agriculturist* is gradually displacing the longer word.

aim This is usually followed by *at* when it means 'to strive' or 'to try', but is now being used more frequently with *to*. It is also followed by *to* when it means 'to intend':

We aim to start tomorrow.

akin This is usually followed by *to* but is occasionally found followed by *with*, a practice condemned by most authorities.

alarm, alarum Both forms were formerly employed without distinction of meaning but *alarum* has now been almost entirely displaced by *alarm* except in one or two set expressions.

albeit Meaning 'although' or 'notwithstanding', this conjunction was only quite recently considered an archaism, but has since received a fresh lease of life:

The army chose a strategic albeit inglorious retreat.

alibi In law this means a defence by an accused person that he was elsewhere at the time when a crime was committed. It is now frequently used to mean an 'excuse' or 'pretext', even by respectable writers, and this colloquial extension of meaning has crept into the definitions given in dictionaries. However deplorable this may be, there appears to be no way of stopping it.

alien As an adjective this was formerly used with the prepositions *from* and *to*. However, in recent years *from* has been almost entirely displaced by *to*.

allege This means 'to assert without proof, to plead in support of' or 'to urge as an excuse', and should not be used as a substitute for *assert* or *affirm*, which have a much more positive sense.

allegory This is the figurative or metaphorical treatment of one subject under the guise of another: the narrating of a story using a symbolic language, usually in order to expound some moral truth. [See also *metaphor*, *parable*, *simile*]

allergic The medical definition is 'physically hypersensitive to certain substances'. In colloquial speech it has been extended to mean having a dislike or aversion. It is better to avoid both *allergic* and its noun *allergy* wherever possible and to substitute phrases using more suitable words such as *dislike*, *antipathy* or *hostility*.

alliteration This is the repetition in a phrase or sentence of words beginning with the same letter or sound in order to create an effect, as in a line of verse or a television advertising jingle.

all of When *all* is used before a pronoun it must be followed by *of*:

all of them, all of us.

When it is followed by a noun the *of* is usually omitted in British English, but may be retained in American English, although frowned on by many American authorities:

all (of) the people, all (of) the girls at my school.

allow of The meaning of this phrase has become restricted to 'leave room for' in much the same way as *admit of*:

The rules do not allow of any exceptions.

all right, alright Although *alright* is commonly found it is not generally regarded as good usage. The only acceptable form is *all right.*

allusion, illusion An *allusion* is a passing or casual reference to something:

He made an allusion to the events of the previous day.

An *illusion* is something producing a false impression or a deceptive appearance:

He cherishes the illusion that everyone likes him.

alone *Not alone* is sometimes wrongly substituted for *not only.* This use of *alone* is now archaic and the word should be restricted to its various meanings as an adjective.

alternate, alternative These two adjectives have quite distinct meanings but are nevertheless frequently confused. *Alternate* means 'following each in succession', 'first one, then the other' or 'every other one in a series':

There will be alternate hot and cold spells.
The two men worked on alternate days.

There is also a verb *alternate* meaning 'to follow one another by turns'.

Alternative means 'affording a choice between one of two (or possibly more) things':

There is an alternative route through the mountains.

Alternative is unfortunately a vogue word which has acquired an extension of meaning and is sometimes used by the ignorant (and by those who should know better) to mean *new*, *revised* or *fresh.* Remember that *alternative* implies a choice.

The same distinctions apply to the adverbs *alternately* and *alternatively.*

They alternately walked and ran.
The journey could be made by steamer or alternatively by aircraft.

although see **though**

altogether, all together These two words are quite often wrongly substituted, the one for the other. *Altogether* means wholly, entirely, completely:

She did not altogether like the new dress.

All together means all at the same time or the same place:

The guests had assembled all together in the drawing room.

amatory, amorous There is some overlapping between the meanings of these two words, but in current usage it is possible to make the following distinction. *Amatory*, meaning expressing love, is frequently applied to something written:

The author of a book of amatory poetry.

Amorous is more frankly concerned with sexual desire:

No girl could resist his amorous approaches.

ambiguity This can arise in a number of ways and is generally the result of clumsy writing. In most cases the real meaning may be quite clear, but sometimes complete obscurity results. The following are some of the most frequent causes of ambiguity.

The incorrect positioning of a word or phrase:

No unnecessary force was used to put an end to the disturbance by the police.

He met his former girl friend out walking with his wife.

The use of words with a double meaning or more than one meaning:

The new secretary worked very happily under the export manager.

The misuse of punctuation:

The manager has only a very small team who are always busy.

This needs a comma after *team*. Otherwise it implies that most of the manager's subordinates do not have enough to do.

Confusion of pronouns: it is unfortunately all too easy to be ambiguous in the use of pronouns.

Mr Jones told Mr Brown that he was prepared to lend him the money, provided he received the guarantees which he had been promised.

It is quite impossible to be sure to whom the two *he's* in the second part of the sentence refer.

ambiguous, ambivalent *Ambiguous* means open to various interpretations or having a double meaning:

To their clear question he gave an ambiguous answer.

Ambivalent, which is a fashionable and much overworked word, is frequently and wrongly substituted for *ambiguous*. It means having mixed or conflicting feelings:

The older members of the staff were ambivalent in their attitude towards the new young manager.

amend, emend *Amend* means to improve or make better:

He was told to amend his ways.

Emend means to remove errors or to correct and is used only in connection with manuscripts or printed matter:

They emended the document to the best of their ability.

America, American These words are commonly used for 'The United States' and a 'citizen of the United States' respectively. Objections may be raised that the term *America* can also be used to cover all North America (*i.e.*, including Canada), and Central and South America. However, *America* and *American* have become so firmly established in their popular senses that nothing can be done to alter the position now.

American usage and spelling Much has been written about the influence of American English on British English. Some Americanisms are deplored as ugly or unnecessary, others seem somehow to fill a gap and to gain ready acceptance. A considerable number of words have in fact become so absorbed into British English that their transatlantic origins are quite forgotten. However, despite this continuous American invasion

British English remains stubbornly resistant in some areas and many words describing ordinary things remain quite different in both countries.

Some of the most important distinctions between British and American spelling are given below. A number of words ending in *-re* in British usage change this to *-er* in American usage:

theater, liter, scepter, somber, caliber, center.

But note British English *meter* (meaning 'instrument') and *filter*.

In American usage many words ending in *-our* in British English drop the *u* in these words and those derived from them:

behavior, behaviorism, candor, color, favor, favoritism, honor, humor, labor, rancor.

But note American *glamour* and the following which are correct in both British and American usage:

clangor, coloration, glamorous, glamorize, honorary, humorist, humorous, odorous, stupor, tremor, vaporize and vigorous.

There are also some differences in certain words containing *c* or *s*. British usage has *licence* and *practice* as nouns and *license* and *practise* as verbs. American usage has *license* and *practise* for both nouns and verbs. Note also the American *defense*, *offense* and *pretense*.

In some words ending in the suffixes *-ed*, *-ing*, *-er*, *-or*, etc., the final consonant before the suffix is left single where in British usage it would be doubled:

leveled, rivaled, libeling, traveler, carburetor, worshiping.

American usage tends to eliminate *a* and *o* from the combinations *ae* and *oe* when British English retains them:

anemia, anesthetic, diarrhea, maneuver, presidium, toxemia.

But note the American preference for the following spellings:

aeon, aesthete, aesthetic.

Other important words which are spelt differently in America are:

aluminum, appall, ax, catalog, caldron, check (British cheque), councilor, counselor, disk, enroll, font (printer's) fulfill, gelatin, glycerin, jewelry, mollusk, mold, molt, plow, program, prolog, skeptic, skillful, stanch, sulfur, tire, woolen.

amiable, amicable Both words are very similar in meaning. *Amiable* is used only when referring to people and means having a good-natured disposition:

He proved to be a most amiable companion.

Amicable means friendly or peaceable and refers to arrangements, settlements and attitudes.

They came to an amicable agreement.

amid, amidst Both words, which are identical in meaning, are falling into disuse, but *amid* is the more common form.

amok see **amuck**

among, amongst There is no real distinction between these two words. *Amongst* used to be found more frequently before words beginning with a vowel, but *among* is now almost invariably the preferred form. [See also *between*]

amoral, immoral *Amoral* means without moral quality or not concerned with morals, or having no moral standards, good or bad, by which one may be judged. *Immoral* means not conforming to a set of moral standards, wicked or evil.

amount, number *Amount* can only properly be used of a material or substance having mass or weight, in fact, anything which can be measured, and should never be applied to things which are divisible into individual units. *A large amount of sheep* is not acceptable and *number* should be substituted for *amount*. It is correctly used as follows:

A large amount of dress material.
A large amount of firewood.

amuck This form is now much more frequently met with than *amok*, and is to be preferred on all occasions.

anacoluthon This rather formidable-looking word describes a common phenomenon in which the structure or grammatical sequence of a sentence is broken:

Let me begin by expressing my thanks to those people who – but I shouldn't have been here in the first place.

analysis, synthesis *Analysis* is the separation of a whole into its constituent elements:

The grammatical analysis of a sentence.

Synthesis, the opposite of *analysis*, is the combination of parts to form a whole:

The production of rubber from petroleum by synthesis.

analyst, annalist There is sometimes a possibility of confusion between these two words. An *analyst* is a person who is skilled in analysis. An *annalist* is one who writes annals or chronicles.

ancient, antiquated, antique *Ancient* is invariably used to refer to a remote past:

The history of the ancient world.

Antiquated means grown old and ill adapted to present use:

An antiquated fire engine.

Antique means belonging to former times and does not, except when used facetiously, have the pejorative sense of *antiquated*:

A lover of antique furniture.

and This is used as a conjunction joining two parts of a sentence. Care must be taken to ensure that the words, phrases or clauses linked by *and* are of the same kind:

He played a fast game of tennis, enjoyed the company of pretty women and good conversation.

The insertion of *and* after *tennis* balances the two parts of the sentence:

He played a fast game of tennis, and enjoyed the company of pretty women and good conversation.

And is often used wrongly with *who* and *which*:

She was a girl of infinite tact and who knew when to keep quiet.

The *and* in the above sentence is unnecessary. The rule is that it can be used with *who* or *which* only if there is a relative clause in the first part of the sentence.

She was a girl whose tact was infinite and who knew when to keep quiet.

Despite widespread belief to the contrary, there is no reason why a sentence should not begin with *and*. Provided it is used with moderation, it can be stylistically very effective.

angry This is followed by *with* when the object of the anger is a person, but by *at* when it is caused by situations or events:

She was angry with her son because he arrived home late.
He was angry at the delay at the airport.

another For the distinction between *each other* and *one another* see *each other*.

antagonist, protagonist These two words are occasionally confused, although their meanings are quite distinct. An *antagonist* is one who is opposed to another in any kind of contest or fight. A *protagonist* is the leading character in a play or novel.

ante-, anti- Similarity in spelling may lead to some doubt about these two prefixes. *Ante-*, which comes from Latin, means 'before in space or time', and occurs in such words as *antecedent*, *anteroom*, and *antenatal*. *Anti-*, which comes from Greek, means 'against' or 'opposed to' and is much more commonly used than *ante*. Examples are:

anti-aircraft, anti-American, anticlimax, antifreeze.

anticipate The valiant efforts of those who have tried to prevent this word from being used simply as a synonym for *expect* or *foresee* have not, unfortunately, been very successful. However, it is better where possible to confine it to its basic meaning of 'to forestall an event' or 'to take action beforehand':

Foreknowledge of the enemy's plans enabled us to anticipate his every move.

A sentence like:

We are not anticipating any trouble

is better expressed as:

We are not expecting any trouble

unless you really mean to say you are not taking any preventive measures.

Anticipate is a case in which the Latin prefix *ante* has changed its *e* to an *i*.

antonym An *antonym* is a word opposed in meaning to another. Thus 'good' is the antonym of 'bad', and 'top' the antonym of 'bottom'. [See also *synonym*]

anyone, any one *Anyone* is a singular pronoun and is followed by a singular verb, pronoun or possessive adjective:

Anyone who takes time off risks losing his job.

It should be spelt as one word except when it singles out a particular person or item. In this instance *any* becomes an adjective and *one* a numeral:

Any one of these books will be suitable.
He has not informed any one of them.

aphorism A short meaningful saying embodying a general truth:

Manners makyth man.

[See also *axiom*]

apiary, aviary These words are occasionally confused. An *apiary* is a place where bees are kept. An *aviary* is for keeping birds.

apocope This is the cutting off of a final letter, sound or syllable of a word to form a new word, as *curio* from *curiosity* and *cinema* from *cinematograph*.

apology, apologia An *apology* is an expression of regret offered for some fault, failure, insult etc. It is, however, also used in the same sense as *apologia*, which is a formal defence or justification of a cause or doctrine.

apostrophe The apostrophe is used to show the omission of letters or figures:

can't (cannot), it's (it is), the early '20s.

The apostrophe is used with *s* to form the plurals of letters, numbers, symbols and words which do not have a plural form or are not easily recognizable as plurals with the addition of just an *s*:

1's, 2's, 5's, p's and q's, do's and don't's.

But note:

M.A.s, M.P.s, G.P.s.

The addition of an apostrophe and *s* is the regular way of forming the possessive case of nouns. In the singular the apostrophe is placed before the *s*:

The boy's book, his daughter's school.

In the plural the apostrophe is placed after the *s*:

His parents' car, the soldiers' uniforms.

When the noun itself already ends in an *s* (or an *s* sound), as in the case of personal names, add *'s*:

Thomas's car, Charles's shop, St. James's Square, Marx's theories, the Jones's Christmas party.

Note that ancient names (Classical or Biblical) ending in an *s* usually add only the apostrophe:

Moses' Law, Sophocles' stories, Xerxes' fleet.

Nouns which form their plural in some other way than by adding an *s*, add an apostrophe and an *s* in the possessive case:

The men's room, geese's wings.

The apostrophe is used after the *s* in phrases like the following involving expressions of time, which are treated as possessives:

Two weeks' time, a five days' journey, two months' holiday.

Do not use an apostrophe with the following personal pronouns:

Its (of it), hers, ours, theirs, yours.

The single exception is *one's*.

apposition This means the addition of a word or group of words to another as an explanation or description. In the sentence:

Gerald Smith, the new managing director, has arrived.

the new managing director is in apposition to *Gerald Smith*.

appraise, apprise *Appraise* means to estimate the worth of or evaluate:

The task of appraising the new candidates had begun.

Apprise means to inform or advise:

The prime minister has not yet been apprised of their decision.

Apprise is a rather formal, not to say pompous word, and one which good writers tend to avoid.

appreciate This undoubtedly useful word has various meanings including 'to form an estimate of the value of something' and 'to acknowledge gratefully'. However, it has in recent times been worked to death in contexts where such verbs as *understand*, *admit* and *realize*, would be far more suitable. In sentences like:

I appreciate that you have taken a lot of trouble

any of the verbs listed above would be preferable to *appreciate*.

apprehend, comprehend Although several of the meanings of *apprehend* are quite distinct from those of *comprehend*, these two words do overlap when they are used in the sense of 'understand'. *Apprehend* is to 'grasp the meaning of', and *comprehend* means to 'have complete understanding of the meaning or nature of something'.

appropriate As an adjective *appropriate* is in danger of being overworked. It is often used where such words as *suitable* or *fitting* would be just as acceptable.

approximate, approximately *Approximate* means 'nearly exact or equal' or 'approaching a great degree of accuracy'. It should not be used as a synonym of *rough* or *roughly* which imply a considerably lesser degree of accuracy. *Very approximately*, which has unfortunately come to mean no more than *very roughly*, should be avoided altogether.

a priori This means reasoning from cause to effect or from a general law to a particular instance without prior study or investigation.

apt, liable In some senses these words are very close and the one is often used where the other would be more suitable. *Apt* and *liable* both mean inclined, disposed or subject to, but *liable* contains a much stronger possibility of unpleasant or disagreeable consequences:

Problems are apt to occur. Serious shortages are liable to result.

Arab, Arabian, Arabic When used as adjectives, these words are now more or less distinct in meaning. *Arab* means 'belonging or pertaining to the Arabs', as in *Arab World*, *Arab statesmen*. *Arabian* is used specifically to mean 'belonging or pertaining to Arabia', as in *Arabian Desert*. *Arabic* refers to the language: *Arabic script*, *Arabic newspaper*, *Arabic numerals*.

arbiter, arbitrator These words are sometimes used indiscriminately but they do have important distinctions of meaning. An *arbiter* is a person who has the sole or absolute power to judge or determine:

The dictator became the arbiter of his country's destiny.

An *arbitrator* is a person chosen to decide a specific dispute:

The government appointed an arbitrator to settle the strike in the steel industry.

arbitrate, mediate *Arbitrate* means to decide a dispute as an arbitrator does. To *mediate* means to act as an intermediary between parties involved in a dispute.

archaism An *archaism* is a word or expression which was once current English, but is no longer acceptable as part of the living language. In the hands of an experienced writer archaisms may be used effectively, otherwise it is best to leave them alone.

aren't I Despite its illogical appearance this is the recognized colloquial interrogative form of *I am*. It is formed by analogy with *aren't you* and *aren't they* and replaces the earlier *an't I*.

arise, rise In the literal sense of 'to get up' or 'to come up' *arise* has been replaced by *rise*. It is used now to mean 'to come into being' or 'to originate' in an abstract sense:

A new problem has arisen.

around, round Although *around* is less frequently met with than *round* it appears in certain set phrases such as *all around us* and *sitting around the table*. It can also replace *about* in expressions of time such as *around five o'clock*.

arouse, rouse The distinction between these words is similar to that between *arise* and *rise*. *Rouse* means 'to bring out of a state of sleep' or 'to stir to action':

Her screams roused the sleeping children.

Arouse is generally (though not always) used in the figurative sense of 'to bring into being' or 'to give rise to':

His erratic behaviour aroused their suspicions.

arrogate see **abrogate**

artist, artiste An *artist* is one who practises the fine arts, in particular painting or sculpture. An *artiste* is one who performs in public, especially a singer or dancer on the stage or on television.

as This is a much overworked word and is frequently used where *because*, *while*, *since*, *for* or *when* would be more suitable. It also results in ambiguity:

He spotted the mistake as he was reading in his study.

This would be better expressed:

He spotted the mistake while he was reading in his study.

and

She felt tired as she was walking up the stairs.

It would be better to say:

She felt tired while she was walking up the stairs.

or:

She felt tired because she was walking up the stairs.

As sometimes appears in phrases like *equally as important*, *equally as cheap*. It is quite unnecessary and should be deleted. It is also superfluous in expressions like *as from* (a certain date) unless reference is made to past time.

When *as* is used to mean 'in the function, role or capacity of' it is important to ensure that it does not become unrelated to its proper subject:

As chairman of the company, you will all, I am sure, agree with me when I say . . .

Logically, although nonsensically, this means that the people referred to as 'you' are chairman of the company. It could be recast as follows:

You will all, I am sure, agree with me as chairman of the company . . .

Another cause of ambiguity with *as* is in expressions such as:

She hates him as much as you.

This can be put right either by saying:

She hates him as much as you do.

or:

She hates him as much as she does you.

ascendancy, ascendant These words have alternative but less common spellings *ascendency* and *ascendent*. Both *ascendancy* and *ascendant* mean a dominating or controlling influence, although *ascendant* has a specifically astrological connotation.

Asian, Asiatic It is advisable to use *Asian* rather than *Asiatic*, either as a noun or as an adjective. *Asiatic* was once more frequent but its unfortunate pejorative overtones make it generally unacceptable today.

assay, essay Neither of these verbs is now frequently used. *Assay* means 'to test or analyse', usually with reference to metals. *Essay* means 'to attempt' or 'to try'.

asset This has been condemned in some quarters as a poor substitute for *advantage* or *resource*, but it now seems to have firmly established itself in the language with the meaning of 'something useful' in addition to its other meanings.

assignation, assignment An *assignation* is an appointment to meet, especially an illicit meeting between lovers. *Assignment* is the transfer or handing over of something or the thing handed over.

assonance In poetry this is a substitute for rhyme where words with the same vowel sounds but with different consonants are used, such as *make* and *tame* or *dream* and *seen*.

assume, presume *Assume* has several meanings, but it is also used as a near synonym of *presume* in the sense of 'to suppose as a fact'. The difference is that *assume* is 'to take for granted' without any evidence, whereas *presume* implies a greater degree of certainty and the belief that something is true.

assurance This is a term used by insurance companies when dealing with life policies as opposed to insurance of property, but the general public does not normally make any distinction, using the term *insurance* on all occasions.

assure, ensure, insure Confusion can arise over the correct use of these verbs. *Assure* means to make confident or reassure, and to insure, especially against death. *Ensure* means to make sure or certain. *Insure* means to safeguard against loss or damage by paying insurance.

as to This phrase tends to appear rather frequently as a clumsy substitute for *about*:

We have no information as to his reliability.

Sometimes it occurs as a completely superfluous phrase:

Doubt has been expressed (as to) whether he is the right man for the job.

atheist see **agnostic**

attend see **tend**

aural, oral These words are usually pronounced in exactly the same way, which may lead to some difficulties in their use. *Aural* means pertaining to or perceived by the organs of hearing. *Oral* means uttered by, administered by or pertaining to the mouth.

autarchy, autarky Although pronounced identically, these two words have quite distinct meanings. *Autarchy* is absolute sovereignty or self-government. *Autarky* is a condition of self-sufficiency.

authentic, genuine There is frequent overlapping between these two words and some authorities make no distinction in meaning. *Authentic* is used particularly of documents and works of art, and implies that they are not false, or copies, and that they really represent what they claim to do.

authoress Feminine designations such as *authoress, poetess* and *sculptress* are now falling into disuse. Women writers have always shown much hostility to the word *authoress*, possibly because it has a somewhat pejorative nuance. *Author* should be used for both sexes without discrimination.

authoritarian, authoritative *Authoritarian* means favouring the principle of subjection to authority as opposed to that of individual freedom:

Authoritarian governments have always been more common than democratic ones.

Authoritative means having due authority or the sanction or weight of authority:

The prime minister issued an authoritative statement about the crisis.

Authoritative can also be used to mean 'peremptory' or 'dictatorial' and in this sense it approaches the meaning of *authoritarian.*

auxiliary verbs These are verbs which are used with other verbs to express distinctions between active and passive and in tense or mood. In the following examples the verbs in italics are auxiliaries:

She *has* made her bed. *Do* you think they *will* come? He *has* been knocked down by a car. I *do* not know the answer. They *may* decide otherwise. You *ought* to stay the night. She *can* come when she likes. He *must* decide quickly.

avail This verb can only be used in a restricted way, the normal construction being to *avail oneself of something*:

They availed themselves of the opportunity for a drive.

It should never be used in the passive as *be availed of*. *Avail* can also take a direct object, but this form is much rarer:

All their attempts availed them nothing.

availability This is a word much favoured in official writing and one which tends to produce obscurity or long-windedness in the construction of sentences.

The availability of these products is extremely limited,

would be better expressed as:

These products are extremely scarce.

avenge, revenge It is not always easy to preserve a distinction between these two verbs. The main difference is that *avenge* and its noun *vengeance* are now usually restricted to the infliction of punishment as a means of achieving justice:

The murder was avenged when the criminal was brought to trial.

Revenge is generally used in the sense of retaliation for wrongs committed by the infliction of pain, emotional or real:

He was determined to revenge the insult he had received.

averse see **adverse**

avocation, vocation *Avocation* originally meant a hobby or something apart from one's regular work. It is now frequently used as an alternative to *vocation* to mean a regular occupation and is in danger of blurring a useful distinction in meaning.

await, wait The usual distinction between these verbs is that *await* is transitive, being followed by a direct object:

We are awaiting your instructions.

Wait is usually intransitive:

He waited for a train for more than two hours.

awake, wake These verbs, together with their alternative spellings *awaken* and *waken*, are often used interchangeably. *Awake* and *waken* are more formal than *wake* and are commonly employed in figurative senses:

To awaken to the realities of life.

Moreover, *awaken* and *waken* can be transitive and intransitive and are preferred in the passive mood:

She was awakened by the sound of gunfire.

Wake, however, remains the basic verb for expressing the idea of arousing from sleep and is the most frequently used of all four. It is also the only one which can be normally followed by *up*.

award, reward An *award* is in law a decision made by arbitrators on matters submitted to them and, by extension, something awarded. A *reward* is something given or received in return for a meritorious action or for services rendered.

axiom This is a universally accepted principle or rule or a recognized truth. [See also *aphorism*]

B

-b-, -bb- With a single-vowelled, single-syllabled word such as *snob*, the *b* is doubled when followed by a vowel, as in *snobbery*. If the *b* is preceded by two vowels, however, or a single vowel followed by an *r*, the *b* remains single:

boob, booby; curb, curbing.

bacillus see **Latin and French plurals**

back formation A word is sometimes created from another which is wrongly – or facetiously – taken to be its derivative. *Typewrite* from *typewriter* and *donate* from *donation*, now acceptable verbs, were probably first introduced ironically, but were later acknowledged as genuine verbs, from which it might be erroneously assumed the nouns had been formed.
Such words are continually being introduced into the language, condemned at first as incorrect or as slang, then later accepted through common usage.

background The dictionary definition, 'the ground or parts situated in the rear', has been extended to cover a variety of contexts so that this has become an overused vogue word. An example of its correct use is:

With his mother always in the background, the marriage was bound to fail.

However, in the instance:

The background of the quarrel was jealousy over a girl,

it would have been better to substitute 'cause', and a sentence such as:

With his background, he could reach the top of his profession

is ambiguous and therefore insufficiently precise. Unless the intended meaning is 'origins', either 'qualifications' or 'experience' would be preferable.

backlog Originally a U.S. term for the log at the back of a fire, it was brought into use as a metaphor meaning a stockpile held in reserve, and is now used almost exclusively in the sense of arrears, or an accumulation of work (such as correspondence) awaiting attention.

backward, backwards *Backward* can be used either as an adjective:

A backward country, the child is backward,

or as an adverb, especially in the United States:

To move backward.

Backwards can be used only as an adverb, and its use in the above example would be equally correct:

To move backwards.

bail out, bale out *To bail out* is usually applied to getting a person out of jail. For removing water from a boat *to bale out* is nowadays considered the preferable spelling, although some authorities contend that *to bail out* is more correct, derived as it is from the Old French *baille*, 'bucket'.

To bale out is also the term used for leaving an aircraft in a hurry.

balance There are dangers in using this word in its colloquial sense of 'the remainder' or 'the rest'. Strictly speaking, it should be applied only when there is a clear indication of comparison, as in this example, where the sums involved could be defined:

When the bills have been paid, the balance of the housekeeping money can be spent on clothes.

Just to say:

He works hard at the office every day, so the balance of his time is his own

is too vague a concept to be of value.

baleful, baneful Both words mean 'pernicious'; *baleful* is also 'full of menacing or malign influences', and *baneful* is 'destructive, poisonous'. It is important to stress that they are interchangeable only in the one sense.

ballad, ballade Both words mean a poem. A *ballad* is essentially of popular origin, simple in form with short stanzas, and often represented as a light, romantic song. The *ballade* is a poem of three eight- or ten-line stanzas with an identical rhyme scheme and an envoy or postscript, the same last line recurring in each stanza and envoy. It can also be a romantic musical composition for piano or orchestra.

balmy, barmy The word for mild, refreshing, soft or soothing is *balmy*. In its literal sense *barmy* means frothy or something containing barm, the yeast formed from fermentation. Figuratively, it is used to mean silly, stupid or mad:

He must be barmy if he thinks he can get away with it.

barbarian, barbaric, barbarous These adjectives have distinct places in everyday usage. *Barbarian* is the most neutral of the three and means rough and uncultured:

The barbarian tribes.

Barbaric describes something that might be done by or owned by a *barbarian*. Its connotations are simple, rustic, crude and unsophisticated but not necessarily violent, and imply amused tolerance rather than condemnation:

Those gaudy ties he wears display his barbaric tastes.

Barbarous, on the other hand, suggests cruelty and violence, the harsh side of barbarian behaviour, and is the antithesis of everything cultured and civilized:

The docking of dogs' tails is a barbarous practice.

baroque In an architectural context this word has a definite meaning, describing a style of architecture developed in 16th-century Italy with bold, contorted forms, heavy decoration and asymmetrical design. It is, however, often applied to other art forms such as music and literature, which has led to a blurring of meaning, since it is not always clear whether the writer is referring merely to the date or period of a work, or using the term in a metaphorical sense to indicate a florid, heavily ornate style.

barrage Originally this was used in the sense of 'curtain' or 'barrier', especially in a military context, 'a *barrage* of fire', or during the war when '*barrage* balloons' became a familiar sight, forming a layer or 'barrier' to keep aircraft at a height where anti-aircraft fire was most effective.
Extended use has brought this word to mean any overwhelming quantity, implying a density through which it is impossible to break, and also in an attacking sense instead of a defensive one, from which it is impossible to escape. Hence, in the following sentence:

After his speech, he faced a barrage of questions,

volley would be a more accurate substitute.

barrister, solicitor A *barrister* is allowed to plead at the bar of any court. A *solicitor* advises his clients and briefs the barrister, preparing the case for him to plead. He can also appear on behalf of his client in a lower court, but only a barrister may plead the case in a higher court.

basic, basically These are vogue words and very overworked ones. They may be quite meaningless, popped into sentences that would survive perfectly happily without them, or they may be used in place of 'fundamental' or 'fundamentally'.

Basically, it's a question of time.

It will remain a question of time with or without *basically*.

It is a basic fact that hedgehogs hibernate in winter.

Here again, the word is superfluous. Omitting *basic* renders the sentence simpler in style and no less informative. But in the following example:

His basic premise was accurate,

the word is used legitimately as an alternative to 'fundamental', since it serves to stress that the premise was the original one upon which ensuing argument was built and from which subsequent conclusions were drawn.

basis Often used by those who enjoy a roundabout way of speaking (see *periphrasis*).

He took a room on a temporary basis while searching for a house

is unnecessarily wordy. The straight adverb is better:

He took a room temporarily while searching for a house.

bathos, pathos *Bathos* is an anticlimax, a sudden leap from the sublime to the ridiculous. *Pathos* is the power of inspiring a feeling of pity or sadness. Confusion arises, however, because *bathos* can also mean a false pathos, or acute sentimentality.

because This is a word which is often misused *because* its purpose is not fully understood. In that sentence the word *because* is a positive link between effect and cause which no other word would provide so strongly. But in the next example:

The reason why he is late is because he missed the train

it is incorrectly used, since it merely repeats the meaning of 'the reason why'. The sentence should read:

The reason why he is late is *that* he missed the train.

Care must also be taken that it is not used in a way that appears ambiguous:

She did not go out that night because she knew he wouldn't like it.

Was it out of deference to his feelings that she refrained from going out, or did she deliberately stay in to annoy him?

When the word is used the weight of the meaning should be borne in mind. By providing a strong link between cause and effect *because* implies greater emphasis on the reason for an action than either *for* or *since*, which treat the reason as subordinate to the main statement and not as the more important part of the sentence. For example, in the sentence:

He usually goes to a match on Saturdays, *because* he is keen on football

for might be a better substitute, and put the other way round:

Because he is keen on football, he usually goes to a match on Saturdays

since might well be preferable.

begin, commence, start Either *begin* or *start* is acceptable in daily use. In most contexts *begin* is perhaps preferable, being a little less suggestive of sudden movement.

Commence should be avoided except in a strictly formal, legal or business context. In daily use it is pompous and unnecessary and smacks of false genteelness.

behalf The idiom *on behalf of* means 'acting for', 'on the part of'.

I am speaking to you today on behalf of the candidate for whom you voted

means that the speaker is standing in or acting for the candidate in question. But

I am speaking on behalf of you all to support the candidate for whom you voted

is wrong if it is for the sake of the candidate the speaker is appearing and not the audience.

beholden The phrase is *beholden to*, not *beholding*, and it means 'indebted to'.

She is beholden to me for introducing her to the man she is going to marry.

behoves This is used only in an impersonal way, meaning 'to be necessary or proper for':

It behoves me to write to him.

It has come to be regarded as a somewhat pedantic expression and is better left alone.

belittle A word which tends to be overused, meaning 'to play down', 'minimize', 'to make small'. There are many other words such as *decry*, *depreciate*, *disparage* or *ridicule* which serve the same purpose with often stricter accuracy.

belly A fine old English word which, for the sake of euphemism, is invariably replaced by the less accurate 'stomach' or, worse, the nursery phrase 'tummy'. Perhaps the pendulum is about to swing the other way: *guts* is returning to daily use with a vigour that once belonged to *belly*.

below, beneath, under *Below* or *under* can in most cases replace *beneath*, except in certain figurative senses:

He considered it beneath his notice

and:

Her remarks were beneath contempt,

or in a poetic or literary context:

They sat holding hands beneath the stars; she sought shelter beneath the trees.

Below implies a comparison, 'lower than', whereas *under* suggests a close relationship, such as in:

The grass under her feet was damp.

Contrast this with:

The grass beneath her feet was damp

and it can be seen that the second example might be more appropriate in a literary context, the former is a factual, prosaic setting. But:

The grass below her feet was damp

presents an image of a pair of feet floating a little way above the ground, or at any rate poised on a steep bank at quite a different level.

beneficence, benevolence These words are apt to be confused. *Beneficence* is 'the act of doing good', 'active goodness or kindness', 'charity'. *Benevolence* is 'the desire to do good', 'goodwill or charitableness'. The first is concerned with the action, the second with the feelings surrounding it.

Thanks to the beneficence of the parish, the church roof was repaired

and:

His benevolence was an outstanding feature of his character.

bereaved, bereft The relationship between these words is close. *Bereft* is generally used with *of*:

Bereft of his senses; bereft of all he owned,

and implies a sudden withdrawal. *Bereaved* is used in a more emotional context, and tends to be a continuing condition:

The bereaved mother was at the graveside,

but it can also be used with *of* in the special sense, 'deprived of':

Bereaved of her children, she turned to go.

beside, besides Apart from its use in poetry, which sometimes cheats for the sake of rhyme, *beside* occurs only as a preposition meaning 'by the side of'.

Beside his brother, he looked very young.

The adverb *besides* means 'in addition to', 'moreover', 'otherwise':

Besides a successful husband, she has wealth and beauty too.

As a preposition it also means 'other than', 'except':

She has no other friend besides you.

between This preposition is often misused. For instance, a choice is made between one object *and* another, not *or* another. Like the word 'after', *between* takes the accusative case:

This secret is between you and me,

not *you and I*, which is just as wrong as saying *after I*. *Between* must link two objects, be they singular words or plural:

He had to choose between each one

is wrong – he cannot choose between 'each' one. The correct line would be:

He had to choose between each one and the next.

Nor is the following sentence correct:

To understand fully, he should read between each line.

It should be:

To understand fully, he should read between the lines.

It is sometimes believed that *between* cannot be used for linking more than two objects, and *among* is substituted. But:

There was agreement between the Chairman, his advisers and other members of the Board

is perfectly acceptable.

There was agreement among the Chairman, his advisers, and other members of the Board

is much less precise, and *among* blends uneasily with the singular *Chairman*.

beware If it is remembered that this means literally 'be wary of' it is not hard to understand that it can be used only in an imperative sense and will, in most instances, be followed by *of*:

Beware of the dog (Be wary of the dog)

or:

Beware lest you fall (Be wary lest . . .)

biannual, biennial These words have distinct meanings. *Biannual* is twice a year; *biennial* means every two years.

bicentenary see **centenary**

bid Except in the context of an auction or a game of cards, to *bid* for something, the past tense of the verb is *bade* and the past participle *bidden*. But the noun, whose original meaning, an offer or the price of one, has now been extended to include an attempt to gain some purpose, is often exploited as a blanket term in headline use:

Prisoners' Bid for Freedom Fails

and

Last Desperate Bid for Peace

and has consequently become devalued.

big, great, large Generally speaking, *big* or *large* imply size, *great* an extreme degree or extension of something. In a few contexts, however, the terms can be interchangeable.
A great man implies a man of high quality or degree compared with other men. *A big man* or *a large man* both convey physical size; colloquially, *big* in this context can also mean 'important':

He's a big man in his field.

Large is more often used than *big* in terms of quantity:

There were a large number of people waiting.

But in the sentence:

There was a large crowd waiting

big could just as well be substituted, since the concept of 'crowd' can be of a single object having a tangible size, as well as a collection of separate units, as in the first example.
There are occasions when *great* is used to convey size in place of *big* or *large*:

Take your great boots out of here

certainly suggests enormity of size, but it is being used ironically in the original sense of 'extreme degree of largeness', and not as a simple factual description.

billion There is an important difference between British and French, German or American usage of this word. In Britain a billion represents one million millions, an amount so vast it is really only of use in an astronomical context. Elsewhere the word means one thousand millions.

blame Most authorities recommend that the expression *blame* something *on* a person should be avoided as an unnecessary elaboration of to *blame* a person *for* something. More acceptable in formal writing would be *to put the blame on* someone *for* something.

blank verse The form in which most of Shakespeare's plays and Milton's *Paradise Lost* are written, consisting of unrhymed iambic pentameter verse. It can, however, be applied to any form of unrhymed verse.

blatant, flagrant 'Flauntingly obvious or undisguised, offensively conspicuous, brazen or barefaced' are some of the dictionary definitions of *blatant*:

He was caught out in a blatant lie.

Flagrant means glaring, notorious or scandalous:

He showed a flagrant disregard for the regulations.

Of the two, *flagrant* invites the greater condemnation.

bloom, blossom In their literal sense these words are close in meaning. A flower can either *bloom* or *blossom*, the apple tree may be in *bloom* or in *blossom* in spring, though *bloom* may imply a completion and *blossom* a state of progress. This is much more marked in a figurative sense, where to *blossom* suggests a development which culminates in a climax:

Under his tutelage, she has blossomed into a gifted artist

and to *bloom* implies that the peak of development has already been reached:

He was in the first bloom of youth.

In these examples the words are distinct and cannot be interchanged.

blueprint Literally, a photographic printing process giving a white print on a blue ground, and used chiefly for copying tracings. In extended use the word has been applied to any kind of plan, formula, design or master copy so that it is now a much overused jargon word. It is best confined to the world of the technical drawing office from which it came.

bogey, bogie, bogy *Bogey* is a term used in golf. It is also an alternative form of spelling for *bogy*, a hobgoblin or evil spirit.
Bogie is a low truck or trolley, especially the pivoted truck which bears the wheels beneath a railway wagon. This, too, is an alternative spelling for a hobgoblin or evil spirit.
Bogy is the usual spelling for a hobgoblin or evil spirit. The plural form of the word is *bogies*.

bona fide Though this is a adverb, meaning 'in good faith', it is more usually treated as an adjective:

He showed me a bona-fide certificate.

The *fides* in *bona fides* is a singular noun and not, as is sometimes supposed, a plural:

His bona fides was questionable.

born, borne *Born* is used only in connection with birth; *borne* is the usual past participle of the verb 'to bear':

He was borne out of the ring by two stalwarts in the corner.

It also occurs as a past participle in connection with birth when used in the active sense:

She has borne eleven children,

and in a passive sense only when followed by the preposition *by*:

The child was borne by a gipsy woman.

But not in the following examples:

She was born in America,

or:

She was born of poor parents.

both Some words and phrases should never be used with *both*. For example, in:

Both the captain as well as the crew were all at sea,

the phrase *as well as* makes *both* redundant and could either replace it:

As well as the captain the crew were all at sea

or the sentence could be altered to read:

Both the captain *and* his crew were all at sea.

Other words with which *both* is unnecessary are *equal*, *at once*, *alike* or *between*. In the examples:

He and his son are both alike in appearance,
She is both equally proud and elegant

the use of *both* is superfluous.

The placing of the word is also important:

He is both concerned with fighting for a cause and achieving justice

is incorrect. The word common to each part of the sentence which is linked by *both . . . and* should always appear before the link itself. In this case it is 'concerned':

He is concerned both with fighting for a cause and achieving justice.

Both implies two objects only, and it is not intended to refer to more. The following sentence is therefore incorrect:

Both John and Mary and Mary's brother went out to play.

However, in the sentence:

Both Adam and Eve and the serpent lived in the Garden of Eden,

both is here linking Adam and Eve as a single human unit and treating the serpent as a separate item. In such a case it would be permissible.

Though it is possible to say either *both of the girls* or *both the girls*, the *of* implies two separate units rather than a single entity, and is usually better omitted.

bottleneck As a metaphor, which is about the only purpose for which it is used, this can be a useful word, provided it is remembered that it represents a constriction and cannot therefore be worsened by enlarging, nor improved by reducing. It can be cleared or removed but neither cured nor solved.

bracket The word *bracket*, associated with mathematical formulae, is sometimes used figuratively to mean 'group' or 'class', an extended use which is euphemistic and dehumanizing:

Most of the pupils were from homes in the lower income bracket.

It should be avoided.

brackets Round brackets or parentheses are used to enclose material in the form of information, explanation, or definition which is additional to the main sentence and which is already complete without it.

Because of the severe conditions (there has been a serious drought in the area for several weeks) the annual flower show has been cancelled.

Punctuation marks such as commas are not used before the first bracket but where necessary may be inserted immediately after the closing bracket:

His pockets contained a grubby handkerchief, a return railway ticket (London to Leeds), and some loose change.

Only if the whole sentence is in brackets should the full stop be included inside:

The Queen reviewed her troops. (This is an annual ceremony.) After the event, Her Majesty returned to the Palace.

The use of square brackets occurs when alien material by another author is interpolated into a text, or there is a deliberate substitution of some words in the original. They are also used when a further parenthesis is required in a passage already enclosed in round brackets, and for mathematical formulae.

bravado, bravery *Bravado* is boasting, swaggering pretence; *bravery* is the real thing – courage or valour.

breakdown This word should never be used figuratively in its statistical sense if there is any possibility of it holding a literal meaning as well:

The breakdown of crime prevention must be brought to the attention of the Commissioner.

This does not necessarily mean that law and order no longer prevail, simply that statistics on the subject must be passed on.

brethren A plural form of *brother*, this is now archaic and used only occasionally, in an ecclesiastical context or in a few technical senses.

British, English It is important to distinguish whether the reference is meant in a wide or a narrow sense. *British* is correct applied to persons or things from Great Britain as a whole:

The British government, the British army, British nationality.

But if speaking of an individual it is better to be specific:

Robert Burns, the Scottish poet; the English novelist, Thomas Hardy.

It must be remembered that for any period before 1707 the term *British* did not exist in a political sense and only English, Scots, Irish or Welsh should be used.

broad, wide Though in many contexts these terms can be interchangeable, there is a distinct difference in meaning in some senses. *Wide* is chiefly concerned with the distance from one limit to the next, *broad* with the expanse of matter between them. In the example:

A broad river flowed between steep banks

the impression evoked is from a viewpoint somewhere in the middle, looking up- or downstream, of a big expanse of water with indeterminate limits. But in:

A wide river flowed between steep banks,

the impression is of a river viewed from the side, where the distance between one bank and the other is the predominant feature – the water between is hardly noticed.

With this analogy in mind the place of each word in various idioms and phrases may be seen. In the following examples:

Broad shoulders, broad leaves, broad outline, broad minded

a degree of expansiveness is being expressed, whether in an actual or a metaphorical sense. But in:

Wide eyes, wide open, giving something a wide berth,

it is the distance involved between the limits imposed that is important, not the area itself.
If the idea expressed is indeterminate, either word may be suitable.

broadcast Since the noun was evolved from the verb and not the other way round, the past tense and the past participle of the verb is *broadcast* and not *broadcasted.*

He broadcast for the first time

and:

The speech was broadcast on all wavelengths.

bulk The meaning of this word is 'magnitude in three dimensions', implying a mass of great size. It can be used figuratively in the sense of 'the greater part of' but it is better not to use it to express numbers, only size:

The bulk of the merchandise was sent on later

implies a weighty mass of some dimensions, but in:

The bulk of the crowd was prepared to wait

'majority' would be a better word to use.

burglar, burgle This is a good example of back formation(*q.v.*), where the verb *to burgle* has been formed from the noun.

burlesque, caricature The dictionary definition of *burlesque* is 'an artistic composition . . . which vulgarizes lofty material for the sake of laughter' and of *caricature* is 'a picture ludicrously exaggerating the defects and peculiarities of a person or things'. Both words are often used in a figurative sense, *burlesque* mostly in connection with acting or performance:

His attempt to conduct the meeting in an orderly manner was a burlesque of the real thing

and *caricature* with appearance and features:

When he left her at the door, his face was a caricature of a disappointed lover.

burn, burned, burnt Though either form of the verb is acceptable in the past tense or as a past participle, *burnt* is more often used in the transitive form, where there is an object:

He burnt his boats behind him

and *burned* when the verb is intransitive:

He burned with desire to possess the diamond.

The adjective is always *burnt*:

When the meal came out of the oven, it was like a burnt offering.

but Used as a conjunction joining two parts of a sentence, *but* implies a contrast with a contradictory element between the parts:

He wanted to go to the station but he did not know the way.

If the contradiction is removed, *but* is no longer relevant:

He wanted to go to the station but he knew the way

is incorrect: *and* would be the logical choice.

Care is needed in using a negative with the construction *but that*:

Who could be sure but that the whole deal was not a trick?

But that already implies a negative and therefore the *not* is redundant.

But what is a colloquialism which should be avoided in sentences such as:

She never goes away but what she returns with a cold.

What should be omitted.

Also superfluous is *however* when used with *but*:

All the world's a stage, but if that is true, however, some of the actors give pretty poor performances.

But may be used quite justifiably to begin a sentence in order to provide a contrast with one that has gone before. It is not true that conjunctions such as *but* and *and* should never be used in this position. However, care should be taken that the construction is not repeated later in the sentence:

But he is not the only one to know how the mechanism works, but the others are not such experts.

Assuming that the sentence is in contrast to one immediately preceding it, this would be better expressed as:

But he is not the only one to know how the mechanism works. The others, however, are not such experts.

by, bye Broadly speaking, *by* is the preposition and *bye* the noun, but there are variations of this general rule. *Bylaw* can be spelt *byelaw*, probably because the word is derived from *byrlaw*, and *bye-bye* comes from *goodbye*, a contracted form of 'God be with you'.

In well-established words the hyphen is usually omitted and the word is written as one, unless there is an awkward juxtaposition of vowels or there is more than one syllable:

byword, bylaw, byway,

but:

by-election, by-product.

C

-c-, -ck- When verbs ending in a *c* occur in the past tense or continuous present they usually take an additional *k* to retain the hard pronunciation:

Let us picnic in the woods,

but:

They were picnicking in the woods.

One exception to this rule is the verb *to arc*, which although pronounced with a hard *c* is spelt *arced*, *arcing*. *Arcked* and *arcking* are given as alternative spellings, but are seldom used.

cacao, coca, cocoa *Cacao* is a small evergreen tree of tropical America from the seeds of which cocoa and chocolate are derived. *Coca* is the name of two South American shrubs cultivated for the stimulating properties of their dried leaves, which contain cocaine and other alkaloids. *Cocoa* is the roasted, husked and ground seeds of the cacao tree. The powder is used as a beverage and manufactured into chocolate.

caesura A literary term in poetry, this is a break or sense pause in the middle of a metrical line. It may cut across the metrical pattern in order to correspond to the rhythm of natural speech.

café Although now naturalized into the English language, this French word should still be spelt and pronounced with an accented *é*.

can, may *Can* indicates a possibility; *may* is used in a permissive sense:

Sarah can go to the party by bus

means that the bus will enable Sarah to reach the party.

Sarah may go to the party by bus

means that Sarah has permission to go to the party by bus. Colloquially, *can* is sometimes used in a permissive sense:

Can I call tomorrow?

cannot, can not *Cannot* is the usual negative form unless there is a particular reason to stress the *not*, when the two words may be written separately. In a sentence such as:

The use of a dictionary can not only promote understanding but also provide instruction,

it can be seen that *not* is part of the correlating phrase *not only . . . but also* and it would therefore be incorrect to attach it to *can*.

can't This contraction of *cannot* is widely accepted in all but the most formal contexts. Such a negative should never be used in a phrase such as:

He can't hardly speak

since a negative is already implied. It should be:

He can hardly speak.

The phrase *can't seem to* is an awkward one and should be avoided:

I can't seem to raise any energy

would be better expressed as:

I seem unable to raise any energy

or:

I can't raise any energy.

canvas, canvass The noun *canvas* is 'a heavy cloth'; the verb to *canvass* is 'to solicit votes, subscriptions or opinions'. *Canvass* is also a noun meaning 'an examination, a close inspection, or scrutiny'.

capacity see **ability**

capitalization Capitals should be used sparingly, and it should be borne in mind that capitalization makes a word more limited in its reference. As a rough guide, an initial capital letter gives a word the quality of a proper name, such as Mary or John, and is usually employed in a specific rather than a general sense. Names of specific organizations should carry capitals, since these are, in their way, proper names:

> The British Medical Association, Royal Academy of Dramatic Art, School of Slavonic Studies, London School of Journalism.

But if no specific organization is mentioned, and the reference is in general terms, then lower case lettering is correct:

> Every country has its own medical association. Many of the universities have recently acquired a college of art, a school of journalism and a school of Slavonic studies.

In a religious context it is customary to treat specific denominations as proper names:

> the Roman Catholic Church, the Orthodox Church, the Presbyterian Church,

but in a more general sense:

> the Christian church, the parish church, the church at the bottom of the street

capital letters not required. When used in a general sense words such as *catholic* (meaning universal in extent), *orthodox*, *heaven*, *hell*, *the devil* and *paradise* remain in lower case, but the *Reformation* or the *Puritan* religious movement of the 16th century are treated as proper names since they are used in a specific sense. This is true, too, of the *Church* as opposed to the *State*, when giving these bodies the status of named authorities and not referring to them in a general sense such as in:

> He was fully occupied in dealing with church and state matters which arose during his time in office.

Political parties are capitalized in the same way when specifically referred to as the *Conservative Party* (the *Conservatives*), the *Labour Party* (*Labour*), and the *Communist Party* (the *Communists*), but when used in a general sense the terms labour, communist and conservative do not need an initial capital.

Again, in a reference to the legislative body of the country, *Parliament* will have an initial capital, and so will the *Government*, meaning the one at present in power, but in a general context neither parliament nor the government – meaning *any* parliament, *any* government – require capital letters:

> As to the next step, Parliament must decide; the Government is the only body in a position to judge the situation.

but:

> It would require an act of parliament to convince that particular group of workers that the government was the proper authority to control the fund.

This differentiation between the general and the specific applies in most contexts. In titles, for example:

> The Queen attended the state opening of Parliament,

but:

> By the 16th century the king of England enjoyed absolute power with very little interference from parliament.

And:

> The Duke of Bedford opened the fete. The Duke then made a speech,

but:

> At dinner she was placed beside a duke of the realm.

There is some support for the custom of dropping the initial capital when only part of the title is used and in a historical context if titles occur frequently, even though the reference is specific. In the above example, for instance:

> The Duke of Bedford opened the fete. The duke then made a speech,

this would be considered equally correct, as would:

> The archbishop was applied to for permission to marry,

or:

> The cathedral was built at Canterbury.

Such variation of the general rules is a matter of taste rather than correctness, but whichever style is adopted it is vital to be consistent within the same text.

Geographical directions in the nature of descriptive adjectives should be in lower case letters, but political or cultural boundaries which imply a proper name for a defined area require initial capitals:

He drove from west to east Africa and through to eastern Asia,

but:

South Africa, East Anglia and Northern Ireland are politically or geographically defined areas.

The North is preferred when referring to the North of England as a specific area; *north of the Wash*, however, is correct in its vaguer geographical sense. Mountains, straits and seas take capital initial letters if they are part of a proper name, such as:

the Straits of Dover, Mount Everest, the English Channel.

The Gulf of Mexico would subsequently be referred to as *the Gulf* – signifying not just any gulf – and the warm stream of water flowing from it across the Atlantic is known as the *Gulf Stream*.

To sum up: capitals are used for nouns placed in a specific context as proper names or titles. In some instances, only part of the title may be capitalized. Provided the writer is consistent, this can be a matter of choice, but it must be borne in mind that ambiguities can arise: *a company secretary* may mean something quite different from *a Company Secretary*, or even *a Company secretary*, and the decision must depend finally on the context.

carat, caret *Carat* is a unit of weight in gem stones, or a measurement of the purity of gold. *Caret* is an omission mark made in written or printed matter to indicate where further material is to be inserted.

carcase, carcass The dead body of an animal. Though both spelling forms are acceptable, *carcass* is to be preferred.

carousal, carousel *Carousal*, with the stress on the second syllable which is pronounced *ow*, means a noisy or drunken feast. *Carousel*, or *carrousel* which is the more acceptable spelling, is a merry-go-round or a tournament with horsemen manoeuvring in formation. The *ou* is pronounced *oo* and the stress is on the last syllable of the word.

case This has become a jargon word. A gift to the sloppy writer, it is frequently used unnecessarily to embroider an otherwise simple sentence:

John was eager to show his skill, but in the case of Mark, he was not so anxious to perform.

The simpler version:

John was eager to show his skill, but Mark was not so anxious to perform

is preferable. And the next example:

In the case of those who have passed the exam, no difficulties will be encountered

would be improved by:

Those who have passed the exam will encounter no difficulties.

But in the following sentences:

The court found there was a case to answer;
In case of illness, ring the doctor;
In a case like yours, I would be the first to complain,

the word has a legitimate place.

cask, casque A *cask* is a barrel-like container made of staves for holding liquids; a *casque* is a word for a helmet, chiefly used in poetry.

cast, caste *Cast* is the spelling of the noun associated with the verb meaning 'to throw'; an object made in a mould or particular pattern. *Caste* is a hereditary social group or rigid system of social distinction.

catachresis The misuse or strained use of words:

It was fortuitous that he was wearing a crash helmet when he fell off

is an example of *catachresis*. Fortuitous means 'accidental', not 'fortunate'.

category, class *Category* is often loosely used to mean *class*, but its definition is more precisely a classificatory division in any particular field of knowledge, especially in science or philosophy. The word *class* refers to a number of persons or things regarded as forming a group. For example:

The domestic cat belongs to the category of flesh-eating mammals,

but:

He joined the class for beginners.

catholic, Catholic The adjective *catholic* means universal in extent, involving all. *Catholic* originally described the whole of the Christian church, but it is now used in contrast to Protestant as a term applying to the Roman Catholic Church.

cause, reason A *cause* is a factor which produces an effect. A *reason* is the explanation or justification for a certain effect being produced. For example:

Ice on the road was the cause of the car skidding,

but:

The reason the car skidded was that he put his foot on the brake when the road was icy.

To say that a cause is *due to* something is repetitive, nor can it be said that a reason is *because* something has occurred:

The cause of the breakdown was due to metal fatigue

is wrong. The sentence should either read:

Metal fatigue was the cause of the breakdown

or:

The breakdown was due to metal fatigue.

And:

The reason he made a mistake is because he was careless

is another example of tautology. The sentence should be:

The reason he made a mistake is that he was careless,

or:

He made a mistake because he was careless.

cavalcade, procession The precise meaning of *cavalcade* is 'a procession of persons on horseback or in horse-drawn carriages', but inevitably, with the advent of the motor car, the word has acquired an extended use to include motorized transport. As a result, it is often used loosely to apply to any kind of *procession* or pageant, and is in danger of being overworked.

cease *To cease fire*, *to cease trading* or *to cease operations* are a few of the phrases in which the word is still sometimes used, but except for some legal and official contexts it has in most cases been superseded by *stop*.

-cede, -ceed, -sede With a few exceptions, all words with this sound at the end are spelt *-cede*. Those which do not obey this rule are *proceed*, *succeed*, *exceed*, and *supersede*, the only one with an *s* instead of a *c*.

ceiling This word is often employed as a metaphor denoting the highest limits that can be reached – a harmless practice, provided it is remembered that a ceiling can be raised or lowered, but not swept aside, extended or increased.

cello Although an abbreviation for *violoncello*, it is so commonly used that it is no longer necessary to precede it with an apostrophe. The plural form of the word is *cellos*, without an *e*.

cement, concrete These words are not interchangeable. *Cement* is the mixture of clay and limestone which, when bound with water, forms an adhesive paste. It is an ingredient of *concrete*, which is formed by the addition of sand and broken stones and bound by water into a malleable consistency which can be set in a mould. *Cement* is also used as an adhesive between other materials, such as tiles or bricks.

censer, censor, censure A *censer* is a container in which incense is burned. A *censor* is an official who examines, and if necessary amends, written material for contravention of existing moral or political conditions, and *censure* is adverse or hostile criticism. The verb *to censor* is to perform the act of censorship, and *to censure* is to criticize or blame.

centenary, centennial Although both these words mean 'one hundred years' and can be interchangeable, the noun *centenary* is more often used in Britain and *centennial* in the United States. One advantage in using *centenary* is that *bicentenary* and *tercentenary* are also established terms. As adjectives, *bicentennial* and *centennial* are the preferred forms.

centre, middle The *centre* implies the central point or pivot of a circle, round which everything else revolves. The *middle* is a less precise term meaning a point or area at an equal distance between two limits. The *middle of the road* is not just one point but a continuous line equal in distance from each side, and the *middle of the room* implies an undefined area around the centre. *To centre round* or *around*, though commonly used phrases, are grammatically incorrect, and should be replaced by *centre on*, or *to be centred in*.

century The word *century* means 'one hundred years', and this always begins on the first year of any given century, so that the last year of that hundred years gives the century its name. Thus 1900 is the last year of the 19th century, and 1901 the first year of the 20th century.

ceremonial, ceremonious The noun *ceremonial* is a rite or ceremony, or a system of rites or ceremonies, and the adjective *ceremonial* pertains to these rites or ceremonies. *Ceremonious* is an adjective describing the observance of rites or ceremonies or formally polite behaviour. Broadly speaking, *ceremonial* is concerned with the ceremonies themselves, *ceremonious* with the people who practise them.

certainty, certitude *Certainty* is an assured fact; *certitude* is a sense of complete conviction. The first is concerned with fact, the second with feelings about the fact.

chance The verb *to chance* is giving way to *happen* in the same way as *cease* is being superseded by *stop*:

He chanced to come upon them standing by the bus stop

is more formal than:

He happened to come upon them standing by the bus stop,

and therefore sounds a little pedantic.

The noun *chance* is sometimes used when *opportunity* would be more appropriate:

It was a chance he knew he should not miss

would be more precise as:

It was an opportunity he knew he should not miss.

chancellery, chancery The *chancellery* is the position or the official residence of a chancellor; *chancery* is a division of the High Court of Justice.

change, alter *Change* has a wider application than *alter*, which implies a modification in one particular only. *Change* can mean a total substitution, or alteration in many respects at once:

He was persuaded to change his habits,

and:

He changed from an amiable, happy boy into a surly, morose adult.

But:

By shaving off his moustache he had altered his whole appearance

is an example of the more limited use of *altered*.

character The dictionary definition is 'the aggregate of qualities that distinguishes one person or thing from another', but this word is often made to stand in for 'kind', 'sort' and 'nature', or used unecessarily in a sentence where a simple adjective would do. For example:

This house is of a spacious character

means:

This house is of a spacious nature

but the simple way of saying this is:

This house is spacious.

charge Originally there was no ambiguity if it were said:

Children in charge of an adult may be admitted free.

But meanings change, and such a sentence now implies that the children are in full control of the adults. This may well be true, but it is probably not what is meant. The sentence should read:

Children in *the* charge of an adult may be admitted free,

for it is the adult who is normally *in charge of* the child.

childish, childlike Both words are defined as 'like or befitting a child', but *childish* is more often used in a slightly derogatory sense, meaning that certain behaviour is suitable only for a child, whereas *childlike* is a term implying admiration and stressing the freshness and innocence of childhood. Examples of the contexts in which these words might be used are:

Such a childish display of temper will achieve nothing,

and:

Her childlike simplicity appealed to all who came in contact with her.

Chinese, Chinaman *Chinese* is the term to use when referring to the Chinese people or the Chinese nation. *Chinamen*, like the slang terms *Chinee* and *Chink*, has a derogatory implication and should be avoided.

choice This word implies an alternative, but it is often loosely used, particularly in advertising copy, in a context which offers no choice at all:

Last opportunity to win the holiday of your choice!

and:

Choice vegetables, freshly picked.

But:

He offered her a choice of three alternatives

is an example of the correct use of the word.

chorale A simple hymn-like tune in slow tempo which is sung by choir and congregation. The emphasis is on the second syllable.

chord, cord *Chord* is a string of a musical instrument, or the sound produced by a combination of three or more harmonious notes struck simultaneously. It is also used figuratively in respect of feelings:

He struck a chord of sympathy in her heart,

and is a technical term in the fields of geometry, civil engineering and aeronautics. *Cord* is a string or small rope consisting of several strands twisted together.

Christian name, first name, forename There is a tendency today to prefer the terms *first name* or *forename* to *Christian name* on the grounds that the person referred to may well not be a Christian. At one time, when all children in the Western world were baptized into some branch of the Christian church, the term *Christian name* had a logical basis, even though many of the names given may have derived from classical or other pagan origins. It seems, however, to be a matter of personal preference rather than one of precept, since long-standing usage has given the term *Christian name* the widest possible application.

chronic A victim of misapplication, chronic is often wrongly used to mean 'severe' or 'deplorable':

The pains in my legs were chronic last night.

Its true meaning is 'of long-standing duration, inveterate or constant', as in:

She was a chronic invalid, and had been unable to walk for twenty years.

circumstances Both *in the circumstances* and *under the circumstances* are acceptable, and there are no grounds for believing that the latter phrase is less correct than the former.

city In general usage a *city* is a very large town, particularly one which is a centre of business and administration. In Britain, however, in its strict sense the word is applied only to those towns which have been appointed by royal charter. Often, though not necessarily, this refers to a cathedral town, which may be of quite a small size. The City of London, for instance, which is the centre of banking and insurance for the rest of the country, is only about a square mile in extent.

clad, clothed Though both words are the past tense and past participle of the verb *to clothe*, the older word, *clad*, cannot be used in so many contexts, but is limited to mean specific kinds of clothing:

He was clad in shining armour

is acceptable, but in:

He was fed and clothed and educated at very little cost to the state

the word *clothed* could not suitably be replaced by *clad*.

claim The meaning of this word, 'to demand as a right or due', has been extended colloquially to replace words such as 'assert', 'allege', 'declare', and 'say', and has lost much of its precision in the process:

He claimed he had seen the thief run off.

He could *allege* or *declare* or even *say*, he had seen the thief, with more accuracy. But:

As the sole survivor of that branch of the family he claimed the legacy

is an example of the word used in its proper context.

clarinet, clarionet Both forms are acceptable, but *clarinet* is now the preferred spelling. The stress is on the last syllable.

classic, classical Though in many contexts these words overlap in meaning, *classic* is more generally used to signify 'of the very first order', 'first class', and *classical*, 'in accordance with Greek and Roman models in literature or art, or later systems of principles modelled upon them'.

Though the term *classic* may be used to mean *classical*, as in:

The house was of classic proportions, with pillars supporting a high portico,

the word is often loosely applied in a variety of contexts in which *classical* could not be substituted and which are in no way connected with Greek or Roman perfection. For example:

It was a classic example of a petty official exceeding his powers,

and:

It was a classic case of whitewashing.

In these two examples 'typical' might be more apt. But in:

This book should become a classic

the allusion is close to the original meaning. Books that are *classics* are those of the highest order, such as might be compared with the models of literature of ancient Greece and Rome. However, music of a similar quality is referred to as *classical*, and the term is used in opposition to 'popular' or 'romantic', as well as applying to that of a particular period.

clause A *clause* is a group of words including a verb and its subject, together with any modifying adjectives or adverbs. If it can stand on its own, making a sentence complete in itself, it is known as a *main clause*. If it depends upon another part of the sentence for its meaning it is a *subordinate clause*.

A sentence can consist of two or more main clauses linked by a conjunction:

The wood was dense, but the trees were not very tall.

A subordinate clause is linked to the main part of the sentence by a relative pronoun or a subordinating conjunction:

My father, who is elderly, is giving up his home.

My father . . . is giving up his home is the main clause, and *who is elderly* is the subordinate clause, *who* being the relative pronoun.

Nero fiddled while Rome burned.

In this sentence *while* is the subordinating conjunction joining the subordinate part of the sentence to the main clause, *Nero fiddled.*

A *clause* is also the name given to each paragraph of a legal document, and each section of an act of parliament while in the preparatory stages.

clean, cleanse Though *clean* and *cleanse* both mean 'to make clean', or 'to remove dirt', *cleanse* should be used only figuratively in a moral, spiritual or ritualistic sense:

Cleansed of his sins, he felt able to return to the world.

The noun *cleanser* sometimes finds its way into advertising copy describing a proprietary brand of household cleaner. This, no doubt, is because it presents an image not just of cleanliness, but also of purity.

cleave There are two distinct meanings of this word. The first is 'to stick or adhere to', 'be attached or faithful to,' the past tense of which is *cleaved*:

He cleaved to his beliefs despite the conflicting evidence.

The second meaning is 'to part by a cutting blow', 'to sever, rend apart, or split'. The past tense is *cleft*, *cleaved* or *clove*, and the past participle *cloven* or *cleft*.

clench, clinch To *clench* is to grasp firmly or to grip: a fist, teeth or hands are *clenched*. To *clinch* is to secure, or fasten together, particularly a nail, by beating down the point. Boxers go into a *clinch*, when they have to be separated, and in a figurative sense a bargain is *clinched*.

clever This word is sometimes misused in the sense of being academically well qualified, erudite, or hard to understand. The true meaning of the word is 'having quick intelligence', 'mentally bright', 'showing adroitness or ingenuity'. For example:

> Thanks to a clever manoeuvre, he extricated himself from a difficult position.

In other words quick intelligence will usually result in academic achievement, but it is the sharp intelligence that the word *clever* relates to, not the result of it.

cliché A trite phrase which 'springs to mind', 'at the drop of a hat', 'in a nutshell' – there are three examples of clichés. Such phrases start life as apt metaphors in a given context but are then adopted by other writers and repeated so frequently and so mechanically that they quickly become overworked and often meaningless. Words, too, become fashionable and are often so ill used that they lose their purpose – 'democratic', 'significant', 'escalation' are examples of vogue words which have lost much of the force of their original meaning and have become trite clichés.

client, customer, patron A *client* is one who seeks professional advice, or who employs the services of a professional expert. A *customer* purchases goods from another, and a *patron* supports another by dealing with him as a *customer*. In the word *patron* there is an implication that he, as a *customer*, is doing the other a favour by 'patronizing' his establishment and buying goods or services from him.

climactic, climatic, climacteric *Climactic* is pertaining to or forming a climax. *Climatic* is relating to weather conditions, and *climacteric* means crucial, pertaining to a critical period, or a year in which important changes are said to occur.

close, shut Some authorities assert that *close* is a genteel euphemism for *shut*. In certain cases this may be true, but there are also specific implications in the two words. In some contexts *shut* signifies a more positive action than *close*, in which there is also a suggestion of enclosure or containment:

He got up and closed the door

implies a closing *in*.

He got up and shut the door

implies a shutting *out*.

clothe see **clad**

cockscomb, coxcomb *Cockscomb* is the comb of a cock, or the pointed cap of a jester which resembles it, and it is also the name of a plant. *Coxcomb* is the word for a conceited dandy.

cohere see **adhere**

coherence, cohesion Both *coherence* and *cohesion* mean the act or state of sticking together, but *coherence* is used more often in a figurative sense, as of thoughts or of verbal statements, whereas *cohesion* is applied to the uniting of objects or substances.

coiffeur, coiffure *Coiffeur* is a hairdresser; *coiffure* is a style of arranging or setting the hair. It can also mean a headdress or head covering.

collective nouns There are different types of *collective noun*. Those that apply to a series of articles collected together, such as luggage, cutlery, clothing and transport are treated as singular and take a singular verb:

The luggage was put on the train.

Some nouns are the same in the singular as the plural and take either a singular or a plural verb according to the sense:

The fish *are* rising

but:

My fish *is* delicious.

Group nouns, known as *nouns of multitude*, may take a singular or a plural verb according to the context. A singular verb is used if the emphasis is on the group acting as an individual unit. A plural verb is used if the emphasis is on the individuals who make up the group:

The jury *has* agreed upon its verdict

but:

The committee *were* unable to come to a decision.

Whichever form of the verb is used, it is most important to be consistent throughout the sentence:

The company *has* agreed that *they* will delay delivery

is incorrect. Either:

The company *has* agreed that *it* will delay delivery

or:

The company *have* agreed that *they* will delay delivery

are acceptable and, since in this context it (the company) is acting as a single unit, the singular version is to be preferred. In the same way, with other group words the choice of a singular or plural verb depends on whether the noun implies a single unit or several members of a group:

The rest of the cake *is* still to be eaten,

but:

The rest of the soldiers *were* forced to retreat.

Three-quarters of the building *is* completed,

but:

Two-thirds of the children *were* unable to read.

With the word *number* itself, *the number* is usually singular, but *a number* is plural:

The number of acts of terrorism *has* shown a steep increase,

but:

A number of students *are* taking part in the demonstration.

This is because in the second example 'a number of students' is a composite subject standing in the place of 'numerous students'. Similarly, in:

Three hundred miles is a long way to come for a funeral,

'a journey of' is implied at the beginning of the sentence, rendering 'three hundred miles' part of a composite subject which takes a singular verb.

collusion This must not be confused with *collaboration*, which has a friendly, benign ring to it. *Collusion* means conspiracy, or a secret agreement for a fraudulent purpose, and there is nothing friendly about it.

colon This punctuation mark is generally considered to be intermediate between the semicolon and the full stop in weight, but with the exception of certain contexts it is not very widely used today.

Its chief purpose is to form a relationship between a general statement and qualifying remarks which follow, each part of the sentence being complete in itself. Indeed, in many cases the colon could be replaced by a full stop with little loss of sense or meaning, though a difference would be seen in the balance of the text as a whole. For example:

> He goes for long walks in all kinds of weather: this may account for the muddy condition of his shoes,

and:

> Most people have some special dislikes in foods: for some it is stewed prunes, for others cabbage.

In both examples a full stop, though grammatically acceptable, would, by dividing the sentences into two, have separated the parts more drastically than the sense demanded. A semi-colon, too, would be a possible substitute, but it also tends to be divisive and would not provide the balancing link so effectively as the colon.

In a similar way a colon is used to introduce a list of items or examples (as in the present text). This is really just an extension of the role already described:

> The company produces four types of motor vehicle: a sports car, a saloon, an estate car and a van,

and:

> The procedure is as follows: dial 999 and ask for the police.

It is also used as an alternative to the comma when introducing direct speech:

> He said: 'I come to bury Caesar, not to praise him.'

comedy, farce, burlesque *Comedy* is the comic element in a piece of drama, a play or film of humorous character. *Farce* stresses the outrageous absurdity of a comic situation or character, and *burlesque* is a caricature or vulgar treatment of ordinary material aimed at provoking laughter. In the United States *burlesque* has the specific sense of a theatrical entertainment of coarse and vulgar comedy and dancing.

comic, comical *Comic* describes the aim, or intention, of causing laughter; *comical* describes the effect. A *comic* actor is one who sets out to perform humorous roles; a *comical* actor is a man whose every word and gesture causes mirth, whether intended or not.

comma The chief function of a *comma* is to separate or set off different parts of a sentence. It should be used to avoid ambiguity, to achieve greater clarity and to prevent a sentence becoming unwieldy, but it should always be used sparingly. Too many commas hold up the flow of thought and are irritating to the reader. There are occasions when the use of a comma is obligatory, some when its use may be a matter of choice, and others where it should not be used at all.

A comma may be inserted between two main clauses linked by a co-ordinating conjunction such as *and* or *but*:

> It has been exceptionally cold today, but rain is forecast for tomorrow.

The comma here is optional. If the two parts of the sentence are fairly short and closely related it is better to omit it.

It is also used to separate three or more clauses, words and phrases in a series:

> She picked up her shopping bag, wheeled out the pram, and set off for the shops,

and:

> She was so desperate for a cigarette she was quite prepared to beg, borrow or steal one.

In modern practice the comma is often omitted before the conjunction connecting the last two items, as in the second example. Whichever course is followed, it is important to be consistent. Commas are used to separate individual adjectives modifying a noun provided they are not related, and could logically be linked by 'and':

> She was a tall, thin, angular woman.

But:

> She was a pretty little thing.

In this example 'little thing' is thought of as a single unit modified by the adjective 'pretty': *and* could not logically be inserted between 'pretty' and 'little', so a comma is not needed. A comma is used following a phrase, clause or word introducing the main clause:

> When the time came to go, he put on his coat.
> Later, he called to see how she was.

One of its most important functions is to set off a phrase or clause in the middle of a sentence:

> My brother, who lives in the city, is a keen photographer.

Here the commas are a form of parenthesis round a clause which is providing additional, but expendable, information about the subject. This is known as a non-restrictive clause: the main part of the sentence:

> My brother . . . is a keen photographer

could very well stand on its own. It is important to ensure that both commas are used in such a sentence; as with brackets, the end of the parenthesis must be shown.

If, however, the same sentence is used without the commas the sense is changed:

> My brother who lives in the city is a keen photographer.

This implies that I have more than one brother. *Who lives in the city* is a restrictive or defining clause distinguishing him from the others, and is therefore essential to the meaning of the sentence, so it must not be separated off by commas. Another example is as follows:

> The doctor who was best known in the town was elected to the committee.

Without the commas this too is a restrictive clause. That doctor was elected because he was the one who was known best. But with commas inserted the sense is altered:

The doctor, who was best known in the town, was elected to the committee.

The clause is now non-restrictive, just providing incidental information about the doctor who had been elected to the committee and who happened to be better known in the town than anywhere else.

A comma is sometimes essential to a sentence in order to avoid ambiguity:

She jumped, the hedge producing unexpected prickles which penetrated her thick skirt.

A comma is not required in a list connected by conjunctions:

He is tall and slim and handsome,

and it should never be inserted between a subject and its verb, even in a long sentence:

The truth of the matter that we are considering in the light of the evidence put before us in court today, is that there is no justification for his behaviour.

The truth is the subject, *is* the verb, and there is no justification for the comma which separates them. It would be preferable to rewrite the sentence if it is felt to be too unwieldy.

commence see **begin**

commitment, committal *Commitment* is a pledge, or the state of being committed to something:

We have a firm commitment every Sunday to drive our neighbour to church.

In other contexts *committal* is often interchangeable, but it is also used in the special sense of committing an offence or of being committed to prison:

His committal to prison was endorsed by the court

and:

The committal of a crime is anti-social behaviour.

common, mutual *Common* is belonging equally to, or shared by two or more people, joint, united. *Mutual* is reciprocal, possessed or experienced by two people or more. On the whole, *common* has a wider application. *Mutual* tends to be thought of as a two-way activity, often restricted to two people.
Mutual should be avoided with words that already indicate reciprocity, as in *mutual agreement*.

Commonwealth of Nations A community bound together by a common allegiance to the British crown and recognizing the British monarch as its head, in which Britain is an equal partner with certain independent nations and their dependencies.

comparative, comparatively These words should be used only when there are two or more things to compare, and not as generalized modifiers of adjectives and adverbs:

He was comparatively slow in learning French.

Slow compared to what? *Fairly* or *rather* would be more suitable substitutes. But:

Of the total number of absentees, comparatively few had genuine excuses.

Here the word is appropriate, since the proportion of those with genuine excuses is being compared with the total number of absentees.

compare to, compare with To *compare* something *to* something else is figuratively to set them up beside each other in order to draw attention to their similarities. To *compare* something *with* something else is to set it against the other object in order to point out their dissimilarities, the implication usually being a derogatory one:

Describing his new girl friend, he compared her to Helen of Troy.

This is complimentary to the girl friend, but:

Compared with Helen, Susan is a non-starter in the beauty stakes

is placing Susan at a disadvantage.

With the verb *compare*, it is important to ensure that the comparison made is a possible one, that like is compared with like:

His work was badly done compared with his neighbour

should read:

His work was badly done compared with that of his neighbour

or:

His work was badly done compared with his neighbour's (work).

comparisons, false see **absolute terms**

compel, impel *Compel* means to force or drive, especially to a course of action. *Impel* also means to drive, or to urge forward, or to incite to action.

There is more strength in the word *compel*, suggesting coercive pressure from outside, whereas *impel* is used more often in a figurative sense, implying the internal pressure of feelings and strong motivation. In the example:

He was compelled to stand against the wall with his hands raised

there is the suggestion of physical force.

She felt impelled to volunteer for extra duty at Christmas.

Here, the driving force is self-motivated.

complacent, complaisant *Complacent* is pleased, especially with oneself, salf-satisfied; *complaisant* is obliging or compliant, agreeable.

complement, compliment *Complement* is that which completes or makes perfect: the full quantity or amount that completes anything, as with *a ship's complement*, meaning the officers and crew required to man a vessel. In grammar the term means a word or words used to complete a grammatical construction, as with an object following a verb:

The girl is tall

Tall is the complement: the sentence is unfinished without it. *Compliment* is an expression of praise or admiration.

complement, supplement A *complement* is that which completes something, and makes up the full quantity or amount. A *supplement* is something added to supply a deficiency and implies an addition to the whole, a reinforcement or extension:

I always give the dog a vitamin pill as a supplement to his rations.

complex sentence A *complex sentence* is one which contains a main clause and one or more dependent or subordinate clauses as well:

She took out a book which she had wanted to read for some time, having seen a review of it.

compound sentence This is a sentence containing two or more main clauses:

It was a brave thing to do and he did not hesitate to do it, but the outcome was quite unexpected.

comprehend see **apprehend**

comprehensible, comprehensive *Comprehensible* is intelligible, capable of being understood. *Comprehensive* is inclusive, having a wide mental grasp, comprehending much, of large scope:

She has a comprehensive knowledge of early English painting.

comprise, include, consist of *To comprise* means to be made up of, encompass, or to be composed of. *To include* means to contain or embrace parts or part of a whole, and *to consist of* means to be composed of, or to be made up of. *Comprise* implies a containment or embracing of all the parts of a whole; *include* suggests that only some of the parts are contained, while *consist of* means that the whole is made up of the sum of its constituent parts:

The course *comprises* the whole spectrum of book publishing, and *includes* illustration research, an important aspect of which *consists of* the selection and commissioning of artwork and photographs.

concave, convex *Concave* is curved outward like a hollow sphere. The opposite is *convex*, which means curved inward like a sphere viewed from the outside, and bulging in the middle. Both terms are applied especially to lenses and mirrors.

concise, succinct *Concise* means expressing a lot in a few words. *Succinct* also means expressing much in a few words, or characterized by brevity, and suggests compactness. With *concise* there is not a word to spare, and *succinct* implies economy in the choice of the words themselves.

condemn, contemn *Condemn* is to censure, or pronounce to be guilty, to compel or force into a certain state of action. *Contemn* is to view with contempt or treat disdainfully.

confidant(e), confident A *confidant* is someone to whom secrets are confided. The word, which is French, also has a feminine form, *confidante*.
Confident is having a strong belief or assurance about something: to be sure of oneself.

confide in, confide to To *confide in* someone is to entrust them with a secret. In the transitive form of the verb one *confides* or entrusts a secret *to* someone.

conjugal, connubial *Conjugal* is an adjective meaning concerning husband and wife. *Connubial* is to do with marriage, or the state of matrimony:

The husband insisted on his conjugal rights,

and:

For forty years they lived in a state of connubial bliss.

conjunction This is the term for a connecting word which joins two words, parts of a sentence or whole sentences together. There are two kinds of conjunction: co-ordinating and subordinating. The co-ordinating conjunctions – *and*, *but*, *or*, *for*, *yet* and *nor* – join words or groups of equal weight:

Horse and hounds.

He knew her name but he couldn't recall her face.

Some are called correlatives, because they are often closely linked:

Neither his wife *nor* his mother knew what to say.

She *not only* plays, *but also* sings.

It is important to ensure that these are correctly placed:

She *both* liked the pink dress *and* the brown one

is incorrect. The correlation is between the two colours:

She liked *both* the pink dress *and* the brown one.

Subordinate conjunctions join a main clause to a subordinate one. They may be of time (*as*, *since*, *before*, *when*), reason (*as*, *since*, *because*, *why*), condition (*though*, *if*, *unless*), purpose (*so*, *lest*, *that*) or comparison (*than*):

You must not climb the ladder lest you fall.

I do not know when I shall be back.

If you are going to the shops, you could buy me some butter.

In the last example, even though it is placed at the beginning of the sentence, the conjunction *if* still does its job of subordinating the clause.

connection, connexion Though both forms are admissible, the former is the more widely used, and is standard in American practice.

In connection with is another of those tiresome phrases frequently used in sloppy English to replace the simple preposition:

I want to speak to you in connection with the matter we discussed yesterday

means:

I want to speak to you about the matter we discussed yesterday.

It is simpler to say so.

connote, denote *Connote* means to signify, but also to imply, or to have associated meanings. *Denote* is to indicate, to be a sign of:

The bristly moustache and upright bearing denote his status as a sergeant; they connote a disciplinarian with a fanatical regard for conformity.

consecutive, successive *Consecutive* is following on in uninterrupted succession one behind the other. *Successive* is also following on one behind the other in order or sequence, but does not necessarily mean next to each other:

When picking the raffle tickets, he chose consecutive numbers. Successive attempts had been made to communicate with the hostages, and some of these had been successful.

consequent, consequential *Consequent* is following as a result, or as a logical conclusion, or logically consistent. *Consequential* is of the nature of a consequence, following as an effect or result. It also means self-important or pompous. *Consequent* is the word usually adopted in the sense of 'resulting':

His speech was deliberately provocative and the consequent uproar was only to be expected,

but *consequential* is correct in the special sense of *consequential damages* or *consequential loss insurance*, which means contingency loss and damage following as the indirect result of something, such as the necessity of taking hotel accommodation when a car has been incapacitated in an accident. In this sense it implies consistency with a result, but not the direct result itself.

consist of, consist in *To consist of* something means to be composed of, to be made up of a material:

Hadrian's Wall consists of nothing more than large stones piled on top of each other.

To consist in means to be contained in, to lie in, and is usually applied in an abstract sense when speaking of qualities:

Success in show jumping consists in acquiring a close understanding with your horse.

consistence, consistency *Consistency* is the form invariably used nowadays. Many dictionaries merely list *consistence* as an alternative.

constrain, restrain *Constrain* is to force, compel, oblige, or to confine forcibly. *Restrain* is to hold back from action, keep in check, keep under control:

She felt constrained to speak her mind and not even his pleading could restrain her.

constructive There is a tendency for this overworked word, the opposite of destructive, to be used solely as a meaningless cliché. *Constructive criticism* has become a euphemism for saying something unpleasant. A suggestion is still the contribution of an idea, whether it is termed *constructive* or not.

consult, consult with *To consult* is to seek counsel for, ask advice of or refer to someone for information. *To consult with* is to consider or deliberate as well as to confer with someone. It is an Americanism to apply the *with* form in the wider context as well. Such an expression should be left to the specific context of a conference in which a topic is deliberated.

contagious, infectious *Contagious* is communicable to others, carrying or spreading a disease. *Infectious* is causing or communicating infection, tending to spread from one to another. The difference between them is that *contagious* means contact by touch, whereas an *infectious* disease is spread by germs in the air that is breathed. Both terms are often used figuratively.

contemporary There is a danger that the true meaning of this word will soon be lost in the confusion of its misapplication. *Contemporary* means belonging to the same time. It can only be equated with 'modern', 'up to date' if that is the time which is under discussion:

I like contemporary furniture

is a perfectly valid statement in the context of the person talking, whenever that was. If, say, Henry VIII had made that remark, he would have been referring to the furniture of the Tudor period – that is, *contemporary* with him.

It was a production of *Romeo and Juliet* in contemporary dress

does not mean a production in modern dress, but in the clothes of Shakespeare's period. To say *they are contemporaries* is to describe two people of the same age group.

contemptible, contemptuous *Contemptible* is despicable, deserving of being held in contempt. *Contemptuous* means scornful, expressing contempt or disdain:

He regarded the suggestion contemptibly

is incorrect. He could regard it *contemptuously*, with contempt or scorn, because he thought it was a *contemptible* or despicable suggestion.

contiguous see **adjacent**

continual, continuous *Continual* is recurring with relentless regularity. *Continuous* is non-stop and unbroken. A telephone might be described as ringing *continually*, because of the number of calls received. Water from a burst pipe would pour through the ceiling in a *continuous* stream.

continuance, continuation, continuity *Continuance* and *continuation* both mean the act or fact of continuing. To continue, meaning the intransitive sense of to last or endure, is a *continuance* of an act; to continue an action, the transitive form of the verb, will produce a *continuation* of it. So:

I hope you will allow a continuance of my tenancy,

and:

The continuation of the serial will be published next week.

Continuity is the state of being continuous, and in a film-making context it has acquired the special sense of consistency.

converse, inverse The adjective *converse* is turned about, opposite or contrary in direction or action:

He is certainly not making money; in fact, the converse is true.

Inverse is reversed in position, direction or tendency, or turned upside down:

I shall announce the winners in inverse order. Third prize goes to…

contrary, converse, opposite *Contrary* is diametrically or mutually opposed; *converse* is turned about, opposite in action or direction; *opposite* is diametrically different, an antonym. With the phrase:

Each cat has nine lives,

a *contrary* statement would be:

Each cat does not have nine lives,

a *converse* statement would be:

Nine cats each have one life,

and the *opposite* is:

No cat has nine lives.

Opposite is contrary, but a *contrary* statement is not necessarily opposite: it will also include shades of lesser meanings.

copulative verb This is the grammatical term for a linking verb, tying the complement in to the subject of a sentence:

He *is* tall.
She has *grown* old.
He *seems* well.

correspond to, correspond with If an object is like something else, it *corresponds to* it. To *correspond with* somebody is to write them a letter.

co-respondent, correspondent A *co-respondent* is the third party in a divorce suit. A *correspondent* is one who writes a letter; also, in a journalistic context, a reporter who specializes in a given subject or area.

corporal, corporeal *Corporal* is of or belonging to the human body. *Corporeal* means bodily, of the nature of matter, as distinct from *spiritual.*

correlatives These are conjunctions that go in pairs: *either ... or, not only ... but also, both ... and.* [See *conjunction*]

cost effectiveness The degree of stability measured by the relationship of costs over returns. This is one of the vogue words at present, more popular than helpful.

could, might *Could* suggests a greater degree of probablity than *might*:

> If he had practised harder, he could have made the English team.

There may have been a possibility but hardly a probability about such a prediction. *Might* would be a better word. But:

> You could get yourself killed, running across that busy road.

That is intended as a statement of probability. *Could* is therefore the correct choice.

council, counsel A *council* is a board or assembly of people convened for deliberation or advice; *counsel* is advice, an opinion or instruction given for directing the conduct of others.

A *councillor* is a member of a council or board; a *counsellor* is an advisor. In the United States it is the word for a lawyer:

> He was elected to the Parish Council, where he proved to be a better counsellor than councillor. For though his counsel was sound enough he was never able to attend the meetings.

counter-productive A very popular vogue word meaning little more than 'unhelpful', but longer.

credence, credit Both words mean belief, but *credit* has many other meanings as well, such as trustworthiness, credibility, reputation, a source of commendation or honour:

She gave no credence to the rumours she had heard about him, but gave him credit for possessing sense enough to have remained an honest man.

credible, credulous, creditable *Credible* is capable of being believed, trustworthy; *credulous* is ready to believe anything; *creditable* is bringing credit, honour or esteem:

The child's story was quite credible and in keeping with the facts, though the old lady was credulous enough to believe anything. But on the whole he had behaved creditably, and made a good impression.

creole This is the term for someone of European descent who is a native of the West Indies or Spanish America.

crevasse, crevice Though similar, these words are not interchangeable. A *crevasse* is a deep cleft or fissure in a glacier. In the United States, it is also applied to a breach in a river bank or embankment. A *crevice* is a crack, rift or fissure in the ground.

crucial Decisive, critical, involving a final and supreme decision are the true meanings of this word, which is often carelessly employed to stand in for 'important'. Such an extended meaning can only have a weakening effect.

cultivated, cultured Literally, *cultivated* is that which is produced or improved by cultivation, such as a plant; figuratively, it means educated and refined. *Cultured* means artificially nurtured or grown, and is a term used especially in the context of scientific and laboratory work.

Figuratively, it means much the same as *cultivated* does in the figurative sense: enlightened, refined. The use of the term 'culture', applied to a race of people and their way of life, has influenced the way in which the adjective is used, and it is often applied in a broader sense than its counterpart *cultivated*:

He is a very cultivated man, interested in philosophy and literature, but then, of course, he comes from a cultured background.

curb, kerb A *curb* is something that restrains or checks, and is the name of the chin-strap or chain which is part of a certain type of horse's bit. It can also apply to the paved edging of a pavement or footpath, though in Britain (not the United States) for this meaning *kerb* is the usual spelling. *Kerb* is also applied to the framework round the top of a well and the fender of a hearth.

Czech, Czechoslovak A *Czech* is a Bohemian and a member of the most westerly branch of the Slavs comprising Bohemians, Moravians and Slovaks. A *Czechoslovak* is a citizen of Czechoslovakia and the word *Czechoslovak* embraces Bohemians, Moravians and Slovaks. *Czech* is, however, used loosely to cover all three groups.

D

-d-, -dd- Single-syllable words ending in *d* double it before suffixes beginning with a vowel if the *d* is preceded by a single short vowel:

bedding, laddie, sadden, maddest.

If, however, it is preceded by two vowels, an *n* or an *r* the *d* is not doubled:

feeding, guarded, loaded, moody, spending.

Words of more than one syllable behave in the same way as single-syllable words if their last syllable is stressed and is preceded by a single short vowel:

embedded, hagridden.

They do not double the *d* otherwise:

impending, rapidity, defended, avoidance.

dangling modifier see **unattached participle**

dare This is a verb with some peculiarities in its use. When it means 'to have the necessary courage or boldness' it has *dare* instead of *dares* as the third person singular in negative and interrogative sentences and also in sentences where the infinitive dependent upon *dare* is not preceded by *to* (although such sentences are usually either negative or interrogative):

He dare not go. How dare she say such a thing?

When *dare* means 'to challenge or provoke to action' the third person singular is *dares* and any dependent infinitive is preceded by *to*:

He dares me to confess everything to my father.

dare say This is usually written as two words and is nowadays almost invariably used only in the first person singular and the present tense.

dash It is advisable to use the dash with great caution. It is too often employed when some other kind of punctuation might have served the purpose much better. The dash can, however, be used legitimately, if sparingly, as follows.

Two dashes in a sentence show that the words enclosed between them are to be read parenthetically, separated off from the rest of the sentence:

His third novel – his last as it turned out – was a failure.

The dash is used in a sentence to explain or expand what immediately precedes it:

These were his greatest achievements – the founding of a successful company, the bringing of prosperity to a depressed region, and the establishment of a better relationship between management and workers.

The dash is used to add a final summing up to a sentence or to gather up the loose ends of a long sentence:

The resources of the Western world, its technological expertise, its capacity for long-term planning, the energy and dynamism of its leaders, its ability to adapt to changing circumstances – all these are at our disposal.

The dash is used to show a change of subject or to indicate that a sentence begun is to remain unfinished:

When he arrived home – but I'd better tell you what happened to his sister first.

data This is a Latin plural and is generally used with a plural verb in English:

The data available are inadequate.

However, there is a growing tendency to consider *data* as a collective noun grouping together individual objects and to attach a singular verb to it:

The data he has accumulated is sufficient for our purposes.

dates It is better to print dates in the sequence day – month – year, i.e., 15 July 1971, 19 December 1861, without commas and omitting *st*, *nd*, *rd* and *th* unless the day is given without the month:

Payment is due on the 10th of each month.
He arrived on 15 May and left on the 20th.

Note that if the sequence month – day – year is used the *st*, *nd*, *rd* or *th* should be included:

December 2nd 1959, October 23rd 1965.

When months have to be abbreviated, as for example in tables, use the following forms:

Jan., Feb., Aug., Sept., Oct., Nov., Dec.

Do not abbreviate March, April, May, June or July unless absolutely necessary for reasons of space.

The apostrophe is omitted in expressions such as 'the 1940s'.

For centuries and millenniums it is better to spell out the numbers:

The eighth century, the fourth millennium, the seventeenth century.

If consecutive four-figure dates fall within the same century the first two figures of the second date are usually omitted:

1820–25, 1914–18, 1730–1840.

Note: 'from 1940 to 1949' or 'during 1940–49' but not 'from 1940–49'.

When using *B.C.* remember that this always follows the figures:

500 B.C., 44 B.C.

A.D. always precedes the figures but it should be used only after one or more *B.C.* dates or to avoid ambiguity:

From 55 B.C. to A.D. 40.

de-, dis- These prefixes, which have a negative or privative force, are put at the beginning of words to create new ones with the opposite meaning. Many authorities have deplored the appearance of such words as *deactivate*, *derestrict*, *disincentive* and *disinflation*, but there is no doubt that they are capable of expressing precise shades of meaning which no other words can convey. The popularity of these prefixes does lead to some rather ugly formations, which, it must be hoped, will disappear in the course of time.

deal Although *a deal of* in the sense of 'a large amount' has been current English for over 200 years it is still considered a colloquialism by most authorities. It is better to say *a good deal* or *a great deal.*

debar, disbar There is some similarity in meaning between these two words, but in practice they are used quite differently. *Debar* means to exclude, prevent or prohibit (an action):

The committee decided to debar from the club all members who had not paid their subscriptions.

Disbar is much more specific in its application, and means to expel from the legal profession or from the bar:

Solicitors found guilty of corrupt practices were disbarred.

decided, decisive It is still possible, although increasingly difficult, to preserve a useful distinction between these two words. *Decided* means 'unquestionable, unmistakeable, resolute or determined':

There is a decided air of importance about him.
The new manager has a very decided manner.

Decisive means 'conclusive, bringing to an end' and is commonly used in phrases like *a decisive battle.* It is, however, beginning to encroach upon the meanings of *decided* in such expressions as *a decisive character.*

decimate This originally meant 'to kill one person in every ten' but has now been extended to cover the destruction in large numbers of people, animals and even crops. It should not, however, be used to mean the complete extermination of anything.

deduce see **adduce**

defective, deficient *Defective* means 'having a defect, faulty or imperfect':

Several parts of the machine were defective.

Deficient is 'lacking in some element or characteristic, insufficient or inadequate' and, although its meaning approaches that of *defective*, it is generally possible to keep the two words distinct:

Their accommodation at the hotel was deficient in every respect.

defensible, defensive *Defensible* means 'capable of being protected or defended, justifiable, or capable of being defended in argument':

Their actions were considered defensible in view of the gravity of the situation.

Defensive means 'serving to defend or protect':

They built a defensive barrier around the camp.

definite, definitive These words are easily confused. *Definite* means 'clearly defined, precise or exact':

They were awaiting a definite reply to their question.

Definitive means 'conclusive or final':

Their offer is a definitive one and must be either accepted or rejected.

deism, theism The difference between these two words is that *deism* means belief in God based on the evidence of reason alone. *Theism* means belief in God which includes supernatural revelation.

delusion, illusion A *delusion* is a mistaken belief that something really exists and cannot be removed by an appeal to reason:

She suffered from the delusion that all her food was poisoned.

An *illusion* is a false mental image which may result from a misinterpretation of something real or from something imagined:

He was under the illusion that he was really quite popular.

demi-, semi- Both prefixes, which are Latin in origin, mean 'half', but *demi-* is found in only a handful of words such as *demigod*, *demijohn* and *demilune*. *Semi-* is much more common and is often used in the formation of new words.

denote see **connote**

depend This verb is normally followed by *on* or *upon*:

Children depend on their parents for support.

However, in colloquial speech and despite the opposition of some eminent authorities *depend* is frequently used without *on* or *upon*, provided it is preceded by *it*:

It depends what you mean by free speech.

dependant, dependent In English usage the noun, meaning 'someone who relies on others for support', ends in *-ant*. The adjective form 'relying on others for support, subordinate or subject to' ends in *-ent*. In American usage *dependent* serves as both noun and adjective.

depositary, depository A *depositary* is a person to whom something is given in trust. A *depository* is a place where something is stored for safekeeping.

deprecate, depreciate These verbs and their derivatives are quite frequently confused. *Deprecate* means 'to express disapproval of or protest against':

They strongly deprecated the use of force to settle the argument.

Depreciate means 'to reduce the value of, belittle' or 'to decline in value':

His shares have depreciated considerably since the stock market crisis.

derisive, derisory These two adjectives can be used interchangeably, but it is possible to make a distinction between them. Both have the sense of 'ridiculing, mocking, or expressing derision', but *derisory* has acquired the additional meaning of 'worthy of derision, causing derision, worthless or insignificant':

The management's offer was considered derisory by the union negotiators.

despatch see **dispatch**

devotee see **addict**

dialectal, dialectic, dialectical *Dialectal* means 'pertaining to or characteristic of a dialect'. *Dialectic* as a noun means 'logical discussion or argumentation', and its adjective can be either *dialectic* or *dialectical.*

dialogue, duologue A *dialogue* is a conversation between two or more people. A *duologue* is a conversation between two people only, especially as part of a dramatic performance.

dieresis This means the separate pronunciation of two adjacent vowels in a word and the term is also applied to the sign placed over them to indicate this separate pronunciation. It is rarely found in English, but is sometimes used in such words as *naïve* and *coöperate*, as well as in a few personal names like *Chloë.*

different There has long been much controversy over which preposition should follow *different*: *to* or *from*. All that can really be said on the subject is that *different from* is the established usage, but that *different to* is quite acceptable. *Different* is also occasionally found followed by *than*, but this particular construction is not to be recommended.

differentiate, distinguish The uses of these two verbs are very similar but not identical. *Differentiate* means to point out precisely and in some detail the differences between two things:

> It is difficult to differentiate between one insect and another when they have so many attributes in common.

Distinguish means to recognize the characteristic features that mark out something as different, but without going into specific details:

> It's not difficult to distinguish between a traffic warden and a policeman.

digraph, diphthong A *digraph* is a pair of letters which combine to represent a single speech sound such as *ch* in *chop* or *ea* in *seat*. *Diphthong* is a term used to describe a composite vowel sound made up of two single vowel sounds as *ei* in *rein* and *ou* in *loud*.

dilemma Its growing popularity has given this word an extension to its original meaning. It is better not to treat it as a synonym for *problem* or *difficulty*, but to restrict its use to describing a situation in which there is a choice between equally undesirable alternatives.

diminish, minimize *Diminish* means 'to make smaller, lessen, reduce, or decrease':

The use of drugs can help to diminish pain.

Minimize means 'to reduce to the smallest possible amount, belittle or underestimate':

Try not to minimize the risks of riding a motor-cycle.

diphthong see **digraph**

direct, directly It is better to keep the meanings of these two words separate when they are used as adverbs in order to avoid misunderstanding, although they tend to be interchangeable. Use *direct* to mean 'straight', 'without any detours':

It told him to go direct to the airport.

Use *directly* to mean 'at once' or 'immediately':

He promised he would be there directly.

Directly is also used as a conjunction meaning 'as soon as'.

discomfit, discomfort *Discomfit* is sometimes used mistakenly for *discomfort*. However, there is really no connection between the two words. *Discomfit*, which is now rather rare, means 'to defeat utterly or rout, frustrate or thwart'.

discreet, discrete Although these two adjectives are far apart in meaning their identical pronunciation and almost identical spelling can be the source of some confusion. *Discreet* means 'prudent, circumspect or cautious'. *Discrete* means 'detached from others, separate, or distinct'.

disinterested, uninterested The confusion between these two words is now so complete that it is difficult to keep them separate. *Disinterested* means 'impartial' or 'not influenced by personal motives':

The committee issued a disinterested report, for they prided themselves on their impartiality.

Uninterested means 'having no interest in':

The students were completely uninterested in what the lecturer had to say to them.

Disinterested is so frequently used by people who ought to know better to mean *uninterested* that those who are trying to preserve a useful distinction in meaning may feel that their task is a pretty hopeless one.

dispatch, despatch The form *dispatch* is still preferred to *despatch* when used as a noun or a verb.

dispersal, dispersion These two words are frequently used interchangeably but it is possible to distinguish between them. *Dispersal* means 'the act of scattering or dispersing':

The dispersal of the mob was possible only after the arrival of police reinforcements.

Dispersion means 'the state of being dispersed' and refers to the condition after the dispersal has taken place:

The widespread dispersion of the mob made it difficult for them to reassemble.

disposal, disposition Although some of the various meanings of these two words are quite distinct, there is some possibility of confusion. *Disposal* has the basic idea of getting rid of something by removing it from one place to another:

The disposal of the refugees was soon completed.

Disposition conveys rather the sense of placing or arranging according to a plan worked out beforehand:

The disposition of the property under the terms of the will.

dissimulate, simulate *Dissimulate* means 'to hide or conceal (something which one has)':

He dissimulated his fear with a show of bravado.

Simulate means 'to make a pretence of having (something which one has not)':

She simulated distress by pretending to cry.

dissociate This verb and its noun *dissociation* are now almost invariably preferred to the alternative forms *disassociate* and *disassociation*.

distinct, distinctive These adjectives are similar in meaning and the one is sometimes wrongly used for the other. *Distinct* means 'definite, unmistakeable, clear to the senses':

There was a distinct smell of gas in the bedroom.

Distinctive means 'characteristic, individual or distinguishing':

The distinctive cry of a hungry baby.

distrust, mistrust These verbs are frequently used interchangeably in the sense of 'to regard with doubt or suspicion' but *distrust* generally implies a much stronger degree of feeling than *mistrust*.

divers, diverse These were originally the same word but have now acquired quite separate meanings. *Divers*, which is rarely used except facetiously, means 'several' or 'sundry'. *Diverse* means 'of a different kind or of various kinds'.

do Apart from its basic meaning of performing an action, *do* is employed in several ways as an auxiliary verb.

It is used to avoid repeating another verb:

He came along past the church, as he did every morning.

In this instance *did* avoids the repetition of *came*, but care must be taken with *do* as a substitute verb. It cannot be used, for instance, to represent the verb *to be* or a verb in a compound tense:

She has read the same books as I have done.

Either substitute *read* for *done* or (better) delete *done*.

Anyone who has been here for twenty years as I have done.

Again either substitute *been* for *done* or delete *done*.

Do is also used to form the interrogative in direct questions:

Did you know he was lying? Do they expect her now?

Do is used in negative sentences with *not*.

I did not know you were here. She doesn't realize what has happened.

Finally *do* is used for emphasis:

I do know what you mean. Do please tell me at once.

donate This is a back formation from *donation*, which has achieved a certain popularity despite the disapproval of some authorities. In most cases it is better to use a simple word like *give*.

double comparatives and superlatives These may still be heard in the conversation of uneducated people, but despite the fact that Shakespeare made effective use of them, they are no longer acceptable English. Do not say *more easier* or *most sharpest*.

double entendre This is the accepted English form of the French *double entente* and has been for three hundred years. Attempts to establish the correct French form have so far proved futile.

double negatives English usage generally frowns upon double negatives, although in the past both Chaucer and Shakespeare used them to enrich the language of their poetry and plays. Expressions like *I never did nothing wrong* are not acceptable, but some double negatives do find their way into the speech of even educated people, especially in sentences like the following:

I shouldn't be surprised if it didn't rain.

Care must be taken to avoid double negatives with *scarcely* and *hardly*, in which the negative force is disguised:

It was impossible to believe hardly anything he said.

doubt The verb *doubt* is followed by *whether* or *if* when it forms part of a positive statement:

I doubt if he will accept. They doubt whether he will come.

When the statement is negative or forms a question, *doubt* is followed by *that*:

I do not doubt that he is right. Do you doubt that they can do it?

doubtful Like *doubt* the adjective *doubtful* is followed by *whether* or *if* when it forms part of a positive statement. When the statement is negative or forms a question it is followed by *that*:

We are not in the least doubtful that we shall succeed.

dower, dowry Originally the same word, *dower* and *dowry* have quite distinct meanings. *Dower* is the portion of a deceased husband's property allowed by law to his widow for life. *Dowry* is the money and goods brought by a woman to her husband on marriage.

draft, draught Both words have their origins in the verb *draw*, *draft* being a phonetic spelling of *draught*. In English usage *draft* can mean 'a drawing or sketch, a preliminary form of something written, a sum of money drawn on a bank'. *Draught* is 'a current of air, a drink, a team of animals used to pull a load'. In the United States *draft* is more widely used and covers some of the meanings listed under English *draught*.

drunk, drunken It is quite difficult to establish a rigid dividing line between the use of these two words. *Drunk* as an adjective is usually placed after the verb as in *he was drunk* but is now frequently found before the noun:

The street was littered with drunk soldiers.

Drunken is normally placed before the noun, as in *drunken dissipation*. One useful distinction is that *drunken* generally describes a permanent or habitual state and when used thus can be placed after the verb:

He was drunken in his habits.

Drunk usually refers to a temporary state as in *drunk and disorderly*.

dry When suffixes are added to this word the usual forms are *drier*, *driest*, *drying*, *drily* or *dryly*. *Dryer*, rather than *drier*, is now more common when referring to a machine for drying things.

due to This is not really an acceptable substitute for adverbial phrases like *owing to* or *because of*. *Due* is an adjective and should accompany a noun. The two following examples are correct:

His death was due to cancer. Errors due to carelessness are all too frequent.

The following example is incorrect:

Due to cancer he was unable to walk.

Unfortunately, the incorrect use of *due to* is rapidly establishing itself in English with the connivance of such official bodies as British Rail or the B.B.C.:

Due to adverse weather conditions ... Due to a technical fault ...

E

each When *each* is the subject of a sentence, either as a pronoun or as an adjective accompanying a noun, it takes a singular verb:

Each has got to pay his share.
Each child receives the same food.

When used as a pronoun with an antecedent it can be either singular or plural. If the antecedent is plural *each* is plural:

The soldiers each have a meal in the canteen.
We each take a small part in the play.

each other, one another Usage now appears to have discarded the rule that *each other* should be used when only two people are involved, *one another* being reserved for three or more. Thus the following is quite acceptable:

The six prisoners were told to help each other with their work.

Each other is treated as a compound word and may be used as the object or indirect object of a verb or preposition:

They dislike each other.
The children sent books to each other.

When the possessive case is used, the form is *each other's* not *each others'*:

They take in each other's washing.

However, the phrase cannot be used in combination when *other* is itself the subject of a verb:

They each knew what the other liked,

not:

They knew what each other liked.

earthen, earthly, earthy *Earthen* means 'composed of earth or of baked clay':

The archaeologists discovered earthen pots from the second millennium B.C.

Earthly means 'pertaining to earth, especially as opposed to heaven':

Not everyone considers this world to be an earthly paradise.

Earthy means 'of the nature of earth, worldly, coarse or unrefined':

His earthy views on the subject embarrassed his sophisticated guests.

easterly *Easterly* is most commonly used of winds in the sense of 'coming from the east'. It can, however, be used to mean 'situated towards the east', but implies previous movement in that direction:

The most easterly outpost of Roman civilization.

In other cases the usual adjectives are *east* or *eastern.*

easy, easily *Easily* is now the normal form of the adverb. *Easy* as an adverb is found in only a few phrases like *to go easy* and *take it easy.*

eatable, edible The main distinction between these two words is that *edible* refers to anything which may normally be eaten, as *an edible plant. Eatable* is used of something which is agreeable to the taste, although *edible* would not be wrong in this context:

The burnt porridge was barely eatable.

echelon This is another word whose growing popularity has led to an extension of its original meaning. It is used now to mean 'a level of command or organization' although its proper sense is 'a step-like or staggered formation of troops'.

economic, economical Economic means 'pertaining to economics or reasonably profitable, offering an adequate return': *economic laws, an economic rent. Economical* means 'avoiding waste or extravagance, thrifty':

Economical ways of budgeting household expenditure.

-ed verb endings see **-t and -ed verb endings**

educational, educative Both adjectives can be used virtually interchangeably, but *educational* is the more common and is applied to education generally: *an educational organization*, *an educational tour*. *Educative* tends to have a more restricted sense of 'serving to educate': *an educative work*.

effective, effectual, efficacious, efficient All these adjectives have similar meanings and all can have the sense of 'capable of producing an effect', but care must be taken to distinguish between them.

Effective means having the power to produce or producing an effect or bringing about a desired result:

At last effective measures are being taken to reduce the crime rate.

Effectual stresses that which actually produces the desired effect:

His conciliatory speech was effectual in ending the tension.

Efficacious means capable of achieving a certain aim and is applied particularly to remedies, treatments, etc.:

Modern drugs are much more efficacious in their treatment of illness.

Efficient refers to the expert use of knowledge, resources etc., to achieve results:

Really efficient managers are hard to find.

e.g., i.e. *E.g.* is a Latin abbreviation meaning 'for example'. It is often confused with *i.e.*, which means 'that is to say', and is used when what follows is an alternative way of saying what went before. The sentences show the correct use of both words:

There were several subjects for discussion, *e.g.* staff holidays, the works canteen, the annual outing.
The man was a palaeontologist, *i.e.* he studied forms of life which existed in previous geological periods.

egoism, egotism Both words are concerned with preoccupation with oneself. *Egoism*, the less common word, means the valuing of everything in accordance with one's own interests and the emphasizing of the importance of the self in relation to other things:

He considered his own egoism to be a philosophical doctrine.

Egotism is boastfulness and self-importance which implies disregard for other's opinions and feelings:

Her egotism angered even her friends.

either *Either* means 'one or other of two' and consequently cannot be used if more than two persons, groups or things are referred to, when it should be replaced by *any*:

either of the twins *but* any of the three boys.

Either is always followed by a singular verb:

Either of the girls has the right to leave.

either . . . or In phrases of this sort the *either* is frequently put in the wrong position. In the following sentence, for example, the *either* is misplaced:

They must either apologize or suffer the consequences.

Since *They must* forms part of the alternative offered by *either* the two words must be placed after it:

Either they must apologize or suffer the consequences.

This misplacement of *either* is common in conversation but should be avoided in writing.

The verb used with *either . . . or* should be singular if there are two singular subjects and plural if both the subjects are plural. However, if one of the subjects is in the singular and the other in the plural, the verb may agree with the nearest subject, but it is better to phrase the sentence so that the plural noun is nearest the verb, which will then be in the plural:

Either the boy or his brother has the book.
Either the mother or her children have to be present.

eke out The proper meaning of to *eke out* is to make something, of which there is only a small amount, go further by adding to it:

They eked out their scanty supply of food with other people's leftovers.

However, *eke out* has acquired an extension of meaning in the sense of 'to contrive to make' in such phrases as *to eke out a living*. This is deplored by some authorities, but seems to have established itself as acceptable usage.

elder, older The comparative adjective *elder* and its superlative form *eldest* are now used almost exclusively to denote priority of birth in a family: *my elder brother*, *my eldest sister*. *Elder* can also be employed as a noun to mean an older person, and survives in the phrase *elder statesman*. Otherwise, *older* and *oldest*, the normal comparative and superlative forms of *old*, are used to indicate someone or something of greater age.

elemental, elementary Although there is some slight overlapping between these two words, they are usually quite distinct in meaning. *Elemental* refers to the power, forces or phenomena of physical nature, especially the four elements of earth, water, air and fire:

The elemental violence of a thunderstorm.

Elementary means 'pertaining to rudiments or first principles':

The teaching of elementary arithmetic in schools.

elision This is the omission of a vowel, consonant or syllable in writing or pronunciation. It is most frequently found with pronouns, auxiliary verbs and in negative expressions:

I'm, let's, don't, they're, you've, shan't.

ellipsis *Ellipsis* is the omission from a sentence of a word or words which would complete the construction or clarify the sense. In the sentence:

The factory was shut and the workers dismissed,

the word *were* is omitted before *dismissed* but can be easily supplied from the context. Some authorities advise against the omission of any verbs necessary for completeness or clarity. The sentence:

Jane is beautiful but her friends ugly

is unacceptable on the grounds that the verb to be supplied after *friends* (*are*) is not the same as the one in the first clause (*is*). However, most authorities would agree on the necessity of not using a single form of the verb to be to do duty as both main verb and auxiliary verb:

The soldiers were in rags and spurned by the crowd.

The *were* omitted before *spurned* is an auxiliary verb and differs from its use as a main verb after soldiers. It should not, therefore, be left out.

Care must be taken over the omission of subordinate conjunctions like *that*, or relative pronouns like *who* and *which*, before dependent clauses. If there is any possibility of ambiguity or even clumsiness the conjunction or pronoun should be retained. The sentence:

Everybody realized he was a liar

is quite acceptable, but:

His decision was they should go ahead immediately

would read better with *that* inserted after *was*.

When using a verb with more than one auxiliary verb be sure that the auxiliary is repeated if necessary:

He can and will work

is quite correct, but:

The remedy which they can and are applying

must be rephrased as:

The remedy which they can apply and are applying.

else It is still sometimes considered an error to use *but* instead of *than* after *else*, so that the phrase *nothing else but a full-scale enquiry* should be *nothing else than a full-scale enquiry*. However, *nothing else but* seems well established in popular usage. The possessive forms are *anybody else's*, *somebody else's*, but when *else* is used with *who* there is some hesitation between *whose else* and *who else's*, although the latter form is now far more common.

elusive, illusory The meanings of these two adjectives are sometimes confused. *Elusive* means 'hard to grasp, express or define', and has the alternative form *elusory*:

Her poetry had an elusive quality about it.

Illusory means 'of the nature of an illusion, deceptive or unreal':

His apparent success in his job was proved illusory when he was forced to resign.

emend see **amend**

emigrant, immigrant An *emigrant* is one who leaves his own country in order to settle in another. An *immigrant* is one who arrives from another country. Thus an *emigrant* and an *immigrant* may be the same person seen at a different stage on his or her journey or from a different point of view.

emotive, emotional Both words can be used to mean 'exciting emotion' or 'appealing to the emotions'. However, in practice a sharp distinction is made between them. *Emotive* is restricted to 'causing emotion' and *emotional* to 'being affected by or expressing emotion'.

endemic, epidemic, pandemic *Endemic* applies to a disease which is peculiar to a particular people or locality. An *epidemic* disease is one which affects a large number of people in a locality, but is not permanently prevalent there. A *pandemic* disease is one which is prevalent throughout an entire region, such as a country or continent.

endorse Some authorities deplore the fact that *endorse* is now used to mean 'to express approval of', notably in the domain of advertising, but this sense does seem to have established itself and is recorded in the more modern dictionaries.

England, English These words are very rarely interchangeable with *(Great) Britain* and *British*, and doubts about their correct use are frequently a source of error and confusion. For English people *England* and *English* have a strong emotional appeal, similar to the feelings aroused in other part of the British Isles by *Scotland* and *Scots*, or *Wales* and *Welsh*. The majority of Englishmen, Welshmen and Scotsman prefer to be called this rather than the collective *Britons*. Moreover, *English* must be used when referring to *English* history and *English* literature. *England* has a patriotic ring to it and Englishmen use it on appropriate occasions even when they may actually be referring to the whole of Great Britain. [See also *British*]

enhance Care must be taken in the use of this verb. It cannot have a person as a direct object in the active form or as a subject in the passive form:

Success has enhanced his prestige

or:

His prestige has been enhanced by his success

are both correct. But one cannot say:

Success has enhanced him

or:

He has been enhanced by success.

enough, sufficient Both words mean 'adequate or equal to what is required'. *Enough* is a more flexible word and can be used as a noun, adjective or adverb, whereas *sufficient* is only an adjective. However, *enough* has its limitations as an adjective. We can say *a sufficient quantity* but not *an enough quantity*. Despite this, *enough* remains the more natural word on most occasions, and *sufficient* may sometimes appear as an over-refined alternative:

Do you have enough money?

is still preferable to:

Do you have sufficient money?

enquire, inquire The spelling *enquire* is now the more normal one in the sense of 'to seek information by questioning, to ask'. However, *inquire into* has the additional meaning of 'to investigate', which provides a useful distinction between these two verbs.

ensure see **assure**

envelop, envelope *Envelop* is the verb and *envelope* (with an extra *e*) is the noun.

epic This is a poetic composition in which a series of heroic events are dealt with as a continuous narrative in an elevated style. By extension it has been applied to a film or novel resembling an epic, and now is used loosely of any play, film or event which is in any way out of the ordinary.

epidemic see **endemic**

epigram This is a witty and pointed saying briefly expressed. The term is also applied to a short poem dealing with a single subject and usually ending with an amusing or ingenious turn of thought.

epigraph, epitaph An *epigraph* is an inscription, especially one on a public building. An *epitaph* is a commemorative inscription on a tomb.

epithet The original meaning is an adjective or other term applied to a person or thing in order to express an attribute. In 'Richard the Lion-Heart', 'Lion Heart' is an *epithet*. The word *epithet* has unfortunately now become a synonym for a term of abuse, which has tended to overshadow its original sense.

equable, equitable These adjectives may be a source of confusion since their meanings are in some respects quite close.

Equable means 'free from variations, uniform', 'tranquil, not easily disturbed': *an equable temperament, an equable climate. Equitable* means 'just and right, fair, reasonable': *an equitable decision.* It also refers to equity as opposed to common law.

equally A frequent mistake is to insert an unnecessary *as* after *equally*. One can say:

Her work was equally good

or:

Her work was as good,

but not:

Her work was equally as good.

Where there is a comparison *as* must stand alone and *equally* can neither accompany it nor replace it:

Good health is as (not *equally* as) important as good pay.

-er, -or The ending *-er* can be added to English verbs to denote one who does (something):

teacher, singer, fighter, buyer, winner.

The Latin ending *-or*, which has the same function as *-er*, tends to be added to verbs which are formed from Latin stems:

actor, confessor, creditor, protector.

Some words of Latin origin, however, end in *-er*:

deserter, dispenser, digester.

Other words can end in either *-er* or *-or*, sometimes with a slightly different meaning:

adapter, adaptor; conjurer, conjuror; resister, resistor.

eruption, irruption An *eruption* is 'a sudden and violent issuing forth, an outburst or a breaking out (of a rash, etc)'. An *irruption* is 'a breaking in', 'a violent incursion or invasion'.

escalate This now very popular verb was formed from the noun *escalator*. It means 'to increase in intensity or magnitude', and although it was not really an essential addition to the English language it appears to have established a firm position.

especially, specially The similarity in spelling and meaning of these adverbs has led to some doubt about their correct use. *Especially* means 'to an exceptional degree' and singles out what is prominent or pre-eminent:

The winter was especially severe that year.

Specially means 'for a specific purpose' or 'to a particular end':

This dress was made specially for her.

The distinction can no longer be observed in the adjectives, *especial* and *special*, since *special* is rapidly displacing *especial*, and even *especially* is losing ground to *specially*.

essay see **assay**

essential, necessary Both words apply to something which is indispensable for the fulfilment of a need. *Essential*, which is a much stronger word, means an absolutely vital condition:

Air is essential to mammals.

Necessary refers to that which is determined by natural laws or results inevitably from certain causes:

Food is necessary to life.

etc. This useful word, an abbreviation for the Latin *et cetera*, meaning 'and others', 'and so forth', is used to indicate that others of the same kind might have been mentioned but for shortage of space:

cats, dogs, horses, sheep, etc.

Etc. is usually preceded by a comma unless only one item has been mentioned before it. It is best not to use it in writing of a formal or literary kind.

ethic, ethical Both adjectives mean 'pertaining to or dealing with morals', but *ethical* is now the more common form, *ethic* being almost exclusively confined to grammar in the *ethic dative*, which refers to a person indirectly interested. In *shoot me a bird* 'me' is an ethic dative.

ethics, morals Both words are concerned with right and wrong and rules of conduct, but their various senses are distinct. *Ethics* is used to mean a system of moral principles, whereas *morals* are concerned with right and wrong in practice.

Ethics is also applied to standards of conduct and behaviour in business:

The ethics of the legal profession.

Morals refer to generally accepted standards of conduct in a society:

The morals of Western civilization.

Morals is also used especially to refer to behaviour in sexual matters. The distinction of meaning holds true for the adjectives *ethical* and *moral*, although here the differences are more blurred. [See also *amoral*]

euphemism, euphuism Although similar in spelling, these two words are entirely different in meaning. *Euphemism* is the substitution of a mild, inoffensive or indirect expression for a blunt one, such as 'mental disorder' for 'insanity' or 'pass away' for 'die'. *Euphuism*, a much rarer word, means an affected, artificial or ornate style of writing or speaking.

evasion, evasiveness *Evasion* means 'the act or practice of escaping something by trickery, an excuse, subterfuge':

An evasion of responsibilities.

Evasiveness is the quality of being evasive:

The evasiveness of his replies aroused our suspicions.

even The correct placing of the adverb *even* in a sentence is very important.

She did not ring on Tuesday

can yield four different meanings with the use of *even*:

Even she did not ring me on Tuesday (she was the most likely to do so).

She did not even ring me on Tuesday (this was the thing she was most likely to do).

She did not ring even me on Tuesday (I was the person she was most likely to ring).
She did not ring me even on Tuesday (this was the day on which she was most likely to ring).

eventuate It is better not to use this rather pompous word when a simpler one will do. *Take place*, *occur*, *happen*, and *come about* are all preferable.

-ever, ever The suffix *-ever* may be added to the words *who*, *which*, *what*, *where* and *how*, which are then written as one word: *whoever*, *whatever*:

Whatever you do try to be home early.

But when *ever* is used for emphasis after interrogative pronouns and adverbs, such as *who*? and *why*? it remains a separate word:

Who ever said that? Why ever didn't you tell me?

every day, everyday *Every day* is an adverbial phrase of time:

He goes to school every day.

everyday is an adjective:

An everyday occurrence, my everyday clothes.

every one, everyone, everybody When the meaning is 'every single one' with the stress on the separateness use the two words *every one*:

He spoke to all those present in the room and every one of them replied.

Every one is also used when referring to inanimate objects:

He wrote ten novels and every one of them was a best seller.

Everyone, when it refers to people who are not singled out, and *everybody* are written as one word. Like *every one* they are followed by a singular verb:

Everyone was cheering, everybody was shouting.

However, these words are in many ways felt to be plural. Although the following is recommended when a pronoun is involved:

Everyone is doing his best,

their best is frequently found, and in the sentence:

Everyone is doing their best, aren't they?

their best seems unavoidable.

evolve The basic meaning is 'to develop gradually by a natural process'. Popular usage has, however, made *evolve* a synonym for such words as *change*, *develop*, *plan* or *devise*, all of which are usually preferable.

except see **accept**

except, excepting *Except* is a preposition and is followed by a noun, pronoun or adverbial phrase:

Except the latecomers, except me, except in the north.

Excepting means the same as *except* and is used instead of it only after 'always', 'not' and 'without':

Not excepting the children, always excepting the pensioners.

exceptionable, exceptional *Exceptionable*, which is a much less common word than *exceptional*, means 'objectionable, open to objection', or 'to which exception may be taken':

We found his wild statements exceptionable.

Exceptional means 'unusual', 'extraordinary' or 'forming an exception':

He showed exceptional courage.

exclamation mark This is a punctuation mark (!) which is placed at the end of an interjection, an exclamatory word, or a phrase or sentence expressing strong emotion, or a wish:

Oh! Help! Heaven forbid! What a way to go! Don't be such a prude! If only we could!

The exclamation mark should be employed very sparingly if it is to be effective and it should not normally be used after an imperative:

Open your books. Shut the door.

Nor should it be used when a question mark is what is needed:

Why in heaven's name did you do that?

exhaustive, exhausting These adjectives are sometimes confused. *Exhaustive* means 'comprehensive', 'thorough':

He published an exhaustive study of Jane Austen.

Exhausting means 'using up or consuming fully', 'draining strength' or 'tiring out':

Digging coal is exhausting work.

explicit, implicit *Explicit* means 'clearly expressed', 'definite', or 'unequivocal':

He refused to do anything without explicit instructions.

Implicit means 'implied rather than openly stated', 'understood':

There was implicit consent in all his actions.

Implicit also means 'unreserved' or 'absolute':

He showed implicit faith in God.

extempore, impromptu Both words apply to something done without proper preparation in advance. *Extempore*, however, is generally used to describe a speech or performance unmemorized or delivered without notes: *an extempore lecture.*

Impromptu is applied to a speech or performance delivered without any preparation or notice:

Despite being called upon on the spur of the moment, he made an effective impromptu speech.

exterior, external These adjectives may be used in the same way but there are some important differences in usage. *Exterior* usually implies the existence of something similar or corresponding which is *interior* – an outer surface which has an inner surface:

The exterior decorations of the wall did not match the interior ones.

Exterior and *interior* can also be used as nouns.
External means 'belonging to the outside' and *internal* 'existing in the interior', but these words do not correspond to each other like *exterior* and *interior*. *External* can apply to things more remote and abstract than *exterior*, as in *the external world*, *external relations*, and, together with *internal*, can be used of medicines: *for external/internal use*.

F

facilitate To make a process less difficult or to help it forward. It is the action that is made easier, and not the one who carries it out who is assisted:

She moved her car to facilitate the parking of the lorry.

facility, faculty *Facility* is ease, advantage, freedom from difficulty, dexterity and also things that make a task easier:

She knitted her way through several sweaters with a facility born of long practice.

Faculty is an ability for a particular activity; an inherent capability of the body, or one of the powers of the mind such as reason, speech or memory:

He had a faculty for languages that was of great assistance in his travels.

factitious, fictitious *Factitious* is artificial, not spontaneous or natural, manufactured. *Fictitious* is counterfeit or false, created by the imagination; in reality, it may not exist at all. It is applied more often to a mental concept than a practical object, especially to products of the imagination.

factitive A grammatical term describing verbs such as 'make', 'render', 'consider', which take the complement of a noun or adjective in addition to the usual object:

I make him angry.
He found me a home.

factor This word is often overworked and widely applied in contexts where a more specific term would be preferable. Its meaning, 'one of the elements that contribute to a given result or have a certain effect', is so generally applicable that it has come to be adopted for every contingency:

One of the factors that make him outstanding is his ability to compromise.

Features would be a better substitute.

A key factor in any industrial dispute is the quality of labour relations.

Element or *constituent* are possible alternatives.

Let me outline for you some of the factors that led to this situation.

Circumstances might be a more accurate word in this context.

fallacy A *fallacy* is a deceptive or misleading belief or false notion. It is not a falsehood, which implies a deliberate act of deception, and cannot be used in its place:

He told her he was not married, but this turned out to be a fallacy

is therefore incorrect.

falseness, falsity, falsehood Both *falseness* and *falsity* express an untruth, a statement of a fact that is erroneous, or incorrectness, but *falseness* also implies treachery and deception, especially in a personal sense. *Falsehood* is a lie, an untrue idea or belief, or a false statement:

When truth is opposed to falsehood, only those in whom falseness resides will refuse to recognize the falsity of their position.

false scent A sentence that can be misunderstood on first reading might be described as providing a 'false scent':

The situation is grave as these figures show only a hint of the true position.

On first sight 'the situation is grave as these figures show' seems to be the complete sentence, but 'only a hint of the true position' makes it clear that the verb 'show' is intended to apply to 'hint' and not to the main clause, 'the situation is grave'. The sentence has therefore to be read twice before the sense becomes obvious.

farce see **comedy**

Far East The countries of East and South East Asia including China, Japan, Korea, the Malay Archipelago and Indochina make up the area known as the Far East.

farther, further Though these words are often used indiscriminately, *farther* is usually applied to a greater distance or space:

The moon is farther away than I thought.

Further is generally used to indicate a greater extent, quantity or time; it also means 'moreover':

We are further committed to implement the decision by the New Year.

fatal, fateful *Fatal* is causing death, destruction or ruin; figuratively, it means of momentous importance, implying doom:

The fatal event took place on Thursday.

Fateful is also of momentous importance, or controlled by irresistible destiny, but although it may be synonymous with *fatal* it may also mean a happy event of great consequence, not necessarily one with a deadly outcome:

At last the fateful day arrived when she walked down the aisle on her father's arm.

feasible The dictionary definition is given as 'capable of being done, effected or accomplished'. In many senses it can therefore be equated with *possible*, but there is a tendency to use it in all senses of *possible*, and of *probable* too, beyond its true capacity:

It is quite feasible that the shares he inherited when he came of age are now worth double.

In this example *feasible* is incorrect; either *possible* or *probable* should be substituted. But in the next example the word is correctly used:

He was convinced that an attempt to overthrow the government by force would be feasible.

female, feminine, womanly *Female* is both a noun and an adjective describing the sex of a plant, animal or human being. *Feminine* is an adjective only, qualifying the condition of being female, and applied only to human beings. *Womanly* is used primarily in opposition to *manly*, indicating possession of qualities that are especially feminine or, sometimes in contrast to girlish, meaning mature.

feminine forms The usual English feminine of nouns of occupation is formed by adding *-ess*:

Host, hostess; actor, actress; warder, wardress.

These particular examples are well entrenched in the English language, but the modern tendency is to avoid such differentiation between the sexes wherever possible, in keeping with the trend towards sex equality. For some occupational words that previously took a feminine form the male form now does duty for both: *sculptor*, *instructor* and *editor* are examples of this group. With other nouns such as doctors or teachers the term 'woman' is simply added to differentiate between them when necessary: *woman doctor*, *woman teacher*, *woman lawyer*.

ferment, foment As a noun a *ferment* is an agent that causes fermentation; figuratively, it means agitation, excitement. The verb means to inflame, agitate or excite. *Foment* is a verb only, meaning to promote the growth or development of, or to instigate or foster, especially in the sense of discord and rebellion. It also means to apply hot water and medication to a body:

The army was in a state of ferment. Rebels had infiltrated their ranks, fomenting discontent.

festal, festive Both words mean 'pertaining to a feast or festival', but *festive* also implies merriment and gaiety, and has come to be associated with such common phrases as 'festive occasion'.

few As a noun *a few* means a small number, *the few*, the minority, and *few*, the adjective, means 'not many':

A few stragglers were left; of these, few were properly clad.
The remaining few had one blanket between them.

fewer, less *Fewer* is correct when referring to numbers, *less* when meaning an amount or bulk quantity:

There are fewer people here than usual,

but:

There is less money about this Christmas.

In the example:

There were large numbers of French and Germans staying at the resort but less British than last year,

the word should be *fewer*.

fictional, fictitious *Fictional* means something that occurs only in fiction, created from the imagination. *Fictitious* is untrue, counterfeit or false.

finical, finicky There is no difference in meaning. Both words are adjectives meaning excessively fastidious or too fussy, but *finical* is the more literary word and *finicky* more frequently used in colloquial speech.

flammable see **inflammable**

flaunt, flout *To flaunt* is to parade or display something conspicuously or boldly. *To flout* is to mock or scoff at, treat with disdain or contempt:

She flaunted her newly won independence by going out of her way to flout every school rule.

flautist, flutist Both words mean one who plays a flute. *Flutist*, though the older word, is now used chiefly in the United States. In Britain *flautist* is the more usual term.

fleshly, fleshy *Fleshly* is pertaining to the flesh or body, and is generally used in the sense of worldly or physical as distinct from spiritual:

Let us set aside all fleshly temptations and concentrate on spiritual matters.

Fleshy means plump, fat, or consisting of flesh:

He was of medium build with thinning hair and a thick-set, fleshy neck.

flotsam and jetsam The phrase *flotsam and jetsam* means the debris thrown out from a ship which either floats on the water (*flotsam*)or is cast up on shore (*jetsam*). Figuratively, it is also applied to the outcasts of society.

following This word is often too easily used as a formal substitute for 'after'. There can be justification for this only when the meaning is fairly closely related to the participle of the verb *to follow*, implying a consequence of an event, such as in:

Following the declaration of martial law, a curfew was imposed.

It has little excuse for appearing in a sentence such as:

Following the talk by Professor Smith, we come to the main item of the programme.

And in:

Following a hunt by police in the London suburbs, a man was arrested in Putney

a false scent (*q.v.*) is created by a curiously circular sentence.

for-, fore- If the meaning intended is 'before', 'in front' or 'superior', the prefix to choose is *fore-*, as in *foreword*, *forecast*, *foreman*. The prefix *for-* comes from an Old Scottish word meaning 'away', 'off', 'to the uttermost', and implies a negative, prohibitive force, as in *forbid*, *forget*, *forlorn* or *forfeit*.

forbear, forebear Both forms are used for the noun meaning 'ancestor', but as *forbear* is also a verb meaning to desist or refrain from, it seems preferable to retain the *e* form for the noun. This usually occurs in the plural:

His forebears were of noble birth.

forceful, forcible *Forceful* means full of force, powerful, vigorous and effective:

He has such a forceful personality he can persuade the committee to vote whichever way he pleases,

and:

He put up a forceful argument.

Forcible means having force, or effected by force or violence:

He gained forcible entry by breaking the window.

forego, forgo *Forego* means to go before, to precede; *forgo* is to do without, abstain or refrain from.

foreign words and phrases These may be divided into three categories: those words and phrases that through common usage have become completely assimilated to the English language, in many cases losing their foreign identity and accents, such as *role*, *omelette*, *concerto*; those that are familiar through daily use, but nevertheless retain their original characteristics, such as *café*, *soufflé*, *protégé*, *au revoir*, and those that may be less familiar but which are sometimes used in a literary context, often by people whose knowledge of the language may be limited. In these cases it is particularly important to ensure that there is full understanding of the meaning of a word or phrase and that they are spelt correctly, with all accents present.

Two examples of common errors are:

I knew exactly where I was – it was a case of *déja vu*.

The word is *déjà* and must be shown with both accents. And in:

Do come back with us for supper. It will just be an *alfresco* meal as we won't reach home till midnight.

Alfresco means 'in the fresh air'; it does not mean 'casual'. Unless they are in such frequent use that they are accepted as part of the English language, as in the first two categories mentioned above, foreign words and phrases are usually indicated in italics.

On the whole, those in the third category are best avoided. Even if you are able to skirt round the pitfalls, their use may place your reader at a disadvantage and might suggest a tendency to show off.

for ever, forever *For ever* should always be written as two words. In the United States, however, the single word is acceptable.

former, latter These are rather clumsy terms restricted to a straight choice between two nouns. It is preferable to use *first*, *second* or *third*, or the *last mentioned*, or, where possible, to rephrase the sentence so that they are unnecessary:

Of the two participants, Mr Ellis and Mr Jones, the former was the taller, the latter the fatter.

A better construction would be:

Of the two participants, Mr Ellis was the taller and Mr Jones the fatter.

forward, forwards These words are often interchangeable but where *forward* is acceptable in most contexts, especially in phrases of time, *forwards* is limited in application. *Forward* is therefore the more widely used word:

It is designed to travel both backwards and forwards

is an example where *forwards* still holds its own, in a sentence indicating movement in a specific direction. But:

In March we move the clocks forward to summer time

is a sentence in which *forwards* could not be substituted.

fragile, frail Both words mean easily broken, but *fragile* implies a brittleness which may be shattered, such as that of glass, while *frail* suggests an inherent weakness, and is used especially of people in a medical sense:

His health was very frail.

Frail can also be used in an abstract sense meaning moral weakness.

full stop The full stop is the most final of the punctuation marks, indicating the end of a complete sentence. It is also sometimes used in place of commas or semi-colons to break up long sentences, or for a deliberate stylistic effect:

He was not in the mood for cheering. Quite the contrary.

And:

The moon, its beams glinting on the water, provided sufficient light for him to see the other man's pale face, tense as he stooped over his sinister task. And then he struck.

In addition the full stop is used after abbreviations except where these end with the same letter as the full word, when in modern usage the punctuation mark may be dispensed with. For example, Doctor James Smith becomes Dr James Smith, but the Reverend John Doe should be abbreviated as Rev. John Doe.

funeral, funereal *Funeral* is a noun which may sometimes be used as a noun adjective, as in:

The funeral arrangements were made by his wife.

Funereal is an adjective meaning pertaining to funerals or anything mournful, gloomy or dismal which might be suggestive of them:

Why did you choose such funereal colours for the hall?

fused participle This is the joining of a noun with a participle to form a single composite subject:

Maggie wearing trousers is an indication that women's lib. is here to stay.

It is a construction frowned on by many purists, but there seems a case for it in certain circumstances in idiomatic English, as in the above example where it is obviously intended as a humorous observation.

G

-g-, -gg- If another syllable is added to words ending in *-g*, the *g* is doubled when a single short vowel precedes it:

Bagged, jogging, bigger.

In most words where the *g* is preceded by a long vowel sound it is also followed by *e* or *ue*, as in *plague*, *league* or *rage*, in which case the *g* is not doubled.

Gallic, Gaelic *Gallic* is pertaining to the French, from Gaul, the ancient name of the region. *Gaelic* is the Celtic language of ancient Ireland and Scotland. As an adjective it means of or pertaining to the Gaels or their language.

Gallicisms The custom of using words of French origin in an anglicized form, or using an English word with an extended meaning borrowed from its French counterpart. [See also *foreign words and phrases*]

gaol, jail Both words mean a prison. Although in Britain both are equally acceptable and *gaol* is still in official use, *jail* is now the more common form. It is the normal spelling in the United States.

gap A term often used in journalism when describing a wide divergence, a rift or discrepancy. There is nothing wrong with this except when it is forgotten that a *gap* can only widen or narrow; it cannot expand or fall:

The gap in our understanding can be easily bridged by closer co-operation

is fine – it is an appropriate metaphor.

The gap between them was aggravated by pettifogging bureaucracy

is not. Aggravation is hardly a quality that can be ascribed to a *gap*.

gender A grammatical term of classification distinguishing the masculine, feminine and neuter categories.

genitive case A grammatical term meaning the possessive case. It can be expressed with *of* or with the use of an apostrophe *s*:

the tail of the dog, the dog's tail.

In general, the apostrophe *s* is confined to people or animals. With inanimate objects the *of* construction is customary, though many objects may take either form:

The car's headlights were bright

is as acceptable in colloquial speech as:

The headlights of the car were bright.

The post-genitive case means phrases such as:

A cousin of my wife's, a book of my father's, a friend of yours,

the last of which illustrates the use of the possessive pronoun. These do not take the apostrophe.

Your friend means a specific person. *A friend of yours* could mean any friend. [See also *apostrophe*]

genius, geniuses, genii *Genius* means the highest level of mental ability, a distinctive character, as of a nation, or a person who strongly influences another. The plural form is *geniuses*. It can also mean the guardian spirit of a place, or two mutually opposing spirits attending someone through life and hence any demon or spirit. In these senses the plural form is *genii*.

gentlemen This is no longer acceptable in a general context, suggesting as it does a 'we' and 'them' division. Put another way, all men are now considered 'gentlemen'. The old forms of class distinction are regarded as anachronisms. As a formal means of address, 'Ladies and Gentlemen', as a notice on a door, 'Gentlemen', and in speech when referring to another in front of him:

I think this gentleman was first,

the word is still correct. Otherwise 'man' or 'men' should always be used.

gerund This is the grammatical term for a verbal noun:

His *working* late was bad enough; what was worse was his *lying*.

When a *gerund* takes a subject, this is in the possessive case: hence the possessive pronoun *his* in the above example. Like a verb, it can be modified by an adverb, in this case *late*.

gibe, gybe, jibe At one time these words were interchangeable, but in modern usage *gibe* is confined to scoff or jeer, taunt or deride, and *gybe* is the nautical term meaning to shift from one side or the other when running before the wind. *Jibe* is an alternative form for both meanings.

gipsy, gypsy *Gipsy* is the usual spelling, although the *y* form is nearer the original meaning (Egyptian). It is more widely acceptable when in the plural *gypsies*.

glance, glimpse *To glance at* is to look quickly or briefly. *To glimpse* is to catch sight of quickly or briefly. The slight difference in meaning is that *glance* is used for the act of looking, *glimpse* for the result of that act. The nouns also correspond to this emphasis.

global At one time this word simply meant shaped like a globe. It has since come to be used as a synonym for world-wide, and hence in a figurative sense comprehensive, all-embracing.

glossary A glossary is a selective vocabulary in which specialized words, usually those of a technical nature, are listed and defined.

goodwill, good will, good-will *Goodwill* is benevolence or favour, especially in a commercial context:

The price offered for the business includes a valuation for goodwill.

When good intent or friendly disposition is meant, *good will* is the correct form:

I believe them to be men of good will.

The hyphenated *good-will* is applicable only in an adjectival phrase such as:

He made a good-will gesture.

Turned round, the sentence would read:

He made a gesture of good will.

got, gotten The use of *got* in a sentence is acceptable colloquial English but not necessarily good literary English. It is useful as an emphasizer, and as an adjunct in a sentence using the abbreviated 'I've' or 'he's':

He's got to go

is much more emphatic than:

He has to go

or:

He's to go,

which would be taken to mean:

He is to go.

But unless it is serving such a positive purpose, indiscriminate use of this word is not good style:

I got a new car

is the past tense, but is sometimes incorrectly used for the present:

I have (or I've) got a new car

is the present form often used in colloquial speech, though unnecessary. The straightforward:

I have a new car

is preferable, certainly in written English.

Too often *got* is used in place of another verb:

I got to London without difficulty.

I reached would be a better substitute.

Gotten is an acceptable word in the United States but not in Britain, except in the phrase *ill-gotten*.

gourmand, gourmet A *gourmand* is one who is fond of good eating and therefore, by implication, tending to greed. A *gourmet* is a connoisseur of good food and wine, an epicure. The first term is often used in a derogatory sense; the second is more complimentary.

grammar, linguistics, syntax *Grammar* may be defined as the features of a language considered systematically, the rules of a language as it is used. The word lacks the precision required today and in modern usage the term *linguistics* is employed to describe the science of language, covering every aspect of it: sounds, inflections, word formation, sentence structure, meaning and spelling. *Syntax*, the pattern or arrangement of words in a sentence showing their relationship to one another, is therefore a branch of linguistics.

gramophone Like *phonograph* (still acceptable in the United States) this word is rapidly becoming obsolete, having been replaced by *record player*. The latest term for it, often incorporating tape and cassette facilities, is *music centre*.

great see **big**

Great Britain The term *Great Britain* applies to England, Scotland and Wales, both in a geographical and in a political sense. The correct term for England, Scotland, Wales and Northern Ireland is the *United Kingdom of Great Britain and Northern Ireland*. The British Isles incorporates the Republic of Ireland as well, and is only a geographical term, not a political one.

Grecian, Greek *Grecian* has in almost all general senses been superseded by *Greek*. It may still be used for certain aspects of art and architecture, and in the special sense of a scholar of the Greek language.

griffin, griffon, gryphon A *griffin* is a mythical monster with an eagle's head and wings and a lion's legs. A *griffon* is a species of vulture, and also a breed of dog. *Gryphon* is an alternative spelling for *griffin*.

grisly, grizzly, grizzled *Grisly* is an adjective meaning gruesome or causing horror. Both *grizzly* and *grizzled* mean grey or grey-haired.

groin, groyne *Groin* is the fold in the body where the thigh joins the abdomen. It is also an alternative but less often used spelling for *groyne*, which is a small jetty built into the sea or river bank to prevent erosion.

guarantee, guaranty, guarantor *To guarantee* means to secure by giving or taking security for, to engage to do something, or to protect or indemnify. The noun means a promise that something is of specified quality, implying an assurance that defects will be put right. A *guaranty* is a pledge accepting responsibility for another's liabilities, or that which is presented as security. A *guarantor* is one who makes or gives a *guarantee* or *guaranty*.

guerrilla This is really a back formation (*q.v.*) from a type of warfare. It now means one who wages this kind of war, a member of a small, independent band of soldiers who harass the enemy by surprise raids.

H

habitable, inhabitable Both words mean 'able to be lived in'. *Habitable* is usually applied to buildings, houses, flats, etc:

Much work was necessary to make the flats habitable.

Inhabitable generally refers to much larger areas:

Desert regions are not usually inhabitable.

half This is followed by a verb in the singular when it refers to a singular noun or pronoun:

Half the town was destroyed.

If the noun or pronoun is plural, so is the verb:

Half of our men were absent.

When *half* is used as a prefix to adjectives, nouns and verbs it is generally hyphenated:

Half-holiday, half-pay, half-pint,

but a *half pint* of bitter. Sometimes it is written as one word:

Halftone, halfway.

hang, hanged, hung When the reference is to capital punishment the past tense and past participle are *hanged*:

The prisoner was hanged at dawn.

Otherwise *hung* is the correct form for the past tense and the past participle.

happen, occur These verbs are to a large extent interchangeable but the following differences should be noted.

Both refer to the taking place of an event, but *happen* is the more common word:

It all happened very quickly.

Occur is a more formal word and is usually more specific in its reference:

The incident occurred on the following day.

harangue, tirade Both words mean 'a long vehement speech', but a *harangue* is usually delivered before an audience:

His lengthy harangue was listened to in silence.

A *tirade* is a denunciation and may be intended for a single person only:

His tirade reduced the girl to tears.

harbour, haven, port All are names of places where ships may shelter. A *harbour* may be either natural or artificially built: *the new harbour on the south coast.* A *haven* suggests a natural harbour where ships may seek refuge from storms, etc. It is also used to mean any place of shelter and safety. A *port* is a place, usually a town with a harbour, where ships may load or unload, although it too can be used to mean a source of refuge: *any port in a storm.*

hard, hardly The usual form of the adverb in its various senses is *hard*:

To work hard, to look hard, frozen hard.

Hardly can be used instead of *hard* in some instances but is best avoided because of the possibility of confusion over its other meaning of 'scarcely' or 'barely'. Remember that when *hardly* is used in the sense of 'scarcely' it is followed by *when* and not *than*:

Hardly had we sat down when it began to rain.

harmony, melody Both words are used to mean a combination of sounds from voices or musical instruments, but there is a difference between them. The *harmony* is a simultaneous combination of notes to form chords. The *melody* is the combination of successive sounds to make up a tune.

have, had Care must be taken to avoid the trap of inserting an extra *have* in certain constructions: *had I have done* for *had I done*, *if she'd have known* for *if she'd known*, and *if I hadn't have seen* for *if I hadn't seen.*

healthy, healthful Both adjectives refer to what promotes good health. *Healthy*, which is the more common word, means both 'possessing health' and 'conducive to health': *a healthy body*, *a healthy climate*.
Healthful is applied mainly to what is conducive to health, wholesome or salutary: *a healthful diet*.

heir apparent, heir presumptive An *heir apparent* is one whose title cannot be made void by any birth. Thus, the eldest son of a reigning monarch is an *heir apparent*. An *heir presumptive* loses his title if an *heir apparent* is born. Consequently the younger brother of a reigning monarch may be *heir apparent* until such time as the monarch has a child.

help The verb *help* is frequently followed by an infinitive without *to*. This usage is quite common when the one who helps participates in the activity of the person who is being helped:

He helped me mend my garage door.

It is never wrong to insert *to* in such instances. *To* should always be included when *help* is separate from the action which follows:

His speech helped them to understand.

The speech did not actually take part in the effort of understanding. Try to avoid the construction *cannot help but* which wrongly combines *cannot help being* and *cannot but be*. *Cannot help being* is preferable:

He cannot help being untidy.

The use of *help* to mean 'to refrain from' or 'avoid' is illogical but is now firmly entrenched in the language:

The spectacle was so ridiculous that we couldn't help laughing.

heritage, inheritance Both words mean something inherited. *Heritage* is that which belongs to one by reason of birth or that which is bequeathed to a subsequent generation by an individual or by a society as a whole:

Our Victorian heritage.

Inheritance is the usual word for any property or possessions which are passed on to an heir:

He received a substantial inheritance from his grandparents.

hesitance, hesitancy, hesitation *Hesitance* is now a rarely used alternative spelling to *hesitancy. Hesitation* is the most common word and more or less interchangeable with *hesitancy*. The only real difference is that *hesitancy* may be said to be the characteristic tendency of a person which gives rise to the *hesitation.*

hiccup, hiccough *Hiccup* is the preferred form. The alternative, *hiccough*, is given in most dictionaries but is strongly condemned by some authorities.

high see **tall**

high, highly Both adverbs are in common use. *High* is more usual when reference is made to altitude, amount, or status:

The cranes were flying high.

To aim high in one's chosen profession

Highly means 'to a high degree' or 'with high appreciation':

A highly amusing episode, to speak highly of someone.

But it can be used with the meaning of *high* in such expressions as *highly placed, highly paid.*

Note that compounds with *high* take a hyphen, but those with *highly* (see above) do not: *high-fidelity*, *high-powered.*

historic, historical These words are frequently confused but their meanings are quite distinct. *Historic* means 'well-known or important in history':

Hastings was a historic battle.

Historical means 'concerned with or relating to history':

A historical novel, historical evidence.

hoard, horde These words are sometimes mixed up. A *hoard* is 'an accumulation of something for future use', as *a hoard of tinned food*. A *horde* is 'a great multitude of people, often an unruly one':

A horde of football fans ran into the arena.

Holland see **Netherlands**

homonym, homophone A *homonym* is a word which has the same spelling and usually the same pronunciation as another but a different meaning, such as *boil* (as water) and *boil* (a painful sore). A *homophone* is a word which has the same pronunciation as another, but a different spelling and meaning, such as *heir* and *air*, *feat* and *feet*. [See also *synonym*]

Hon. This is an abbreviation for both *honourable* and *honorary*. *Honourable* is a title prefixed to the Christian names of younger sons of earls and all children of viscounts and barons, to the names of certain High Court justices, and to some others. It is also used inside the House of Commons when one M.P. is referring to another. *Honorary* describes the unpaid holder of an office and is invariably abbreviated: *the hon. secretary*.

hopefully As the adverb formed from *hopeful*, *hopefully* means 'in a hopeful mood'. In recent years, however, it has acquired a new use which, though deplored by some authorities, has made its way into the dictionaries. *Hopefully* now has the additional sense of 'it is to be hoped':

Hopefully, we will finish work by tonight.

hotchpotch, hodgepodge Most dictionaries give both forms but the first is now the preferred spelling. The form *hotchpot* is a legal term, but even this has the alternative spelling *hotchpotch*.

how This is both an adverb and a conjunction, and care must be taken to avoid ambiguity when it is used as a conjunction. A sentence like:

They told me how they had managed to complete the job in four hours

may be a simple statement, in which case *how* should be replaced by *that* or omitted altogether. On the other hand if *how* means 'in what manner' or 'the way in which' it is perfectly acceptable.

however, how ever When *however* is used as a conjunction meaning 'nevertheless' or 'yet' it is separated by a comma or commas from the rest of the sentence which it modifies:

However, they decided to go at once.
They decided, however, to go at once.

When *however* is used as an adverb meaning 'to whatever extent or degree' or 'in whatever manner' it is not separated by a comma:

However hard he tried, he never succeeded.

As an interrogative adverb in direct and indirect questions it is written as two words and is used for emphasis:

How ever did you succeed in getting up so early?
We wondered how they ever managed to complete the job.

human, humane Both adjectives refer to what is characteristic of human beings, but their meanings are now quite separate. *Human* can refer to the good and bad in mankind: *human kindness, human weakness*, or to man as opposed to God: *human frailty, divine compassion.*

Humane, which was once interchangeable with *human*, is now restricted to the idea of being tender and compassionate towards the sufferings of others:

Humane treatment of the injured, humane feelings.

hyphens Much can be written about such a complicated subject as the use of hyphens. To hyphenate too much is as bad as to hyphenate too little. The following are some guidelines which the general reader may find useful.

The hyphen is normally used with a composite adjective:

a light-coloured suit, a poverty-stricken family.

It is not normally used to join an adverb to an adjective which it qualifies:

a tastefully furnished room, an ever increasing amount.

It is used with the adverbs *well*, *better*, *best*, *ill*, *worse* and *worst*, and any other adverbs which might not be recognized as such:

A well-known actor, an ill-advised move.

However, when the compound adjective or adverb plus adjective are used predicatively, *i.e.*, after the verb, the hyphen is omitted:

His suit is light coloured, the actor was well known, the move would be ill advised.

There are many compound words which hover uneasily between complete separation, a hyphenated form and one word:

pile driver, pile-driver; book-binder, bookbinder.

All that can be said is that the more commonly such a compound is used the more likely it is to be printed as one word:

bullfighting, watchmaker, doorkeeper.

Other compounds, originally printed as two words or hyphenated, have through frequent use become one word:

eyelid, blackbird, armchair, bedroom, electrostatic, thermonuclear.

Some compounds are still written with a hyphen in order to avoid an ugly combination of vowels and consonants, to make the pronunciation clear, or to distinguish between two different meanings:

micro-organism, anti-icing, damp-proof, re-emerge, re-cover (to cover again), re-form (to form again).

There is little consistency in the use of hyphens with prefixes. Some prefixes, like *all-*, *ex-*, *non-* and *self-* are normally hyphenated to the word with which they are compounded:

all-embracing, ex-serviceman, non-self-governing.

Others, like *anti-*, *co-*, *counter-*, *neo-*, *pan*, *pre-* and *post-* are normally joined to the main word unless this begins with a capital letter or produces an awkward combination of vowels:

antifreeze, coedition, neocolonialism, predecease, posthaste, Pan-American.

The prefixes *mis-* and *re-* are almost always spelt without a hyphen. The prefix *by-* may be spelt with or without a hyphen: *bypass*, *by-product*.

The following suffixes are usually hyphenated:

-all (know-all), -elect (president-elect), -odd (twenty-odd), -off (rake-off, spin-off), -to (lean-to).

The following suffixes do not generally require hyphens:

-down (showdown), -fold (fivefold), -goer (cinemagoer), -less (endless), -like (childlike), -over (takeover), -wise (lengthwise).

Note that *-like* usually has a hyphen when the word to which it is attached ends in an *l*, as in *snail-like*.

A hyphen is used in spelling out numbers between 21 and 99:

thirty-five, eighty-eight, two hundred and ninety-two.

It is also used in fractions:

one-third, two-fifths, three-quarters.

I

I The trap into which the unwary fall is to say 'you and I' or 'you and me' in the wrong context:

This piece of information is just intended for you and I

is wrong, and so is:

You and me had better leave it to the experts.

In the first example, the two pronouns are both objects of the preposition *for* and are therefore in the accusative case, so they should be *you and me*. In the second example both pronouns are the subjects of the sentence and are therefore in the nominative case, which means that *you and I* are the correct forms.

The simple way to decide is to strip away all but the bare essentials. It then becomes obvious that '. . . is for I' simply wouldn't do, nor would '. . . me had better leave'.

The idiomatic *It's me* is so widespread that it is generally acceptable, though most authorities recommend that in formal writing the correct form *It is I* should be used. However, given the nature of the words themselves it is highly unlikely that they would occur in a formal context. Nobody would ever say *It's I* in speech and so it would not appear in reported speech. The argument would seem, therefore, to be specious.

-ible The *-ible* suffix occurs in adjectives derived from Latin words ending in *-ibilis*, such as admissible, credible, collapsible, flexible, indigestible, legible, visible, and several others.

-ic, -ical Some of the adjectives ending in *-ic* and *-ical* have different meanings, such as *economic*, 'pertaining to the production and distribution of wealth' and *economical*, 'avoiding waste or extravagance'. Others, such as *poetic* and *poetical*, are interchangeable. In many instances the *-ic* form may also be a noun and when this is the case it is preferable to differentiate by using the *-ical* form for the adjective and to keep the *-ic* form for the noun.

-ics When referring to a subject suitable for study nouns ending in *-ics* are singular:

I am taking mathematics for my A levels, because it is my best subject.

But in a more generalized context they will take a plural verb:

Economics offer a gateway into politics, which are the best means of wielding influence in public life.

idiom The Greek word has been translated as 'a manifestation of the peculiar', and the dictionary definition is 'a form of expression peculiar to a language, especially one having a significance other than its literal one'. Idiomatic English is very much concerned with usage. It is English as it is spoken every day, and its conventions and phraseology have become established by practice. That is not to say that an idiom is necessarily ungrammatical. It may well be correct, but have taken a short cut. Or it is simply a colourful metaphor, apparently arbitrary and incapable of being literally interpreted. It is the idioms of a language that are so hard for a foreigner to learn:

Not a single flight was taking off – the weather had seen to that.

Not a single is an idiomatic way of saying 'no flight'. *The weather had seen to that*: how could the weather 'see' anything? Though seemingly quite illogical, the phrase *seen to* meaning 'accounted for' in such a context is a well-established idiom.

i.e. see **e.g.**

if, whether *If*, used in place of *whether*, can be ambiguous:

Let me know if you would like a lift to the station.

Does this mean that he should be contacted only if a lift is required?

Let me know whether you would like a lift to the station.

In this sentence it is clear that he should be informed whether a lift is required or not – it leaves no room for doubt.

if and when It is seldom necessary to use both *if and when* in a sentence:

We can expect a reduction in income tax if and when the Conservatives return to power.

In this sentence either *if* or *when* would be acceptable. The use of both together should be avoided.

ill, sick In general *ill* occurs only predicatively:

She was very ill.

If *sick* were substituted here it would mean she was vomiting. But in:

She was a very sick woman

ill could not take its place. *Sick* is the term used when speaking of a sick person, sick list, sick benefit, sick leave, and in idiomatic phrases such as *to go sick*. Though the general term is *ill health*, the word has also the secondary meaning of bad or evil, so that used in this context it is being equated with bad health.
American usage is different. The two words are interchangeable, *ill* being used for the more serious complaints and *sick* for a simple ailment like a cold. *Ill* may also be used attributively: in the United States it is usual to speak of an *ill person*.

illegal, unlawful, illegitimate, illicit *Illegal* is against the law of the land. *Unlawful* may be against the law or what the law intends, but it can also apply to religious or moral laws. *Illegitimate* is outside the law, not in accordance with or sanctioned by law, often used with particular reference to birth out of wedlock. *Illicit* means not permitted or authorized, but this does not necessarily mean by law – it could simply be describing a breach of school rules.

illegible, unreadable *Illegible* refers to the quality of the handwriting or the printed words, which may be impossible to decipher. *Unreadable* refers to the contents of the text as a whole, which may be too technical, learned or ill conceived to be understood. Or just too boring. That which is *illegible* will, of course, be *unreadable*.

illicit, elicit These two words are sometimes confused because they sound alike. *Illicit* (see above) means not permitted or authorized. *Elicit* is to draw or bring out, or to evoke:

> Perhaps his sister will be able to elicit the truth about his illicit activities.

illusion see **delusion**

illusory see **elusive**

image This is a vogue word which has become fashionable since the power of television has emphasized the need for politicians and moguls of industry to present themselves to the public in the best possible light. People in the public eye have become conscious of the *image* that they project, and the word has acquired a fresh significance.

imaginary, imaginative *Imaginary* is an image created in the imagination, having no existence in reality. *Imaginative* is having the faculty for creating such images or mental pictures:

> Her work was highly imaginative, yet it was possible to believe in the existence of her imaginary characters.

imbue, infuse, instil *Imbue* is to impregnate or inspire. *Infuse* is to cause to penetrate. *Instil* is to infuse slowly into the mind or feelings, to insinuate. It is possible to *imbue* someone with something, such as enthusiasm, or enthusiasm can be *infused* into him, but he cannot be *infused* with it. Modern dictionaries give 'inspire with' as one of the definitions of *infuse*, an indication of the common loose usage of these two words.

Enthusiasm can also be *instilled into* a person. Again, he cannot be *instilled with* it:

Joe was imbued with excitement. He tried to infuse some of his enthusiasm into Bob. But Bob remained indifferent, however hard Joe tried to instil some life into him.

immanent, imminent *Immanent* means remaining within, inherent, or taking place within the mind and having no effect outside it:

The faculty of imagination is immanent to human progress.

It is a little-used word, occurring most frequently in a theological context.

Imminent means impending, or about to occur.

The threat of a breakdown in negotiations was imminent.

immature, premature *Immature* is not fully developed. *Premature* is coming into existence or maturing too soon:

Premature shoots are likely to be damaged by frost because they are immature.

immigrant see **emigrant**

immoral see **amoral**

immunity, impunity *Immunity* is exemption from any natural or usual liability, especially susceptibility to disease. It can also mean special privilege. *Impunity* is exemption from punishment or ill consequences.

impassable, impassible *Impassable* applies to that which cannot be passed over or through. *Impassible* is incapable of suffering pain or harm, or of displaying emotion. The word is seldom used, having been superseded by impassive.

impel, induce *Impel* is to drive or urge forward or to incite to action. *Induce* is to lead or move by persuasion or influence:

He felt impelled to take an active part in union affairs, believing that his example would induce others to follow.

imperative mood A grammatical term for the mood of command:

Stop! Raise your arms above your head. Now bend down and touch your toes.

Each of these commands is in the *imperative mood.*

imperial, imperious *Imperial* is of or pertaining to an empire, an emperor or empress, of a commanding quality or aspect, very fine or grand. *Imperious* is domineering, dictatorial or overbearing; also urgent or imperative. At one time the words were almost synonymous, stemming as they do from the same Latin word meaning 'commanding':

His imperious behaviour is an offensive reminder of the imperial circles in which he used to move.

implicit see **explicit**

imply, infer, insinuate *Imply* is to signify, indicate or suggest without expressly stating:

He implied that the bank knew the position from the beginning.

Infer is to draw a conclusion from, to derive by reasoning. It is therefore possible to *infer* that something is true by the evidence that has been *implied*:

It is reasonable to infer that the bank acted as they did because of what they knew.

To *insinuate* is to suggest or hint slyly, to instil something into someone's mind subtly by underhand means. It is even less explicit than to *imply*, and is often used in a derogatory sense:

He insinuated that the bank had not acted very creditably.

impractical, impracticable see **practicable**

impromptu see **extempore**

in-, un- As a rough guide, the negative prefix *in-* applies to Latin-based words and to most of those ending in *-ible* and *-ent*:

Inessential, inexact, incredible, ineligible, incoherent.

With some exceptions, such as *incapacitated*, words ending in *-ed* and *-ing* take the negative prefix *un-*.

in, at *In* is the more general term, *at* the preposition for the specific. When thinking of a place as a district or area *in* would be the preposition to choose:

I live in the village of Middleton,

meaning that I live within the area the village occupies. But to say:

I live at Middleton

means that I am identifying Middleton as a particular pinpoint on a map, a specific place at which I live within a wider area. Thus *in* a city, because it is a vague term implying a large district, but *at* No. 6 Acacia Avenue, a given point in that city.
In the same way, I could be said to work *in* a department store (any department store) but *at* James Smith Ltd, a particular department store, *in* the sports department (anywhere in it) but *at* the sports counter, one specific place in the department.

inability, disability *Inability* is lack of ability, power or means, which may be a temporary condition:

His inability to pay should have been foreseen.

Disability is lack of power or ability due to a physical or mental defect, and is usually a situation of long standing.
Inability, which means that someone has been rendered unable to fulfil an obligation, may be a result of a *disability*, a physical factor which impairs capacity to carry out such an obligation:

Because of his disability he could not travel by train, which accounts for his inability to attend the board meeting.

inapt, inept *Inapt* means not apt or fitted, without aptitude or capacity. *Inept* also means not apt or fitted. It is the term preferred when applied to what is unsuitable or out of place, and also implies clumsiness. *Inapt* is more usually confined to lack of aptitude or capacity.

incapable, unable Both words mean lacking ability or power to do something. The chief difference is that *incapable* is usually applied to a long-standing condition, *unable* to a specific situation:

He is incapable of expressing himself clearly, so it is not surprising that he was unable to make himself understood at the meeting.

incredible, incredulous *Incredible* is too extraordinary to be possible or that cannot be believed. *Incredulous* is sceptical, showing disbelief:

As she unfolded her incredible story, her audience became increasingly incredulous.

incubus, succubus An *incubus* is an imaginary demon who was supposed to have intercourse with sleeping women, and a *succubus* is a female demon who was supposed to have visited sleeping men. *Incubus* is the more familiar word, because it has come to mean anything that weighs oppressively on one like a nightmare.

inculcate, indoctrinate *Inculcate* is to impress on someone by repeated statement, to instil in or teach persistently. *Indoctrinate* is to instruct, especially in a doctrine, to imbue someone with information or principles.

It must be remembered that it is the ideas that are *inculcated* into a person, whereas the person is *indoctrinated* with the ideas:

From earliest childhood religious principles had been inculcated into her, so that she had become indoctrinated with the ethics of a rigid code of morality.

indicative mood This is the most important mood of English verbs. It is the mood of fact, a statement, as distinct from the imperative mood (command) or subjunctive (conditional):

Look! (*imperative*) I see a flying saucer (*indicative*), as clearly as if it were standing (*subjunctive*) where you are now.

indict, indite *Indict* is to accuse or charge with an offence or crime. *Indite*, a rarely used word, is to compose or write, especially a speech or poem. Both words are pronounced in the same way.

indifferent Originally this word meant 'impartial'. Other dictionary definitions are 'without interest or concern, apathetic, neutral in character, neither good nor bad'. From the last definition it has come to mean 'not very good', and this has supplanted the original meaning of 'impartial':

He was an indifferent judge of character and his opinion was often biased.

At one time such a sentence would have been nonsense, since an 'impartial' judge cannot be biased. Today it simply means that he was not a very good judge of character.

One is *indifferent to* a circumstance, not *for* it.

individual The proper use of this word is in contrasting a single person with a group:

The local bird society has supported our conservation efforts, though certain individuals have criticized our methods.

It is often used colloquially, however, as a term of contempt or facetiousness. The first can be detected in the tone of the above example, and the second is exemplified in:

Into the room walked an extraordinary individual. He was clad from head to foot in shining blue plastic and there were dangling antennae attached to his head.

indoor, indoors *Indoor* is the adjective:

Card playing is a pleasant indoor pastime,

and *indoors* the adverb, meaning in or into a house or building:

You will have to play indoors. It is raining hard outside,

or:

You will have to go indoors. It's raining quite hard now.

induction, deduction *Induction* is the process of drawing a general principle from certain specific facts. *Deduction* is assuming the truth of a specific fact because of a known set of general principles:

I have never come across a male tortoiseshell cat, so it seems a fair induction that tortoiseshell cats are generally female,

and:

Since tortoiseshell cats are invariably female, it would be an obvious deduction that the next tortoiseshell cat that I meet will be a female.

industrial, industrious *Industrial* is pertaining to industry or productive labour. *Industrious* is hard working or diligent. The first is applied to the processes of industry, the second to the people concerned with it.

ineffective, ineffectual see **effective**

infamous, notorious *Infamous* means detestable, shamefully bad, having an extremely bad reputation, but not necessarily widely known. *Notorious* is widely known for unfavourable reasons, but not necessarily evil ones. [See also *famous, notorious*]

infectious see **contagious**

infer see **imply**

infinitive The infinitive can be either the subject or the object of a sentence:

To understand (*subject*) is to believe (*object*).

It should not be used in a sentence where the gerund is clearly required:

> The custom of shopkeepers to label their goods in decimal quantities can be very confusing.

The infinitive in this sentence should be replaced by *of labelling*. Equally incorrect is the 'dangling' infinitive:

> To achieve a high record, concentration and determination are required.

Somebody must require them – 'concentration and determination' cannot achieve the record by themselves. The correct sentence should read:

> To achieve a high record, *a man* requires (or *one* requires) concentration and determination.

[See also *split infinitive*]

inflammable, flammable, inflammatory *Inflammable* is capable of being set alight, combustible, (figuratively) excitable. *Flammable* means the same thing and is interchangeable, but *inflammable* is in more general use, especially in its combustible sense. *Inflammatory* means tending to inflame, kindling passion or anger, and is used almost entirely figuratively.

inflict see **afflict**

inform, information An overworked word, *inform* is too often employed as a formal way of saying 'tell', especially in commercial jargon:

> I have to inform you that your licence has been withdrawn.

To inform someone *to* do something is not possible. He can be informed *that* he should or must do something, or he can be informed *of* an event.

For your information is another glib phrase. This is acceptable if it does indeed mean 'just for information – don't do anything', but it is often used as an officious way of passing on a directive:

> For your information the form XYZ must be completed in triplicate by the end of January.

informant, informer An *informant* is one who informs or gives information. An *informer* also gives information, but the word is used more specifically to apply to someone who passes on incriminating evidence to a prosecuting officer. The information given by an *informant* is not necessarily about anyone else, though it may well be of an illicit character:

It is supposed to be a Cabinet secret, so I can't tell you the name of my informant.

ingenious, ingenuous *Ingenious* is having inventive faculty, skilful in contriving or constructing:

His plan for solving the city parking problems is very ingenious.

Ingenuous is free from restraint or dissimulation, artless or innocent:

Her open, ingenuous manner was the chief quality for which she was chosen.

Ingenuity is the noun for *ingenious*, and ingenuousness the noun for *ingenuous*.

inhabitable see **habitable**

inherent, innate *Inherent* is existing in something as a permanent and inseparable element:

A talent for mimicry is an inherent part of the comic's job.

Innate means inborn, existing from birth. It also means part of the essential character of something:

Because of her innate shyness she found it hard to communicate with the children.

inheritance see **heritage**

inhibit, prohibit *Inhibit* is to restrain, hinder or check:

He was inhibited from expressing himself too freely by the presence of several women.

Prohibit is to forbid by authority, to prevent or hinder:

It is prohibited to spit.

Although some of the meanings overlap, in general *prohibit* is much stronger than *inhibit* and presupposes the possibility of authority to enforce it.

inmost, innermost These words, both meaning situated farthest within or most intimate, are interchangeable, but *inmost* is the more usual choice, especially in the figurative sense.

innuendo In common usage *innuendo* is an indirect intimation, usually derogatory, about a person or thing. It also has the specific meaning in law of a parenthetic explanation in a pleading, and it is from this, the original definition, that the extended meaning in common use has evolved.
The plural is innuendoes.

in order that This construction should always be followed by 'may' or 'might':

He drove slowly in order that she might follow.

In this example the phrase serves to emphasize the purposefulness of the sentence '. . . *in order that she might* (be able to) *follow*', but in many instances the simpler construction *that* or *so that* is preferable:

They came early in order that they might get good seats

sounds a little pedantic.

They came early so that they could get good seats

is a more natural way of expressing it.

inquire see **enquire**

in so far This should always be written as three words, not one, but it is not a very desirable expression, and tends to lead to wordiness. It is usually better replaced by *although*, *except that* or *so far*:

He did not agree to the proposal, save in so far as he was prepared to make a few marginal concessions.

Although would be a better substitute here, replacing *save in so far as.*

insolate, insulate *Insolate* is to expose to the sun's rays, to treat by exposure to the sun. *Insulate* is to cover or surround something, especially an electric wire, with non-conducting material.

instinct, intuition *Instinct* is an inborn pattern of activity, innate impulse or natural inclination. Figuratively, it is a natural aptitude or gift for something:

Migrating birds find their way by instinct.

Intuition is direct perception of facts independently of any reasoning process:

How she knew you were coming I don't know – it must have been her feminine intuition.

institute, institution An *institute* is a society or organization for carrying on particular work, especially of an educational, literary or scientific nature:

Classes are held at the institute every evening of the week.

An *institution* is an organization or establishment for the promotion of a particular object. It is also an organized pattern of group behaviour or any established law or custom:

The institution of beating the bounds goes back to pagan times.

instructional, instructive *Instructional* is pertaining to the act of teaching or education. *Instructive* is also conveying instruction, knowledge or information, but whereas the emphasis of *instructional* is on the process of imparting the knowledge *instructive* deals more with the quality of the information imparted:

It was a very instructive lecture, but you would expect a high standard for an instructional course of this kind.

insure see **assure**

intelligent, intellectual *Intelligent* is having a good understanding or mental capacity, quick to grasp. *Intellectual* is appealing to or engaging the intellect. An *intelligent* person is not necessarily *intellectual.* He may have great mental capabilities and a quick understanding but be wholly uninterested in academic matters and things of the mind. Conversely, however, an *intellectual* person is likely to be *intelligent*, since without the capacity for understanding, mental exercise is unlikely to appeal to him:

> He is extremely intelligent, showing a quick grasp of essentials, but his intellectual commitment appears to be minimal: he prefers sport.

Intellectual has come to have a derogatory sense in social terms, implying a superiority to others who are not so occupied with things of the mind.

intense, intensive *Intense* is existing in a high degree, acute, strong or vehement, especially of feelings:

> His intense anxiety about his wife's safety is understandable.

Intensive means characterized by intensity, concentrated or thorough. It has special application to treatment in medicine and to increasing effectiveness in agriculture: *intensive treatment*, *intensive cultivation.* It is also applied to grammar, indicating expressions of emphasis or force, as *self* in *himself.*

inter-, intra- Both these prefixes occur in Latin words, *inter-* meaning 'between' or 'among', as in *interdenominational*, *interrupt*, *interfere*, and *intra-* indicating 'within', as in *intramural*, *intravenous*, *intracellular*.

interface A surface regarded as the common boundary of two bodies or spaces. It is becoming a vogue word increasingly in use as a metaphor, and as such is in danger of being overworked.

interject, interpolate, interpose *Interject* is to throw in abruptly between other things in a conversation:

I went shopping for new shoes today – by the way, there's a sale on at Marsh's – and managed to get just what I wanted.

Interpolate is to introduce new material between other things in a text or manuscript, especially deceptively or without authorization.

Interpose is to place something between, cause to intervene, or to put in a remark in the middle of a conversation:

They interposed a gauze curtain between the audience and the stage so you couldn't really see any details.

interjection A part of speech used to express delight, anger, surprise and other emotions. It is independent of the rest of the sentence, to which it bears no grammatical relation. Examples are:

Heavens! Rubbish! Good gracious!

in to, into When used as a straightforward preposition *into* is written as one word:

They opened the front door and went into the house.

But if the sense demands a separate adverb and preposition, it must be written as two words:

She took the post in to him as soon as he arrived.

This is also the case when *to* is attached to an infinitive:

He left the envelope in to be collected later.

intransitive and transitive verbs The term *intransitive* applies to those verbs that need no object; the action is confined to the subject alone:

He is sleeping.

The verb applies only to the subject *he*. It is not doing anything to anyone or anything else, and can stand alone.

A *transitive* verb is one that requires an object to complete its sense:

He opened the book

In this sentence the action moves from the subject *he* to the object *the book*. By itself the phrase *he opened* is meaningless without *the book*.

inverted commas see **quotation marks**

involve This has become a rather ineffective vogue word. Originally it could be defined as envelop or enfold, and it then came to mean implicate, especially in a crime, or to entangle (someone), to entail, include or contain. It is often used quite unnecessarily in a sentence which could stand equally well and more positively without it:

It is estimated that the work involved will take approximately ten days.

Here *involved* is quite superfluous.

In sloppy writing it is frequently chosen in place of a word with a more precise meaning:

Nothing can be countenanced which might involve labour problems at a later date.

It would be a more appropriate choice if *lead to* were substituted for *involve*. And in:

Snow was blocking many roads but the motorway was not involved,

affected would be preferable.

involve, entail *Entail* shares the meaning of include or contain with *involve*, but it also means to impose as a burden, and has a special legal sense of limiting inheritance to a specified line of heirs:

The estate was entailed, so she was unable to touch the capital.

inward, inwards *Inward* is the adjective describing something that is situated within, directed towards the inside or interior. It can also be an adverb, though this is less usual:

She stared out of the window, lost in inward thought.

Inwards, the adverb, can be equated with inwardly, and means towards the inside, as of a place or body, or in the mind or soul:

It was easy to identify his footprints, with the toes turned slightly inwards.

irony This is a mild form of verbal humour in which the speaker says one thing but means another, sometimes to the confusion of his listener:

The Express Delivery service have been extraordinarily generous. They have allowed me a refund of half the cost of postage of the parcel they didn't deliver.

The speaker obviously considers the delivery service anything but generous, and his enlightened listeners will recognize his *irony*.

Socratic irony is pretending ignorance in discussion in order to expose the weakness of the other's argument. *Dramatic irony* is the ignorance of the characters in a dramatic situation when the audience knows more than they do:

But Jemima, I love you and only you!

says the hero, but the audience has just watched him cavorting with another woman in the previous scene.

The idiomatic phrase *irony of fate*, which is much overworked, refers to a twist of circumstances which renders an action futile or ridiculous.

-ist Some words offer the choice of ending in *-ist* or *-alist*: for example, *educationist* or *educationalist* are both acceptable. On principle, unless there is a sound etymological reason for using *-alist*, the shorter form should be preferred: *horticulturist* rather than *horticulturalist*, and *agriculturist* rather than *agriculturalist*. In some cases, however, the longer version is firmly established in general use, for example *conversationalist* instead of *conversationist*.

italics This sloping typeface should be used judiciously in printed matter to emphasize or single out one word or short phrase which, for some reason, requires special attention in a sentence. Its effect is equivalent to underlining in handwriting or typescript. It may indicate a word which would be stressed vocally:

He can't tell *me* what to do,

or contrast two words together, or set out the title of a book or play, taking the place of the untidier inverted commas. It is also used to distinguish foreign words and phrases which have not yet become fully assimilated to the English language:

Being reprimanded like that has damaged his *amour-propre.*

To overuse the device of emphasis is to diminish the importance of the rest of the text, and this will cause irritation to the reader. It is reminiscent of Queen Victoria's habit of underlining lengthy passages in her letters.

its, it's *Its* is the possessive pronoun and, like *yours*, *hers* and *theirs*, does not take an apostrophe before the *s*:

The bird fluttered its wings and settled on the branch.

It's is the abbreviated form of *it is* or *it has*. Because the *i* has been omitted from *is* and the *ha* from *has*, the apostrophe is necessary to indicate the missing letters:

It's cold outside, but it's stopped raining.

-ize, -ise For some verbs of Greek and Latin origin the French suffix *-ise* is preferred by many people to *-ize*: *realise* rather than *realize*, for example. But in American practice and in that of many respected authorities the *z* spelling is given preference. It must be remembered, however, that words which do not have Greek origins must retain the *s*, and many common verbs such as advertise, surprise, chastise, supervise, revise and televise come into this category.

J

Jacobean, Jacobin, Jacobite *Jacobean* describes anything belonging to the period of James I of England. A *Jacobin* was a member of a famous club of French revolutionaries started in 1789, and *Jacobite* was the name given to adherents of James II of England and his descendants after his overthrow in 1688.

jail see **gaol**

jargon, commercialese, journalese The proper meaning of *jargon* is a language peculiar to a particular trade or profession. But in extended use the word has come to be applied to any pretentious form of writing that uses a quantity of long words, euphemisms and cumbersome phrases, often quite meaningless, in an attempt to impress or lend weight to an ordinary sentence. *Commercialese* is commercial jargon, a peculiarly sterile form of it:

> We are in receipt of yours of the 14th inst. in respect of which we beg to inform you that we are expediting the matter as urgently as possible and we remain your obedient servants . . .

Journalese is journalist's jargon, particularly evident in headline copy:

> Councillor Presses Reform in Rate Probe

and:

> Gross Negligence Charges Minister.

This kind of verbal shorthand in which clichés play a prominent part occurs all too often in the body of the text.

jetsam see **flotsam and jetsam**

jocose, jocular Both words mean given to or characterized by joking, or facetious. Perhaps *jocose* is a little more ponderous than *jocular*, suggesting rather heavier humour, whereas *jocular* is humour in a lighter vein, almost waggish.

judg(e)ment Both spelling versions are acceptable, but *judgement* is the preferred form, in line with other words containing a mute *e*, such as *abridgement* and *acknowledgement.*

judicial, judicious *Judicial* pertains to judgement in a court of law or the administration of justice. *Judicious* means using or showing good judgement, wise or sensible.

junction, juncture *Junction* is the act of joining, a combination, or the state of being joined. It also has the special sense of a station where railway lines meet and cross. *Juncture* applies especially to a point in time, a critical moment being a critical *juncture*, though it can also mean the joining point of two bodies.

jurist, juror A *jurist* is one who professes the science of the law or who is versed in law. A *juror* is a member of a body of people sworn to deliver a verdict in a case.

just To say:

It is just exactly five o'clock

is an unnecessary repetition. Either *exactly* five o'clock or *just* five o'clock is quite sufficient.

The use of the word in such expressions as *I'm just fine*, meaning truly, positively, is an Americanism which is now acceptable in Britain as a colloquialism, but not in formal English. Otherwise it is a widely used adverb meaning only a moment before:

He has just gone,

or exactly, precisely, as in:

That is just what I meant.

juvenile, puerile *Juvenile* is young, or intended for young persons. *Puerile* means childishly foolish or trivial, an extension of its original meaning 'of or pertaining to a child or boy'.

K

kerb see **curb**

ketchup This is the accepted British spelling of this word, but in the United States it is sometimes spelt *catsup* or *catchup*.

kind It seems to be generally agreed that the phrase *those kind of things* is acceptable in colloquial speech but better avoided in written English. Ideally, the singular pronoun should be used with the singular noun *kind*, but since this can sound awkward – *that kind of things* – it is better to rephrase it as *things of that kind*, or keep the whole phrase singular, *that kind of thing*. Quite unacceptable in written English, though often used colloquially, is *kind of* used as an adverb:

He was kind of awkward.

kneeled, knelt Both forms are correct for the past tense and past participle.

knit *Knitted* is the past tense when applied to the weaving of fabric on knitting needles. In other senses, especially abstract ones, the past tense and past participle is *knit*:

The views they shared knit them even closer in a common bond.

kowtow, kotow Although *kotow* may be nearer the original Mandarin Chinese, *kowtow* is the more generally acceptable form of the word, with equal stress on both syllables.

L

-l-, -ll- When a verb ends in an *-l* preceded by a single vowel the *l is* doubled, regardless of stress, if another syllable is added:

channel, channelled; tunnel, tunnelling; revel, revelling.

An exception is *parallel, paralleled.*

The *l* remains single when preceded by two vowels or a vowel and a consonant:

reveal, revealing; curl, curling; boil, boiled.

The present or infinitive form may finish in a single or double *l*. As a general rule it is usually a *ll* if preceded by *a*, single if any other vowel precedes it:

enthrall but instil; recall but extol.

An exception is *appal.*

In nouns and adjectives the *l* is doubled when followed by *-er*, *-ed* or *-y*:

leveller, metalled, literally,

but not before *-ish*, *-ist*, *-ism*, or *-ment*:

existentialism, fulfilment, finalist, foolish.

Compound words often drop the second *l*, as in:

almost, already and skilful.

In American usage, unlike English, the *l* follows the normal rules of stress and is not doubled when the stress falls on the first syllable:

travel, traveler, traveled, traveling; level, leveler, leveled, leveling.

lacuna see **Latin and French plurals**

laden This is the past participle of the old word to *lade*, and is little used now except in such phrases as *a heavily laden lorry.* It has in most cases been superseded by *loaded.*

lady, woman As a term for differentiating sex, *woman* should be used in preference to *lady*, which is a genteelism to be avoided.

For example, *woman* doctor, *woman* barrister, and:

This job is not suitable for a woman.

An exception is made, however, if the person referred to is present, when *lady* is used as an expression of courtesy:

Would you let this lady through, please?

The term *lady* is little used now to describe a social category, carrying as it does snobbish implications which are unacceptable today. It may occasionally be employed to emphasize the superiority of a post such as a *lady housekeeper*, but is not recommended. However, when a group of women at a formal meeting are being addressed the term *Ladies* is still used as a courtesy.

lama, llama A *lama* is a Buddhist priest from Tibet. A *llama* is a South American mammal.

large see **big**

last, latest *Last*, meaning final, occurring or coming after all others, refers chiefly to position, though it can also mean final in time. *Latest* refers only to the most recent in time:

The last turn to appear was the best in the show,

and:

This is the latest fashion in Paris,

meaning that it is absolutely up to the minute, the most up to date.

late Care must be taken when using this word that it cannot be interpreted to mean 'dead':

The late editor of the paper was a man of strong principles

may mean either that he has moved to another job or that he has died. If it is intended to mean the former, it would be better to say *previous* in this context.

lath, lathe A *lath* is a thin strip of wood used with others to form the base for supporting tiles or plaster on a ceiling, wall or roof. A *lathe* is a machine used for wood- or metalwork.

Latin and French plurals In some words it is customary to retain the Latin forms for the plural. For example *species*, not specieses, *crises*, not crisises, and *emphases*, not emphasises. In others the choice is open. Both the English and the Latin forms are acceptable, and often the only criterion is the context in which they will appear. For a text of popular appeal the English form is preferable: *indexes* rather than *indices*, *formulas* rather than *formulae*, *radiuses* rather than *radii*, and *aquariums* rather than *aquaria*, but in a text intended for scientific or scholarly purposes the Latin forms would be preferred. Use the English plural in cases of doubt.

Not all words ending in *-us* should automatically take *i* in the plural. *Hippopotamuses* is the accepted plural and not hippopotami. We refer to the *buses* (omnibuses) running late, and not the busi. Like octopus, *hippopotamus* is from a Greek word, not Latin, and *omnibus* is the Latin dative plural, meaning literally 'for all'.

French words ending in *-eau* take the plural *-eaux*, though in almost all cases the anglicized form *-eaus* is also acceptable, and it is becoming increasingly common to see the *s* form preferred. Again, choice should depend on the context, and the degree of anglicization is based largely on the frequency with which the word is encountered in the English language:

> beaux or beaus; tableaux or tableaus; plateaux or plateaus.

latter, former, last The *latter* should be used only in contrast with the *former* when the choice is between two items comparable in kind. These terms cannot be applied to just one noun simply in order to avoid repeating a word:

> He plodded on steadily, making his way down a steep path. The latter was slippery with recent rain.

This is incorrect. *The latter* should be replaced by *This*.

To use these terms in respect of more than two choices is also wrong:

> When Tom, Dick and Harry started to sing everyone stopped to listen. The former had a resonant, pleasing voice.

Who had a resonant voice, Tom or Dick?

Mary Ann went shopping on Friday. She bought a dress, a coat, two pairs of shoes and a handbag, the latter in real leather.

Last is the word that should have been here instead of *latter*, or alternatively *last-mentioned.*

As a general rule, it is preferable to avoid using the terms *former* and *latter* and instead to refer to *first* and *last.*

laudable, laudatory *Laudable* is praiseworthy, commendable:

It was a laudable piece of work.

Laudatory is expressing or containing praise:

The reviews were laudatory in their comments on the play.

lawful, legal *Lawful* is allowed by law, not contrary to law. *Legal* is established or authorized by law, connected or concerned with the law or its administration:

I don't know what the legal position is. He was carrying out his lawful business when the police arrested him.

Of the two words *lawful* is merely permissive, whereas *legal* is more positive. *Lawful* can also be applied to moral laws; *legal* refers only to the laws of the land.

lawyer, attorney, notary A *lawyer* conducts suits in court or gives legal advice and aid. Both a barrister and a solicitor are *lawyers.* An *attorney* is someone appointed or empowered by another to transact business for him. In the United States, however, the word is synonymous with *lawyer.* A *notary,* or (to use the full term) a *notary public,* is someone who attests to deeds or writings and certifies their authenticity, usually for the purpose of passing copies on abroad. [See also *barrister*]

lay, lie These verbs are probably mistreated more frequently than any others in the English language.

To *lay* is to put or place something in a prone position. It is a transitive verb: it must have an object:

Lay your cards out on the table.

In this sentence *your cards* is the object of the verb *lay*. The present participle is *laying*:

He is laying his cards out on the table.

The past tense and past participle is *laid*:

He laid his cards out on the table,

and:

He has laid his cards out on the table.

Note the spelling, *laid*: no such word as *layed* exists.

To *lie* is to recline in a prone position. It is an intransitive verb: it does not take an object, but can stand alone:

In summer it is delightful to lie in the sun,

and:

Sometimes in summer I lie in the sun.

The present participle is *lying*:

In summer nothing is more delightful than lying in the sun,

and:

She has been lying in the sun, and now I am lying beside her.

The past tense is *lay*, and it is this which leads so often to confusion with the present tense of the transitive verb:

For much of the time last summer she lay in the sun.

The past participle is *lain*:

He has lain idle for quite long enough.

There are many idiomatic and colloquial phrases with special meanings using the transitive verb *to lay*: to lay in, lay off, lay out, lay siege to, lay waste, and lay down (your weapons, or some other possession). It will be seen that all these phrases require an object.

The verb *to lie*, meaning to tell an untruth, is quite a different word and is seldom confused. The past tense and past participle are *lied*, the present participle *lying*.

leading question This is a question which is so worded that it leads the recipient on to give the answer which the questioner wants. Contrary to belief, it does not mean a hostile or important or principal question but one so worded that it incorporates a strong suggestion, a device which is often attempted in a court of law:

> *Question:* You had at no time met the deceased in the week prior to his death, had you?
> *Answer:* No, sir.

The expression is loosely used to mean an unfair question or one difficult to answer.

leap The past tense and past participle may be either *leapt* or *leaped*. Both are correct, but on the whole *leapt* is the preferred form in Britain.

learn Both *learnt* and *learned* are acceptable as the past tense and past participle. However, since there is an adjective *learned*, it avoids confusion if *learnt* is chosen as the preferred form for the verb.

least *Least*, the superlative form of *less*, is used in phrases such as *at least* and *least of all*. There is occasionally confusion about whether *least of all* or *most of all* is appropriate, depending on the negative or positive quality of the sentence:

> I do not like the idea of a man calling at the door and asking questions, most of all a council official.

With the negative slant of this sentence the correct phrase should be *least of all*, since I would like even *less* the idea of a council official calling than any other man.

leastways, leastwise *Leastways* is a colloquialism unacceptable in formal speech or in writing. *Leastwise*, which is now almost obsolete, is no less colloquial.

legend, myth A *legend* is a story which has been handed down by tradition, and for which there is no firm basis in fact, though it may be popularly accepted as true. A *myth* is also a traditional story, but one which is invented, often in an attempt to explain natural phenomena in terms of supernatural beings. It is sometimes used figuratively to describe an untruth:

That story he told us about being offered a marvellous job was a complete myth.

legible see **readable**

legislation, legislature *Legislation* is the act of making laws. The *legislature* is the law-making body of a country or state, as Parliament is in Britain.

lengthways, lengthwise Either form is acceptable.

lengthy, long *Long* is of considerable or great extent either of time, scope or distance, and has a widespread application. *Lengthy* is used more specifically for the duration of a speech or the extent of a written text, and implies a degree of tedium.

-less Added to nouns, this suffix forms adjectives to indicate 'without' whatever the noun means:

hopeless (without hope), formless (without form), colourless (without colour).

In some cases the suffix is applied to verbs, as in *tireless*.

less see **fewer, less**

less, lesser Both *less* and *lesser* are in origin comparative forms of *little*. *Less* is an adverb (*less* easy, *less* complicated) and an adjective, when it can be employed both attributively and predicatively: *less butter is available* or *there is less*. *Lesser* can be used only as an attributive adjective:

A lesser evil; lesser troubles.

lessee, lessor The *lessee* is the person to whom a lease is granted and the *lessor* is the one who grants the lease.

lest The correct construction following *lest* is *should*:

The newspaper did not print his name and address lest he should be inundated with unwelcome callers.

The alternative is the pure subjunctive, now regarded as rather old-fashioned:

I always leave the light on, lest he be frightened by the dark.

let A common mistake is to use the wrong case for the personal pronoun in a construction such as:

Let you and I make up our differences.

This should be *let you and me*, since both pronouns are the objects of the verb *let*.

The phrase *let alone*, though frequently used, is a colloquial one:

I can't keep my present garden tidy, let alone one twice its size.

In a formal context *much less* would be a preferable phrase. It is also better to say *leave the child alone* rather than *let the child alone*, which is acceptable only as a colloquialism in informal speech. But *to let go* is as correct as *to leave go*.

letter forms The formalities with which business and other letters used to be presented have to a large extent been superseded by simple, direct formulas which are universally applicable. No longer is it deemed necessary for an official to sign himself 'I am, sir, your obedient servant', nor is it any longer customary to begin a business letter with 'We beg to acknowledge recepit of your favour of the 14th instant', though both examples may still be encountered.

Briefly, a formal letter between strangers should start with *Dear Sir* or *Dear Madam*, *Dear Sirs* or *Mesdames*, and end with *Yours faithfully* or *Yours truly*, though the former is to be preferred. In less formal letters the recipient can be addressed by name, *Dear*

Mr Smith, and the letter should end with *Yours sincerely*. This formula may be used even with strangers if a degree of friendliness is desired.

Letters to friends and acquaintances may start *Dear Mary* or *My dear Mary*, *Dear John* or *My dear John*. Older people still sometimes use the surname alone and address an acquaintance as *Dear Smith*, but this is now considered rather old fashioned and is no longer customary, especially between younger people. Letters to friends and acquaintances may be ended *Yours ever*, *Yours affectionately* or, simply, *Yours*.

To summarize: if a letter begins *Dear Mr Smith* it should never end *Yours faithfully* but always *Yours sincerely*. Similarly, a *Dear Sir* letter should not end with the more intimate *Yours sincerely*, but should terminate in *Yours faithfully* or *Yours truly*.

Do not finish a letter with an unattached clause:

Looking forward to an early reply,
Yours faithfully.

If this formula is to be used it should include a verb:

Looking forward to an early reply,
I am
Yours faithfully.

Better still, it should be rephrased into a complete sentence:

I look forward to an early reply.
Yours faithfully.

Formal invitations may be worded in the third person:

Mr and Mrs John Smith request the pleasure of the company of Mr and Mrs Tom Jones at . . .

This demands a reply in exactly the same style:

Mr and Mrs Tom Jones have pleasure in accepting the kind invitation of Mr and Mrs John Smith to . . .

and the rest of the wording can be copied from the original invitation. A refusal might be couched in the following terms:

Mr and Mrs Tom Jones thank Mr and Mrs John Smith for their kind invitation to . . . but regret that they are unable to accept owing to a previous engagement.

Note that the third person pronoun should be used throughout and not *we* or *your*.

liable see **apt**

libel and slander Both words mean defamation of character. *Libel* is defamation in a form that is permanent such as the written or printed word, pictures or broadcast material. *Slander* is a malicious or defamatory statement or report in the form of speech only.
In bringing an action for *slander* proof must be offered that damage has actually been caused. There is no such obligation with *libel*, and to be able to prove the truth of the libel or establish that it was 'fair comment' is a good defence.

liberality, liberalism *Liberality* is generosity, the quality of giving freely. *Liberalism* describes liberal principles, especially in religion or politics, emphasizing freedom from tradition and authority. When applied to the principles of the Liberal party in politics, denoting a specific philosophy, *Liberalism* should be written with a capital *L*.

licence, license *Licence* is the noun, *to license* the verb. In the United States, however, *license* is the usual form for both the verb and the noun.

lifelong, livelong *Lifelong* means lasting a lifetime. *Livelong* means long to the full extent, whole or entire, and is used only in the expression *the livelong day*.

light The verb *to light* has two separate meanings: (1) to illuminate or ignite, and (2) to get down or descend, to come upon or fall on a place or person. The past tense and past participle for both verbs is either *lighted* or *lit*. Of the two, *lit* is the more usual form:

As soon as she entered the room her eyes lit upon the open book,

or:

I have lit the fire,

but *lighted* is the usual adjectival form:

Somebody dropped a lighted match.

lightening, lightning *Lightening* is the lessening of a weight, *lightning* the flash of light in the sky caused by electrical discharge.

like Colloquially, this word is often used as a conjunction in constructions such as:

The man was not qualified to teach mathematics like his predecessor was.

Though common in speech, this should be avoided in writing, the appropriate word *as* being substituted. In the United States this construction has been carried a step further to replace *as if*:

He ran down the road like he was chased by a thousand devils,

but in Britain this is regarded as a vulgarism.

Like is acceptable as a *prepositional adverb*:

He is behaving like a child,

but in:

Like the man before him, mathematics was his special subject

it is incorrect, for the two subjects compared are incompatible. *Mathematics* is not like *the man*. The sentence would be better rephrased:

Like the man before him, he specialized in mathematics.

This misrelationship is a common mistake of careless writing, not confined only to *like*.

Pronouns following *like* are in the accusative case, *like you and me*, not *like you and I*.

like (verb) A construction frequently encountered is *would like to*:

There is one passage in the article that I would like to change.

If the verb *like* is removed, the sentence is correct:

There is one passage . . . that I would change,

but with *like* included *should* is the correct form (see *shall*, *will*, *should*, *would*):

There is one passage in the article that I should like to change.

likely Only in dialect or archaic speech, especially in Scotland and Ireland, is *likely* found on its own without a qualifying *very*, *most* or *more*:

He will likely call tomorrow

sounds quaint to our ears and is not generally acceptable.

He will most likely call tomorrow

is quite correct.

limit, delimit To limit is to restrict by fixing limits or boundaries to something:

The extent of his pruning is limited by the height to which he can reach.

To *delimit* is to demarcate, to fix or mark the limits:

Let us delimit the distance he has to run with a white cross.

limited The meaning of this word has been extended beyond its proper province. Though not necessarily wrong, it is often used to stand in for other more suitable adjectives:

With limited resources the authority is limited to undertaking only a limited number of projects

could easily be written as:

With scarce resources the authority is restricted to undertaking only a few projects.

It is sometimes used as a euphemism to soften a much harsher meaning:

He is a man of limited means = he is poor.

The child was of limited intellect = he was backward.
The company's resources are limited = they're losing money.

This device has its uses, but can be overdone.

linage, lineage *Linage* is alignment, or the number of lines of written or printed matter. *Lineage*, which is pronounced as three syllables, is lineal descent from an ancestor.

lineament, liniment *Lineament* is a distinctive characteristic or feature of a face or body. *Liniment* is a liquid preparation for rubbing into the skin, especially in the treatment of bruises.

liqueur, liquor A *liqueur* is a strong, sweet alcoholic drink such as curaçao. *Liquor* refers to spirits such as brandy or whisky, though in the United States it may also apply to any alcoholic drink.

litany, liturgy A *litany* is a ceremonial form of prayer consisting of supplications with responses. *Liturgy* is a form of public worship, a particular arrangement of services.

literally This has become a word of emphasis which is all too often misapplied. It should never be used in a figurative sense, unless it is intended to indicate that what might be taken to be metaphorical is – *literally* – true:

I literally rolled about on the floor with laughter.

If this is really the case, the word is well used. If the speaker did not, in fact, lie down on the floor and roll over and over, the word should have no place in the sentence. But:

I literally screamed at him

carries the truth of hysteria and does its job of emphasis in the right place.

litotes This is a Greek word for the device by which an affirmative is expressed by the negative of its opposite, having the effect of a modest understatement. For example:

That's not a bad likeness, is it?

and:

She was not unattractive in a quiet sort of way,

meaning that she was rather fetching.

little, small Perhaps these words can best be differentiated by pairing them with their opposites, *big and little*, *large and small*, *much and little*. *Little* refers to size, duration or extent:

Little dog, little child, little time, little noise.

It is also widely used figuratively:

Little hope, little scope, little wonder,

and in these senses it contrasts with *much*, qualifying the amount or degree.

Small is a word of dimension, of limited size or quantity:

Small room, small size, small tree, small amount.

It too is used figuratively, and in some expressions overlaps with *little*:

Small thanks, small wonder, small consolation,

but on the whole each has its place in accepted idiomatic use.

loaded see **laden**

loan Once this word was in general use as a verb, but it was supplanted by *lend*. It survives in the United States, but in Britain it is not acceptable. *To lend* is the correct verb and *loan* is just the noun.

loath, loathe, loth *To loathe* is the verb meaning to feel hatred or intense aversion for. *Loath* is the adjective, meaning averse, unwilling or reluctant, and *loth* an alternative spelling, once the usual form but now less favoured than *loath*:

Although I always loathed the colour, I am rather loath to part with this dress, old though it is.

locality, location A *locality* is the geographical designation of a place, spot or district, without reference to the people or things in it. A *location* is a place of settlement or residence, or something occupied. The difference is largely in the association of people with the word *location*.

locate, find To *locate* is to discover the place of, to establish in a place or situation; to settle:

Can you locate the exact spot where the murder took place?

To *find* is to come upon by chance, or to recover something.

loose, loosen To *loose* is to free from restraint, to release:

If you loose his lead, he'll come to heel when you call.

To *loosen* is to slacken or relax, to make less tight. It is also sometimes used to signify undo or let go, but this is an extension of meaning which blurs the distinction between *loose* and *loosen* and should be avoided. It must, however, be borne in mind that *to loose* is only rarely encountered.

loose, lose These verbs are sometimes confused because of their similar spelling. The past and present participles of *loose* are *loosed* and *loosing*, and those of *lose* are *lost* and *losing*.

loud, loudly *Loud* is both an adjective and an adverb, and *loudly* is an adverb. *Loud* is usually used in reference to sound volume, though *loudly* also occurs in this context:

If you play it loud, the neighbours will hear.

Loudly is the form for the figurative sense of clamorous or vociferous:

He complained loudly when they cut off his allowance.

lustful, lusty *Lustful* is full of lust or passion. *Lusty* is characterized by healthy vigour, hearty.

luxuriant, luxurious *Luxuriant* is abundant in growth, producing abundantly. *Luxurious* is characterized by luxury or sumptuousness.

lyric, lyrical In poetry *lyric* is having the form and musical quality of a song and characterized by an ardent expression of feeling. Colloquially, *lyrics* mean the words of a song.
Lyrical is almost synonymous with *lyric*, but is also used more loosely to describe a general mood of euphoria:

She became quite lyrical in her praises.

M

-m-, -mm- Single-syllable words ending in *m* double it before suffixes beginning with a vowel if the *m* is preceded by a single vowel:

crammed, ramming, drummer, slimmest.

If it is preceded by two vowels or a vowel and an r the *m* is not doubled:

aiming, doomed, roomy, charming.

In words of more than one syllable the same rule applies as for single-syllable words if the last syllable is stressed:

overbrimming, undimmed.

Otherwise they do not double the *m*:

systematic, envenomed, ransoming, victimize, emblematic.

However, words ending in *-gram* do double the *m*:

diagrammatic, epigrammatic.

madam, madame *Madam* is the polite form of address for a woman. *Madame*, the French equivalent of the English *Mrs*, has the plural *mesdames*, which is still occasionally used in English as the plural of *madam*.

magic, magical Although the meanings of *magic* and *magical* are to a considerable extent interchangeable, a distinction can be made. *Magic* is almost exclusively concerned with the realm of the supernatural and is usually placed before the noun:

A magic carpet, a magic wand, magic forces.

Magical, on the other hand, is used mainly attributively (that is, following the verb) and tends to be employed more loosely to mean 'like magic':

The change was magical. The twilight appeared magical. A magical moment. A magical voice.

Mahomet, Mohammed *Mahomet* is the traditional English spelling of the name of the founder of Islam. In recent years this has been giving way to *Mohammed*, which has the merit of being closer in pronunciation to what the Arabs call him. The purists insist on *Mahammad* since the vowels *e* and *o* do not exist in Arabic, but *Mohammed* seems to be the most acceptable form for the time being. Similarly *Mohammedans* must now be preferred to *Mahometans*.

main clause In a sentence containing several clauses the main clause is the basic sentence, on which the other clauses depend, and which can stand by itself:

When they arrived, although it was blowing fiercely, the sun was shining brightly.

In the above sentence *the sun was shining brightly* is the main clause.

major This word has lost most of its original force as a comparative but is in danger of being overworked because of its popularity in some quarters. It is frequently used when such words as *chief*, *principal* or *important* would have been more suitable.

majority This has several senses and it is important to distinguish between them. First of all *majority* is used to mean most or the numerically greater part:

His work makes an appeal to the majority of mankind.

It should not, however, be used of something which is not divisible numerically. Do not say:

The majority of this book is unreadable.

Majority also means a group of voters in agreement forming more than half the total number:

The majority decided to go ahead with their reforms.

Finally *majority* is the number by which votes cast for the leading candidate exceed those cast for the next in line:

His majority was so small as to be barely useful.

In this use of *majority* it is always followed by a singular verb, but in the other examples listed above it may be followed by either a singular or plural verb. The verb is normally plural when it refers to a collection of individuals.

malapropism This is the misapplication or misuse of words which have a similar sound or spelling but are widely divergent in meaning, usually producing a comical result:

The patient was to have an explanatory (read *exploratory*) operation.

male, manly, masculine *Male* is always used with reference to sex, whether of human beings or other forms of life:

Male animals in herds protect the females.

Manly means possessing the noblest qualities to be found in man:

His manly show of defiance in the face of adversity was an inspiration to us.

Masculine refers to those qualities that are supposed to be characteristic of the male sex:

He was noted for his masculine enthusiasm for the outdoor life.

mandatary, mandatory When used as nouns both words mean a person holding a mandate, the first being the more common form. However, when used as an adjective *mandatory* means 'obligatory' or 'permitting no option':

Attendance at the union meeting is mandatory.

mankind *Mankind* is always followed by a verb in the singular:

Mankind has not tolerated such treatment in the past.

mannered *Well-mannered* and *ill-mannered* are preferred by some authorities to *good-mannered* and *bad-mannered*, but the latter two seem to be steadily gaining ground.

many a This phrase is always used with a singular verb, although *many* by itself always requires the plural:

Many a good man has been ruined in this way.

marginal This has become such a favourite with some writers, who use it to mean 'slight', 'slightest' or 'small', that it is in danger of losing its basic sense. *Marginal* means close to a border, edge or dividing line, and so uncertain. Thus it is correct to talk about *a marginal constituency*, whose voters are likely to choose their candidate by a narrow margin.

marquess, marquis Both spellings are acceptable, but *marquess* has now established itself as the most popular amongst the English nobility who hold that rank.

marry see **wed**

marten, martin The *marten* is a North American mammal. *Martin* is the name given to any of various swallows.

mask, masque A *mask* is a covering for the face, especially one worn as a disguise. A *masque* was in times past a form of entertainment consisting of pantomime, dancing and song. It can also be spelt *mask*.

massive This is another word which has unfortunately become rather too fashionable in its figurative sense. It is used where a whole host of other adjectives would be more suitable, including *huge*, *widespread*, *vigorous*, *intense* and *powerful*. Avoid it in such phrases as:

> A massive assault on the problems of the Third World

and find a more fitting alternative.

masterful, masterly At one time these words were very close in meaning and there is still some confusion about their correct use. *Masterful* means showing the qualities of a master or dominant person, authoritative or domineering:

> The prime minister showed a masterful disregard for his opponent's angry protests.

Masterly means showing a high degree of skill in the performance of any activity:

The young pianist gave a masterly display of his talents.

materialize This word has been much overworked in recent years. It has several useful meanings including 'to assume material form' or 'to make physically perceptible'. It should not be used as a substitute for *happen*, *occur* or *take place*.

mathematics There is some doubt whether this should be followed by a plural or singular verb. It is generally followed by a singular verb when it is thought of as a science:

Mathematics is an important item in the school curriculum.

The plural is frequently used when reference is made to someone's specific knowledge of the subject:

She is good at games but her mathematics are weak.

Even here, however, there is uncertainty and the verb after *mathematics* may be influenced by a following singular noun:

Mathematics is his weak point.

maunder, meander These words are often incorrectly taken to be alternative forms of each other. *Maunder* means 'to speak in a rambling, foolish or incoherent way'. *Meander* means 'to wander aimlessly' or 'to proceed by a winding or indirect course'.

maxim A *maxim* is the expression of a general truth, especially in relation to conduct. [See also *aphorism*]

maximize This is another word which has suffered from overexposure. It means 'to increase to the greatest possible amount', but is often used as a substitute for *increase*, *enlarge*, *heighten*, etc.

may, might *May* is an auxiliary verb which is used to express possibility, probability or permission:

I may be able to work on Friday (possibility or probability).

May I go to the cinema tonight? (permission).

It is important not to confuse *may* with *can*, which implies ability or power to do something, although in colloquial speech *can* is frequently substituted for *may* in the sense of permission. *Might* is the past tense of *may* and is used with the same meanings:

He said he might be able to work on Friday.
The child asked if she might go to the cinema.

When *may* is used in the past tense with a perfect infinitive, it implies that there is still a possibility of something being so:

The prisoner may have been captured.

However, if the sentence is changed to:

The prisoner might have been captured,

then the possibility of his being captured existed in the past but does so no longer.

maybe, may be This is finding increasing favour as a synonym for *perhaps*. When used as a verb it must be written as two words:

It may be that I shall have to stay late.

me The use of *me* instead of *I* in such expressions as *it's me* and *it was me* now appears to have been accepted by most authorities. However, when *it's me* is followed by a clause beginning with *who*, educated speakers tend to revert to *I*:

It was I who discovered that the lock was broken.

means When this signifies 'resources or income', it takes a plural verb:

My means are not sufficient for a holiday abroad.

When it means 'method' it can be either singular or plural:

They found a new means of communication.
Several means are being tried out.

meantime, meanwhile When these words are used as adverbs *meanwhile* is generally preferred. However, of the expressions *in the meanwhile* and *in the meantime* the latter is more common.

medieval, mediaeval The first spelling is now more usual, although many people still prefer *mediaeval.*

medium, mediums, media When *medium* is used to mean a person through whom some supernatural agency is manifested the plural is always *mediums*. In other senses of the word either *mediums* or *media* are acceptable, but *media* seems to be gaining ground, no doubt because of its status as a vogue word.

meet, meet with To *meet* generally means 'to come into contact with, to encounter, become acquainted with':

I met the new teacher at the station.

To *meet with* has the sense of 'to undergo, experience or be subject to':

His efforts to improve matters met with much criticism.

melted, molten *Melted* is the past participle of *melt*. *Molten*, which is an alternative form, is now used only as an adjective applied to substances which are considered hard to melt: *melted butter* but *molten metal*, *molten lead*.

mendacity, mendicity *Mendacity* means 'the practice of lying'. *Mendicity* is 'the practice or condition of being a beggar'.

mental, mentality Both these words have acquired perjorative meanings. The basic sense of *mental* is 'pertaining to the mind', but it also means 'foolish or mad', although this particular slang use appears to be dying out. *Mentality* has undergone a similar downgrading and is frequently employed in a derogatory sense to describe a certain kind of character or disposition:

He had the mentality of a man who was unable to think for himself.

metaphor A *metaphor* is a figure of speech in which a term or phrase is applied to something to which it cannot literally refer in order to suggest a resemblance. In such phrases as:

> He proved to be a tower of strength, she spoke with tongue in cheek, he made an acid remark,

a man cannot literally be a tower nor a woman literally speak with her tongue in her cheek nor a remark be literally composed of acid. However, we accept such literary conventions because when properly used they enrich the language we speak and write. Pitfalls lie in employing the same metaphor too often, so that it becomes a cliché, such as *leave no stone unturned*, *grinding to a halt*, and many others. Another danger is the mixed metaphor, in which two or more images are confused, often with ludicrous results:

> Now that we have buttered our bread we must lie on it.

There is also the hazard of moving from a literal meaning to a metaphorical one:

> The even distribution of material has been made possible by the reduction of bottlenecks.

meticulous This means 'solicitous or finical about minute details'. Since it always implies excessive or undue care it should not be used as a synonym for such words as *careful*, *scrupulous* or *exact*, which have a more favourable connotation.

metre, meter These two words are sometimes the source of confusion. *Metre* is a basic unit of linear measurement now used in most countries. It is also used to mean 'a poetic measure or the arrangement of words in regularly patterned lines of verse'. When referring to linear measurement *metre* has the adjective *metric*. When it applies to verse the adjective is *metrical*. A *meter* is an instrument that measures and is frequently found in compound words like *thermometer*, *tachometer*, etc. This spelling is also used for the various poetic *metres*, as in *hexameter*, *pentameter*, etc.

Middle East This rather vague term was at one time used to describe lands as far east as Afghanistan, India, Tibet and Burma. It now tends to be confined to the countries at and beyond the eastern end of the Mediterranean, including Egypt, Syria and the Arabian Peninsula.

might see **may**

mileage, milage Some authorities claim that the *e* in *mileage* is an unnecessary one, since it does not affect the pronunciation. However, the spelling *mileage* is the preferred one in most dictionaries.

militate, mitigate *Militate* (*against*) means 'to work or operate against':

Unforeseen circumstances militated against the success of our plans.

Mitigate means 'to lessen, moderate or make less severe' but is quite frequently used by mistake for *militate*:

This unfortunate incident ought not to mitigate (read *militate*) against my chances of getting the job.

It is used correctly as follows:

Her gentle words successfully mitigated his anger.

million This is generally spelt without an *s* when it stands for a definite number:

Six million men; more than two million died.

When used vaguely to indicate a large amount, it usually adds an *s*:

Millions of times, thousands of millions of people.

The *s* is also used when *million* refers to money, even when a definite number is involved:

They estimated that the property was worth four millions.

minimal This means 'pertaining to the least possible or smallest'. It is a popular word and tends to be overworked, being frequently used where *slight* or *small* would be more suitable.

minimize see **diminish**

minimum This is another vogue word which is commonly misused. It means 'the least quantity or amount possible' and is often used where *a little* or *a small amount* would be more acceptable, as in:

The child gave only a minimum of trouble.

minority Like *majority* this occasionally causes some confusion. One meaning is 'the smaller part or number', or 'a number forming less than half the whole':

This film was appreciated only by a minority of those present.

Do not use *minority* to mean 'a few' or 'a very small number of' as in:

The police were called to investigate only a minority of cases.

Remember that a *minority* can be quite a large number, provided it is less than 50 per cent of a total. *Minority* is also used in the sense of a smaller group or party as opposed to a *majority*:

The minority on the council protested in vain against the new housing programme.

Minority may be followed by either a singular or plural verb, but the verb is usually plural when *minority* is considered as a collection of individuals:

A minority of the shareholders have strong objections.

mis- It is now normal practice not to hyphenate words made with this prefix, even when the word it is attached to already begins with an *s*:

misspell, misstatement.

misplaced modifiers These are words whose connection with the word they modify is not clear, thus leading to ambiguity. They include adverbs such as *only*, *nearly*, *hardly*, *scarcely*, *just*, *even* and *quite*. In a sentence like:

He only told her what he had seen

it is not clear what the speaker means. If he means

He told her what he had seen (and nothing else),

then the sentence should be recast as follows:

He told her only what he had seen.

[See also *only*]

Miss, Misses The correct plural of *Miss Brown* is the *Misses Brown*. However, although it may still be used on formal occasions the *Miss Browns* is now the usual plural.

mistrust see **distrust**

modifiers, dangling see **unattached participle**

Mohammed see **Mahomet**

momentary, momentous Despite similar spellings these adjectives have very different meanings. *Momentary* means 'lasting only very briefly':

He caught a momentary glimpse of a very beautiful woman.

Momentous means 'of great importance or having far-reaching consequences':

His decision was a momentous one for the future of the world.

monarchical, monarchic, monarchal *Monarchical* and *monarchic* are virtually interchangeable in their meaning 'of a monarch or characterized by monarchy', although *monarchical* is the much commoner form. *Monarchal* means 'befitting or having the status of a monarch' and carries an aura of pomp about it.

moneys, monies Both forms exist as the plural of *money* but *moneys* is the generally more acceptable form.

monogram, monograph A *monogram* is a character or device consisting of two or more letters combined or interlaced to make a design. A *monograph* is a treatise on a particular subject.

monologue, soliloquy Both words refer to a 'prolonged talk or discourse made by a single speaker'. However, whereas a *monologue* is usually intended to be heard, *soliloquy* means talking to oneself when alone or thinking out loud, regardless of whether anybody may be present. A *monologue* also means a form of dramatic entertainment by a single speaker.

moral, morale *Moral* means concerned with right conduct or the distinction between right and wrong:

It is impossible to ignore moral considerations in your treatment of people.

Morale, which is derived from a French word, *moral*, means the condition of mind which enables people to show courage, confidence or cheerfulness under difficult conditions:

He was amazed at the high morale of troops under fire.

morals see **ethics**

more The expression *more than one* is followed by a singular verb, despite being to all intents and purposes plural:

More than one boy was killed in the accident.

Otherwise verbs used with *more than* are in the plural:

More than ten men are involved in the plot.

Be careful not to try and form comparisons using *more* with adjectives which are already comparative such as *more prettier*, or with adjectives which cannot take a comparative form, such as *more superior*, *more unique* or *more perfect*.

mortgagor, mortgagee These words are often mixed up. The *mortgagor* is the person who mortgages his property, *i.e.*, the one who pledges his property in order to receive the loan. The *mortgagee* is the person to whom the property is mortgaged, *i.e.*, the one who lends money on the security of an estate.

Moslem, Muslim *Moslem*, the more traditional English spelling, is being displaced by *Muslim*, which is in fact a more accurate representation of the Arabic pronunciation. Both *Moslem* and *Muslim* add an *-s* to form the plural.

most, mostly Both *most* and *mostly* are adverbs and *mostly* is sometimes wrongly used in place of *most*:

It was the cyclist who was most (not *mostly*) to blame for the accident.

Mostly means 'for the most part' and is correctly used as follows:

By evening the work was mostly completed.

Most is also used in colloquial speech as a substitute for *very*, but is best avoided in writing:

He gave a most interesting account of his travels.

motivate, motivation These words first came into prominence in the domain of psychology and psychiatry, where they have a useful function to perform. However their increasing popularity has been at the expense of more suitable words such as *move* or *impulse*.

mow The past tense of this verb is *mowed* and the past participle *mown* or *mowed*. When the past participle is used as an adjective *mown* is the preferred form: *mown grass*.

MS, MSS *MS* is the contracted form for *manuscript* and *MSS* for *manuscripts*. However, since *MS* is always pronounced 'manuscript', it should be preceded by *a* and not *an*.

much, very As a general rule *much* is used with participles and *very* with adjectives: *much admired*, *much emphasized*, but *very bad*, *very pleasant*, etc. Some participles which have lost their verbal force are treated as adjectives and take *very*:

very pleased, very tired, very interested.

much more, much less These phrases are frequently a source of confusion. The general rule is that *much more* is used in an affirmative sentence:

It is hard enough to understand him, much more sympathize with him.

Much less frequently occurs in sentences which in fact require *much more* and many people would be tempted to use it in the above example. *Much less*, however, must be used only with negative sentences:

We did not even hear them, much less see them.

mucus, mucous Remember that *mucus* is the noun and *mucous* the adjective, *mucus* being defined as 'a secretion of the *mucous* membranes'.

mulatto A *mulatto* (plural *mulattos* or *mulattoes*) is the offspring of parents one of whom is white and the other a Negro. [See also *creole*, *quadroon*]

Muslim see **Moslem**

must This auxiliary verb implies necessity, obligation, or compulsion. Originally a past tense, it is now used only in the present:

Soldiers must obey orders.

Weaker obligations are expressed by the auxiliaries *ought to* and *should*. [See also *ought*, *shall*]

mute e The spelling of words or suffixes formed from words ending in mute *e* (silent or unpronounced *e*) has always been a source of confusion and uncertainty. The rules, to which there are unfortunately many exceptions, are as follows.

A mute *e* at the end of a word is retained before a suffix beginning with a consonant:

tamely, homeless, blameworthy, judgement (also spelt judgment), acknowledgement (also spelt acknowledgment).

but note the exceptions *truly*, *duly*.

A mute *e* at the end of a word is dropped before a suffix beginning with a vowel: *loving*, *proving whitish*. However, *e* is retained to prevent *c* or *g* becoming hard before a following *a* or *o*:

changeable, changeover, peaceable, traceable.

There are, in addition, a number of words such as *rateable* and *ratable*, *mileage* and *milage* in which alternate spellings exist. [See also *spelling*]

mutual see **common, reciprocal**

myth see **legend**

N

-n-, -nn- In a single-syllabled word followed by a suffix a final *n* is doubled if the vowel before it is a short one, as in *sun*, *sunny*, but not if the vowel is long, such as in *yawn*, *yawning*. With words of more than one syllable the same rules apply when the stress is on the second syllable, as in *beginning*, *refrained*, *remaining* or *buffoonery*, but the *n* does not double even after a short vowel when the stress is on the first syllable, as in *deafened*, *threatening* or *kittenish*.

naive This is now the accepted anglicized spelling of the French word *naïve* (masculine *naïf*). The nearest English meaning to it is ingenuous, unsophisticated or showing natural simplicity. It is a useful word, since there is no exact equivalent in English.

napkin, serviette *Serviette* is a term frowned on by many people as a genteel euphemism for *napkin* which, though an honest word, has a wider application with some less pleasant associations.

nationalize, naturalize To *nationalize* is to bring under the control or ownership of a nation, and is a term applied chiefly to land or industries. To *naturalize* means to confer the rights and privileges of citizenship on a foreign national. It is also applied to the introduction and successful adaptation of animals and plants to a region so that they thrive as if in their original natural surroundings.

native(s) Applied as a generic term to foreign nationals, especially those of Africa and Asia, the word is offensive, implying a patronage reminiscent of the days of colonialism. It is acceptable, however, if used in its specific sense, which could not be interpreted as disparaging:

He returned to his native land (he returned to the country where he was born),

and:

He was a native of France/Britain/Ireland/India,

or:

Only a native (of this town) would know his way through the back streets.

nature This is one of those words adopted by lovers of verbosity to deck out their adjectives:

It was a journey of an exploratory nature

would be more simply expressed as:

It was an exploratory journey,

and:

The dress she wore was of a diaphanous and flimsy nature

simply means:

She wore a diaphanous, flimsy dress.

But in the example:

The nature of his illness was never disclosed

the word is being used in its proper context.

naught, nought *Naught* is the archaic form, occasionally used in a poetical context, and *nought* is used in a strictly numerical sense:

Naught availed her, though she begged for mercy

and:

It's like a game of noughts and crosses.

near, nearly The adverbial use of *near*, for *nearly*, meaning 'almost', 'all but', is rarely used, except in dialect:

He was near exhausted

is more likely to be rendered as:

He was nearly exhausted

or:

He was near exhaustion.

nearby, near by *Nearby* is an adjective:

He called at the nearby farm for milk

and *near by* an adverb:

He called at the farm near by for milk.

But in modern usage *nearby* may also be accepted in an adverbial sense in place of *near by*.

Near East This is no longer a specific term, but a loose geographical definition incorporating the Balkan States, Egypt and the countries of South West Asia (Turkey, Lebanon, Syria, Israel, Jordan, Saudi Arabia, etc.).

need Confusion sometimes arises with this word, which occurs both as a verb and as a noun. The verb appears in:

He needs a new coat,

and:

A new coat is needed for winter.

In the construction:

He needs to have a new coat

the verb takes the infinitive in the usual way, but the negative:

He does not need to buy new clothes

can be expressed:

He need buy no new clothes.

Here the verb becomes an auxiliary like *must* and does not require the *to*. This is also true of a question:

Need he buy new clothes?

In the sentence:

He needs must purchase a coat

needs is an adverb meaning 'of necessity'. It is an archaic term used only occasionally in this context.

As a noun, *need* appears as:

He has need of a new coat

or:

He is in need of a new coat.

need, want *Need* is used in an objective sense; *want* is subjective. To become educated, a child may *need* to go to school. At the same time, the child may not *want* to go to school.

Colloquially *want* is sometimes substituted for *need* in the sense of 'ought to':

He wants to be careful he does not lose his wallet.

negatives Before condemning the double negative out of hand, it should be remembered that in some countries a repetition of negatives throughout a sentence serves to strengthen the negation, and at one time our own language followed a similar course. However, in modern usage two negatives are regarded as cancelling each other out and resulting in a positive:

I don't know nothing about it

means that I *do* know something about it. Even in educated speech it is very easy to slip unwittingly into a contradiction:

She said she had found nothing to make her doubt that it wasn't true.

The negative *that it wasn't true* should be a positive *was true* for the sentence to make its point.

If the first part of a sentence is negative, care must be taken that the rest of the sentence is consistent with the writer's intention:

No men will be recruited during the winter months but will be signed on in early spring.

The second part of the sentence has no subject of its own and is referring back to *no men*, which was clearly not intended. A fresh subject is needed – perhaps 'new recruits'.

Nobody wanted to go home by bus and agreed to take a taxi instead.

Nobody agreed? Again, a new subject is needed: *everyone* agreed.

The placing of the negative is important. In:

It is not believed to be a matter of choosing between fact and speculation but of making up our minds on the basis of probabilities

the main verb *it is believed* applies to the whole sentence and the negative to part of the sentence only. Here, by governing the main clause it reverses the meaning of the second part of the sentence:

It is not believed to be a matter of . . . making up our minds on the basis of probabilities.

The sentence should read:

It is believed to be not a matter of choosing between fact and speculation but of making up our minds on the basis of probabilities.

neither . . . nor If both the subjects joined by this correlative conjunction are singular, they will take a singular verb:

Neither the boy nor his dog was harmed.

If one of the subjects is singular and one plural, the verb may agree with the nearer subject:

Neither the captain nor his men were prepared for the attack

or:

Neither the men nor their captain was prepared for the attack.

However, it is more usual and sounds more natural to place the plural noun next to the verb and to use a plural verb, as in the first example.

More than two subjects may be included:

The answer was neither animal nor vegetable nor mineral,

but in:

Neither children, nor cats nor dogs nor any other kind of pet is welcome here.

It should read cats *or* dogs, since the meaning implies one category in which these terms are alternatives to each other and are not therefore correlated separately to the other subjects in the sentence.

Netherlands, The This is the proper name for the kingdom of Holland, the adjective for which is Dutch.

never Literally, this is 'not ever', and is used to emphasize a negative sentence:

I should never have allowed him to go.

This is stronger than:

I should not have allowed him to go.

However, it must be remembered that as a negative it should not be used with another one:

Nobody, however hard he tries, can never believe what I've been through

is therefore incorrect. For *never* substitute *ever*. The same rule applies in:

I promise I shan't never do it again

which would be better expressed as:

I promise I shall never do it again.

never so, ever so Once accepted in normal speech, *never so* was replaced by *ever so* in a construction such as:

She refused to listen to his protestations, spoke he never so gently.

This construction, too, has fallen out of use and today *ever so* occurs chiefly as a colloquial expression, frowned on as a vulgarism, and used in the sense of 'very':

I am ever so sorry.

nice One of the original meanings of this word was minute, fine or subtle, as of a distinction, or requiring delicacy or precision. Its commonest use today is as a blanket term meaning amiably pleasant, agreeable, delightful, or refined. It has been so overused and its meaning so broadened that it is almost valueless – ironic that a word once implying precision should now represent the opposite, and provide us with a vague, bland expression of pleasure. As a term of approval it is therefore best avoided.

nom de plume These French words, of which the literal translation is 'pen name', are the term for a writer who wishes to remain anonymous and uses a false name. The true French term for the same thing is *nom de guerre* (literally, 'war name').

nomenclature This is not just another more impressive word for 'name', but a word meaning a set or system of names of terms, such as is used in scientific or other fields requiring classificatory terminology. For example:

A club has just been started under the nomenclature of the Rosebery Committee Youth Association

is incorrect. A proper context is:

Linnaeus established the binomial system of scientific nomenclature.

non- A negative form which is often too easily used in place of a genuine word. There are many examples where it has a legitimate use because there is no single word as an alternative:

Because of the non-appearance of the star, the show was cancelled.

But in:

His non-positive approach was a handicap,

'negative' would be a preferable substitute.

none This pronoun may take a singular or a plural verb, according to which sense is most logical. So in a sentence such as:

He made us all stand up in turn; none of us was spared

none means 'not one' and therefore indicates a singular verb. But in:

Of the events which followed none are worth recording

none here means 'not any', referring to the events, and should therefore be followed by a plural verb. But applied to a collective term such as an amount or quantity, *none* in the sense of 'not any' would take a singular verb:

None of the money was spent.

non-restrictive see **restrictive**

nonsense The idiomatic use of this word:

This is nonsense

has long been accepted. What has been less readily assimilated is the use of the word with the indefinite article:

He made a nonsense of the test and had to take it again.

But events have overtaken the purists and this development of the idiom is now in such common use that its incursion into the language is unlikely to be repelled.

non-sequitur Literally, 'it does not follow'. This term means a statement or argument which does not relate to the premise which has gone before it:

She is a beautiful girl, so she is going to be a film star.

The second statement is not necessarily a consequence of the first.

nor Following neither, *nor* should always be used, just as *or* should always follow either. But in a negative sentence where the verb governs the whole sentence *nor* can have the effect of a double negative:

The purpose of education is not to stuff the heads of children with facts, nor with the doctrines nor prejudices of their teachers.

In this sentence *or* should be substituted.

However, if the verb with its negative applies to only one part of a sentence the second part must be reinforced by the negative *nor*:

He had little sense of achievement at the end of the day's work, nor did he have much in the way of material reward.

Where the verb is positive and the negative is attached to only one part of the sentence *nor* is attached to the other negative alternatives:

The use of a car is justified not just on the grounds of seniority, nor of distance nor time saving, but simply on account of expediency.

northerly see **easterly**

nostalgia, homesickness *Nostalgia* is defined as a longing and desire for home, family and friends. It has also acquired the additional meaning beyond homesickness of a yearning for times that have passed and this is the sense in which it is increasingly used. The meaning of *homesickness* is confined to the longing and desire for home, family and friends.

not There is nothing wrong with the idiomatic construction:

All women are not fools

but it is simpler to say:

Not all women are fools,

and easier to grasp the meaning at first glance.

The deliberate use of two negatives in a construction to convey a positive message is a peculiarly British quirk, having the effect of a gross understatement:

He exerted a not inconsiderable amount of energy in screwing up his courage to pop the question,

and:

She was not wholly unprepared for it.

Too much of this kind of irony can, however, easily become tedious. Used in an exclamation:

Not you again!

the force of the negative is in its positive meaning, equivalent to saying, 'So it's you again!'

Other idiomatic constructions where the sentence may be started with *not* are:

Not that I was one of them, but I understood how they felt,

and:

He called for volunteers and was greeted with silence. Not a man replied.

notable, noted *Notable* is worthy of notice, distinguished or prominent. *Noted* is celebrated or famous. In general, *notable* is applied to events or things and *noted* to people.

not only . . . but also A common error with this type of correlative conjunction is that it is often misplaced:

She must realize that not only are we interested in her present career but also in her future prospects

should be rephrased to read:

She must realize that we are interested not only in her present career but also in her future prospects.

The second sentence is better balanced. Each of the correlating conjunctions *not only . . . but also* is followed by a matching phrase, and the verb (*are interested*) is common to both. The important point to bear in mind is that the verb should come before the two correlating phrases since it governs both.

If one subject is singular and the other plural, the verb may agree with the subject nearest to it, though to avoid awkwardness it might be preferable to rephrase the sentence:

Not only the pupils but also their teacher has the right to express an opinion.

The more usual and natural-sounding way of expressing this would be to transpose the singular and plural nouns and use a plural verb:

Not only their teacher but also the pupils have the right to express an opinion.

notorious, famous *Notorious* means widely and publicly known for unfavourable reasons:

With his notorious weakness for drink, he soon spent all his money.

Famous is celebrated, renowned or well known for favourable reasons, though it may be used ironically:

One of the most famous of all generals was the Duke of Wellington.

It can also be used colloquially to mean excellent or first rate:

We had a famous night out on Saturday.

noun The modern tendency to use nouns as adjectives is deplored by some writers, especially in cases where there is a perfectly good adjective already in existence:

His home circumstances were unsatisfactory.

Domestic would be a better adjective than *home*. But since, as in that example, the alternative –

The circumstances at his home were unsatisfactory

– is often lengthier, there is quite a strong argument in support of the noun adjective, provided it does not result in ambiguity. This is especially liable to occur in newspaper headlines:

Police Chief Focus of Attack

Is this referring to the chief of police? Or are the police the chief focus? The ambiguity in such a headline has done its work, however, if it makes us look twice. The danger is that this kind of headline journalese tends to be used excessively in everyday speech. *The world food situation, the railway workers' strike, the Government Services Department report* – the proliferation of noun adjectives appear in longer and longer phrases until they require unravelling to make sense. A judicious use of the word 'of' would simplify them all.

number A common mistake is to use a plural verb when the subject is singular but the rest of the sentence is plural:

The attraction of the birds are chiefly in their songs.

It is *the attraction* that is the true subject of this sentence and the verb should therefore be singular. When two single subjects are offered as alternatives, the verb must remain singular, because they are independent of each other:

He must decide whether his wife or his sweetheart takes precedence in his affections.

But if one subject is singular and the other plural, the sentence can either be rephrased to avoid awkwardness, or the verb can follow the nearest subject:

He must decide whether his wife or his children come first.

Nouns of multitude are those words such as 'group' or 'party' which represent a collection of people as a single unit, and can be treated as either singular or plural. Where the group acts as one person, a singular verb may be preferable, but if it is thought of as a collection of individuals the plural form is better:

The committee decided it would meet again on the following day,

but:

The union were ready to call a full-scale strike.

The word *number* itself takes a plural verb if it suggests several units:

A number of children were playing in the snow,

but a singular verb if it refers to an amount or a total:

The number of people going abroad for holidays is higher than ever before.

numbers In general reading matter, numbers and fractions should be expressed in words, not in figures, unless particularly long or complicated. Twenty thousand may be written out, but it is preferable to present 20,345 in figures. Time may be expressed either way. Dates should be written in figures. Except in dates, where the name of the month is included, words and figures should never be mixed, and a sentence should never begin with a figure. This should always be spelt out.

O

O, Oh The interjection *O* is used only in poetry. *Oh* occurs in all other cases, usually followed by a comma, except in phrases such as 'Oh dear!', or 'Oh no!':

> Oh, look at that lovely moon!

object, objective The words both mean an end towards which efforts are directed, or something aimed at, but *object* has several wider meanings as well, other than abstract ones, and can also denote purpose:

> The object of the game is to see who can get the highest number of goals.

Originally a military term, *objective* is best reserved for a goal to be aimed at, an aim to be achieved:

> His first objective is to win the support of the people, his next to win the support of the Government.

obliqueness, obliquity Both words mean the state of being oblique, but *obliquity* is more often used in a figurative sense meaning moral delinquency or mental perversity.

oblivious The meaning of this word is forgetful, without remembrance, not unaware or unconscious, with which it is often equated:

> He was oblivious of the anger expressed on the faces of those behind him.

This is incorrect. *Unconscious* would be a more appropriate word here.

> Oblivious to the rain that cascaded down, he watched, fascinated, as the bird fed her young.

This example is nearer the true meaning, but strictly speaking the correct preposition is *of*, not *to*.

obnoxious, noxious The original meaning of *obnoxious* is exposed or liable to harm or evil, but the more widely used sense today is objectionable, offensive or odious.

Noxious is harmful to health or, in a figurative sense, morally harmful, pernicious.

observance, observation *Observance* is the action of conforming to, obeying or following, or a celebration by proper procedure, ceremony or rite:

The observance of a cease-fire is vital to the peace negotiations.

Observation is the act of noticing, perceiving or watching; that which is learnt by observing. It can also mean a remark or comment:

Your observation about the weather could have a bearing on my own observations made in the bird sanctuary last spring.

In this example the word has been used in two of its senses.

obsolete, obsolescent Obsolete means no longer in use, discarded, out of date:

The hansom cab is an obsolete vehicle.

Obsolescent is tending to become out of date, passing out of use:

The piston-engined plane is obsolescent.

Obsolete is a stage beyond *obsolescent*.

obstacle, impediment *Obstacle* is something that stands in the way of progress:

Her mother's opposition to the marriage was an obstacle still to be overcome.

An *impediment* implies a physical defect, such as a speech disorder, an obstruction or hindrance:

Lame though he was, his impediment did not prevent him from undertaking a strenuous job.

occupant, occupier An *occupant* is one who is occupying a place, seat or compartment. An *occupier* is one who occupies living or office premises. The first suggests a temporary occupation, the second, one of a more permanent nature.

occur see **happen**

oculist, optician An *oculist* is a doctor who specializes in examination and treatment of the eye; an ophthalmologist. An *optician* is one who makes and sells glasses according to the prescriptions of an oculist. However, although he is not medically qualified an *optician* may also be competent to prescribe glasses for correcting defects of vision.

odious, odorous *Odious* is hateful or detestable. *Odorous* is having or diffusing an odour, especially a fragrant one.

-o(e)s Most of the commonest words ending in *-o*, such as *tomato*, *potato*, *hero*, *cargo*, take an *-e* in forming the plural: *potatoes*, *heroes*, *tomatoes*. So do words of a single syllable, such as *does* in 'does and don'ts', *noes* in 'yeses and noes' and *goes*. Words which occur less frequently in the plural, shortened words like *photo*, words in which the *-o* is preceded by a vowel, foreign words, especially of Italian origin, and many long words ending in *-o* do not take an additional *-e-* but invariably finish in *-os* in the plural. Some examples are:

concertos, photos, memos, folios, manifestos.

of This preposition is sometimes carelessly used when, in a complex sentence, a clause is introduced by one preposition and requires linking to another. A secondary use of *of* has perhaps just occurred and it is mistakenly repeated in place of the correct word:

She will be of most value to us for her knowledge of French and *of* her ability to speak fluently and clearly in public.

For should be substituted here for *of*.

It is also sometimes misplaced:

His chief ambition was the acquisition of a good job and of finding a comfortable home.

This should be amended to *the finding of* a comfortable home. Never say *off of*. This is a vulgarism which is quite unacceptable:

He took it off of me

should be:

He took it from me.

official, officious The adjective *official* means pertaining to an office of trust or authority, authorized or possessing authority. *Officious* is pressing one's services upon others obtrusively:

I don't mind being told what to do by an official steward, but I refuse to be bossed by an officious underling!

O.K. This is a colloquialism that is universally accepted either in its initial form or spelt out as *okay*, but it should not be used in formal speech or writing. In a commercial context it is acceptable as an adjective, verb and noun.

olden This adjective is used only in the limited context of *olden days*.

Old English, Anglo-Saxon Both terms refer to the English language of the period before A.D. 1100.

older see **elder**

Olympian, Olympic *Olympian* is pertaining to Mount Olympus, home of the gods of ancient Greece. *Olympic* refers primarily to the Olympic games, though it can also mean the same as *Olympian*.

-on Some words ending in *-on* which are derived from Greek take *-a* in the plural, for example *criterion* and *criteria*, *ganglion* and *ganglia*, *phenomenon* and *phenomena*. With others, though an *-a* suffix would not be wrong, the English *-s* ending is usually employed, as in *skeletons*. Other words such as *tendon*, *nylon* or *siphon* take a different form in Greek and therefore should always be given the *-s* plural in English.

one Words compounded of *one* should be written:

anyone, everyone, someone, oneself, no one.

Some accidents can happen with the use of this pronoun:

One of the trains which runs to Waterloo has been cancelled.

This is wrong. The pronoun *which* is referring to the trains, so the verb of the subordinate clause should be in the plural:

One of the trains which run to Waterloo has been cancelled.

Another incorrect stentence is:

One of the longest, if not the longest, song was eliminated.

If the sentence is reduced to its bare essentials it will be seen to read: *One . . . was eliminated.* One what? *Of the longest . . . song.* This must clearly be amended to *songs.*

One may also be used as a pronoun either numerically:

There were one or two things I had to do,

or impersonally, standing in for a person or people in general:

One must work in order to live,

or as a 'false' personal pronoun, replacing the first person *I*:

One likes to feel one has been able to make a tiny contribution to this marvellous cause.

This last practice is condemned as an affectation and should be avoided.

If *one* has been used in a sentence it must not be changed halfway through to another pronoun:

It was bad enough to have one's shortcomings exposed, but to have to admit ignorance on my own pet subject was humiliating.

Either *one's* should be replaced by *my*, or *my* should give way to *one's* again.

One's is the only pronoun to take the apostrophe in the possessive case.

one another This is the correct form to use when referring to more than two people, for whom *each other* (*q.v.*) would be appropriate:

The two of them eyed each other suspiciously,

but:

All the members of the team helped one another to perfect their tactics.

However, in common usage *each other* is often used colloquially in this context.

In the possessive case it must be remembered that *one another* remains in the singular:

They helped to perfect one another's tactics.

ongoing This is a colloquial term which seems to have originated in the United States. It has become a vogue word meaning 'continuing', which is freely used in commercial circles in Britain. Provided it is not destroyed by overuse, it could become as useful a part of the English language as its opposite number *oncoming*:

The ongoing success of the company's export effort is reflected in the figures.

only This word is perhaps misplaced more frequently than any other. Its position in a sentence governs the entire meaning, as these examples will demonstrate:

Only she was wearing a bikini on the beach (nobody else was).
She was only wearing a bikini on the beach (ambiguous – could be 'Just imagine! That's all she was doing', or she was wearing nothing else, or it was just on the beach that she was wearing a bikini).
She was wearing only a bikini on the beach (and nothing else).
She was wearing a bikini only on the beach (and nowhere else).
She was wearing a bikini on the beach only (and nowhere else; possibly it was the only place where she was wearing anything at all).

It is not always best, however, to be too pedantic. What looks right and seems the position most acceptable in common usage for the sense intended may well be the most suitable, provided the meaning is absolutely clear and unambiguous.

onomatopoeia The formation of a name or word by imitating the sound associated with it: *buzz*, *cuckoo*, *clop*, for example, or of a phrase suggesting the sound:

'... murmuring of innumerable bees'.

on to, onto There has been disagreement for a long time between those who prefer to write this as two words and those who believe it should be one, and it remains a matter of choice. When it occurs as a separate adverb suggesting movement and as a preposition it must be regarded as two words, and written separately:

After visiting Coventry, he went on to Birmingham.

Onto should not be used unnecessarily if either *on* or *to* will do alone:

He put his gloves on the table

is quite sufficient. To say:

He put his gloves onto the table

implies that he moved them from somewhere else, and is a more deliberate action. But:

He drove on the motorway

has quite a different meaning from:

He drove onto the motorway,

and to make the distinction when necessary is perfectly valid.

onward, onwards *Onward* is both an adjective and an adverb and is more commonly used than *onwards*, which is an adverb only.

operator, operative An *operator* is a worker skilled in operating a machine. An operative, also a worker, is skilled in some branch of work, especially productive or industrial. *Operative* is a more loosely applied term and it is also a jargon word which, used as an adjective, has come to mean most effective or important:

In any society cooperation and mutual respect are vital to its success, and the operative word is respect.

Such usage is best avoided.

optimistic, pessimistic *Optimistic* was originally used to describe someone who believed that good ultimately predominates over evil, and *pessimistic* someone who thought that everything in the world naturally tends to evil. Both words have extended their meanings considerably. They are now vogue words, *optimistic* having come to mean disposed to take a favourable view of things and *pessimistic*, inclined to take the gloomiest possible view:

I am very optimistic about the Company's prospects for the coming year,

and:

The Chairman takes a pessimistic view about the country's prospects of curbing inflation.

optimum This is another vogue word suffering from overuse, especially in its figurative sense, and consequently in danger of losing its precise meaning – the best or most favourable conditions for the growth or reproduction of an organism. As an adjective it has come to be loosely used to mean 'best':

That model is the optimum in luxury at such a price.

But in the example:

A large, modern factory and up-to-date machinery offer the optimum conditions for successful expansion

there is a good case for it: in a figurative sense, the word is not far from its original meaning.

or In a sentence such as:

I am not old nor stupid

or could equally well be substituted for *nor*. The sentence can be read in two ways – either *I am not old, nor am I stupid*, or *old or stupid* could simply be regarded as interchangeable alternatives, in which case *or* is correct.

Sometimes *or* is incorrectly substituted for *and*:

No advantage or no profit will result from this transaction.

This implies that either there will be no advantage or there will be no profit, but not that there will be neither. *And* should be substituted for *or*, or alternatively it should be rewritten as *no advantage or profit*.

-or Many nouns, particularly those ending in -ate, which are derived from a Latin verb, end in *-or* instead of the English *-er*:

placate, placator; dictate, dictator; liberate, liberator.

Others also take the *-or* ending:

collector, protector, director,

and some have alternative endings, *-er* when applied to people and *-or* for inanimate objects:

adapter or adaptor; conveyer or conveyor.

oral see **aural**

ordinance, ordnance An *ordinance* is a decree or command, an authoritative rule or law. *Ordnance* is cannon or artillery, or military weapons of all kinds.

orient, orientate The *Orient* is the name given to the East, applied to countries east of the Mediterranean, from the archaic word *orient* meaning east. It also means the lustre of a pearl. The verb *to orientate* is to place so as to face the east, or to place something in any definite position in relation to compass points or surroundings. It is also sometimes used figuratively. The verb *to orient* means the same thing, but is little used in Britain. In the United States, however, it is preferred.

Oriental, Eastern *Oriental* refers to those lands east of the Mediterranean. *Eastern* can apply to the eastern part of any country or continent. When used as proper names both words should be written with a capital letter, but as technical or geographical terms these adjectives are written with small initial letters:

The eastern part of Britain is flatter than the west.

ornate, ornamental *Ornate* is elaborately adorned, sumptuously splendid. *Ornamental* means used for ornament or decorative.

oscillate, osculate *To oscillate* is to swing to and fro like a pendulum. Figuratively it means to fluctuate between opinions and purposes. *To osculate* is to kiss, to bring into close contact.

other The phrase *on the other hand* is sometimes used where *on the contrary* is required. *On the other hand* introduces a supplementary statement to a first statement, whereas *on the contrary* proposes a contradiction:

> The yield was hardly a lavish one; on the other hand, it was lower than usual.

This sentence clearly demands *on the contrary*. But:

> He could see that she was feeling the cold. On the other hand, she made no complaint.

Here the phrase is correct. There is nothing contradictory about the second sentence, which is complementary to the first.

In a sentence such as:

> He could do no other but accept the part he was offered,

but should be replaced by *than*.

otherwise A fault which is widely perpetrated is to use *otherwise* where *other* or *others* would be preferable:

> Those who support libraries, teachers or otherwise, must bear a share of the costs,

and:

> Not all the union's supporters, Labour or otherwise, agree with the decisions made.

In the first sentence a straight substitution of *others* for *otherwise* should be made. The second example might better be expressed as:

> Not all the union's Labour or other supporters agree with the decisions made.

When meaning *or else*, the word *otherwise* is sufficient alone:

> You must have a ticket or otherwise you won't get in.

Or is superfluous here. The sentence should read:

You must have a ticket, otherwise you won't get in.

ought Never say *you didn't ought to.* It is a vulgarism. *Ought* is the past tense of an old verb to *owe*, and it cannot be used with an auxiliary verb. The negative is simply *ought not to*. The verb must be followed by an infinitive, and is therefore incorrect expressed as:

He ought but doesn't want to pay,

which should be rephrased to read:

He ought to pay but doesn't want to.

Ought is stronger than *should*, expressing more of a general moral judgement, whereas *should* is simply a pious hope.

-our, -or Words with an *-our* ending such as *humour*, *valour*, and *vapour* lose the *u* if their adjectives end in *-ous*:

humorous, valorous, and vaporous,

but the *u* is retained for adjectives ending in *-able*, such as *honourable* or *favourable*.

In American usage such words are spelt without a *u*: *honor*, *color*, *favor*.

outdoor, outdoors The adjective is *outdoor*:

I like an outdoor swimming pool,

and the adverb is *outdoors*, as in *Let's eat outdoors*, but many consider the three-word phrase, *out of doors*, preferable to this.

outstanding This word can easily lead to ambiguity with its two meanings, 'prominent, conspicuous' or 'remaining unsettled, unpaid':

The figures are rather high but the quarterly report is outstanding.

Is it late? Or is it sensational? *Still outstanding* would clarify one of the meanings.

outward, outwards *Outward* is both an adjective and adverb, pertaining to what is seen or apparent, or to the outside of the body, or proceeding towards the outside:

Don't judge him by his outward appearance.

It is used in a wide range of senses, especially figuratively. *Outwards*, the adverb, is used chiefly in its literal sense of towards the outside, out:

He moved outwards from the curb, just as I was about to pass.

overall What has always been a versatile word, with its use as a noun meaning a garment, an adverb meaning all over, and an adjective describing the extent of a measurement, has now become a popular vogue word which is often used indiscriminately and meaninglessly:

She was elected with an overall majority of 47,

and:

The overall character of the area is rundown and derelict,

and:

After touring the factory, he made a short report to the Director giving his overall impressions.

In each of these examples the only contribution the word has made to the sentence is to fill up space.

overflow The past tense and past participle of this verb is *overflowed* not *overflown* or *overflew*. These are the past participle and past tense of *overfly*.

overlay, overlie *Overlay* is the past tense of *overlie* which, though transitive, corresponds to the verb *to lie* (*q.v.*). The past participle therefore is *overlain* and the present participle is *overlying*:

Heavy clouds have overlain the mountains all day.

There is also a transitive verb *to overlay*, meaning to lay something over something else. This corresponds to the verb *to lay* (*q.v.*), and the past tense and past participle is *overlaid*, the present participle *overlaying*:

She is overlaying the edges with a narrow embroidered ribbon.

overlook, oversee To *overlook* is to fail to notice or perceive, or to disregard. It also means to view from a higher position. To *oversee* is to supervise or manage, to observe without being seen.

oversea(s) There used to be a singular form *oversea* in use as an adjective, but this has been superseded by the plural form *overseas*, which is also an adverb:

The overseas branch is doing remarkably well.

overtone, undertone Both these words, taken from a musical analogy, are used metaphorically: *overtone* to suggest that a word or phrase means more than is apparent, and *undertone* to express a feeling that beyond the words, there is still a wealth of meaning left unsaid.

owing to, due to Too often *owing to* is used clumsily in place of *because*, *since* or *as*. On the other hand, as a preposition it is a better phrase than *due to*, which is creeping in on its preserves:

Owing to a signal failure, trains will be running 20 minutes late.

P

-p-, -pp- Single-syllable words ending in *p* double it before suffixes beginning with a vowel if the *p* is preceded by a single vowel:

mapped, slapping, foppish, sloppy.

If it is preceded by two vowels, a vowel and an *m* or a vowel and an *r* the *p* is not doubled:

peeping, sharply, heaped, looped, stamping.

In words of more than one syllable the same rule applies as for single-syllable words if the last syllable is stressed:

unmapped, enwrapping *but* unstamped.

There are however some words of more than one syllable which do not obey the rule. *Handicap*, *kidnap*, *worship* and some others are not stressed on the last syllable but nevertheless double the *p*:

handicapped, kidnapping, worshipper.

palaeo-, paleo- This is a Greek prefix meaning 'old' or 'ancient'. The form *palaeo* is preferred in British English, although *paleo* is the more common spelling in American English.

panacea This does not mean a remedy for a particular disease or an infallible cure, but a remedy for all diseases.

pandemic see **endemic**

pandit, pundit In India a *pandit* is a 'learned man' or 'scholar'. The spelling *pundit*, which is an alternative form, is now used to describe anyone who claims to be an expert or a specialist in a particular subject.

panic This verb has the present participle *panicking* and the past tense and past participle *panicked. Picnic* forms its present participle and past tense in the same way.

para- There are two prefixes with the form *para*, one of Greek and one of Latin origin. The Greek prefix, meaning 'beside', 'beyond', or 'aside', is used in words like *paradox*, *paraphrase* and *parallel*. The Latin prefix, meaning 'guard against', occurs in *parachute*, *parapet*, and *parasol*.

parable A short allegorical story designed to convey a truth or moral lesson. [See also *allegory*]

paradox This is a seemingly self-contradictory or absurd statement that yet expresses a truth.

paragraph This is a distinct section of written matter dealing with a particular point or topic. There are no rules for deciding the lengths of a paragraph, but it is important that it should link together related sentences, dealing in a unified manner with a single theme. If the paragraph becomes too long, it is sensible to split it up. On the other hand, paragraphs can be made quite short if each one deals with a separate topic.

parallel This verb does not double the *l* when suffixes are added: *paralleling*, *paralleled*, making it an exception among verbs ending in *-l*. [See also *-l-*, *-ll-*, *spelling*]

parameter This is another word whose popularity has led to a distortion and oversimplification of its very specialized meaning in mathematics. It is frequently used as a synonym for *boundary*, *limit* or *framework*, any of which is preferable.

parentheses see **brackets**

parody A *parody* is a humorous or satirical imitation of a literary work. Its purpose is frequently to ridicule the writer of the original by making fun of his work, but the imitation of another's style or mannerisms is often used to launch an attack upon an entirely different target.

parricide, patricide The similarity in spelling is sometimes a source of confusion. *Parricide* is the more general word and means the murder of a parent or anyone to whom reverence is due. *Patricide* is the act of killing one's father.

partially, partly There is some overlapping between these two adverbs, but they are not really interchangeable. *Partially* means 'to a certain or limited extent':

> His opera was only partially completed at the time of his death.

Partly means 'as concerns one part' or 'not wholly':

> The letter was written partly in ink and partly in pencil.

Whereas *partly* could be substituted for *partially* in the first example, *partially* would be quite wrong in the second.

participles The English verb has two participles, the present which ends in *-ing*, and the past which may end in *-n* or *-en* in strong verbs and *-ed*, *-d* and *-t* in weak verbs. The participles are used to form compound tenses of verbs, the present participle forming the present continuous, *I am talking*, and the past participle the perfect tense, *I have talked*. Both present and past participles can be used as adjectives as in *a winding road*, *a stolen car*. They are also employed to form an adjectival phrase which qualifies a noun or pronoun in the main clause:

> Watching the children, he forgot about his troubles.
> Exhausted by his long vigil, the soldier fell asleep.

For the common error of the misrelated or unattached particle see *unattached participle*.

particular This useful adjective is sometimes used as a superfluous addition to a demonstrative adjective like *this* or *that* in such phrases as:

> We have nothing to add at this particular juncture.

part of speech This is the term given to the function that a word performs in a sentence. There are eight parts of speech: noun, pronoun, verb, adjective, adverb, preposition, conjunction and interjection, and each has an entry in this book.

passed, past The verb *pass* has *passed* as its past participle:

The time had passed very quickly.

The form *past* is used whenever the past participle is employed as an adjective:

During the past three months.

passive A verb is *active* if the subject performs an action, but *passive* if the subject receives an action or has an action performed upon it. In *the dog bites a boy* the verb is active but in *the boy is bitten by a dog* it is passive. The passive tends to be used in impersonal constructions, often to an excessive degree and in an apparent attempt to avoid personal responsibility: *it is regretted* and *it is thought*, where *I regret* or *we think* would be preferable. Another construction to be avoided is the double passive which always appears clumsy:

The plans which were proposed to be discussed.

past participle see **participles**

pathos This is the quality in art, literature and music which arouses feelings of pity or sympathetic sadness.

peaceable, peaceful Both adjectives are similar in meaning and to some extent interchangeable. *Peaceable* is 'disposed to peace or inclined to avoid strife' and is usually applied to people, their actions or feelings:

Peaceable intentions, peaceable folk.

Peaceful, which means 'characterized by peace, tranquil', is rarely applied to people and refers to situations, scenes, periods and activities:

A peaceful reign, a peaceful life.

pendant, pendent A *pendant* is a noun meaning 'a hanging ornament, as a necklace'. *Pendent* is an adjective meaning 'hanging' or 'suspended'. Confusion arises because *pendant* has the alternative spelling *pendent*, and *pendent* can be spelt *pendant*.

peninsula, peninsular *Peninsula* is the noun and *peninsular* the adjective, as in *The Peninsular War*.

people When used to mean the body of persons constituting a tribe or nation, *people* used generally to be followed by a singular verb. However, although it has its own plural, *peoples*, it now takes a plural verb:

The people of England are not easily intimidated.

In all its other senses *people* is followed by a plural verb.

per This Latin preposition has its uses in such phrases as *per annum*, *per cent*, where it is followed by another word in Latin. It should not be employed as a substitute for *a* or *an* in expressions like *two pounds per hour* or *thirty miles per hour*, although its use with English words is acceptable in *per day*, *per head*, *per person*, *per week*. *Per* should not be used instead of *by* in sentences like:

They sent the parcels per rail.

per capita This does not, strictly speaking, mean 'per head' but refers to a method of distributing property among a number of people or a payment made according to the number of people, an agreed amount being allowed for each. However, its meaning 'per head' or 'each person' is now firmly entrenched in the language in such phrases as *per capita income* and *consumption of alcohol per capita*.

percentage Do not use *percentage* to mean 'some' or 'a number of' as in:

This method has proved reliable in a percentage of cases.

Percentage should be used only to indicate the relationship of one number to another and is really meaningless unless preceded by an adjective such as 'low' or 'high'. [See also *proportion*]

perceptible, perceptive *Perceptible* means 'capable of being perceived', as in:

A perceptible difference of colour.

Perceptive means 'having the power of perceiving, quick to perceive':

He proved to be a perceptive writer.

perfect The adjective *perfect* is an absolute expression and cannot usually be preceded by *more* and *most*, since one thing cannot, strictly speaking, be *more perfect* than another. However, it has gained acceptance in the sense of 'coming close to perfection' in such phrases as:

You could not find a more perfect friend,

although care should be taken over its use.

perfect infinitive This is sometimes wrongly used after a perfect tense in such expressions as:

They would have liked to have watched the film.

Only one verb needs to be in the perfect tense and the sentence should be recast in one of two ways, depending on whether the action is viewed from the present or past:

They would like to have watched the film (present).
They would have liked to watch the film (past).

However, the use of the perfect infinitive after verbs like *seem* or *appear* can be justified:

They seemed to have found what they wanted.

In this instance *to have found what they wanted* refers to something which happened before the time indicated by *seemed*. The perfect infinitive is wrongly used in the following example:

I meant to have seen him yesterday.

Here the *to have seen* does not refer to a time prior to *meant* and the sentence must be:

I meant to see him yesterday.

periphrasis This means a roundabout way of speaking or writing and is to be avoided:

He made her the object of his most tender affections

means no more than:

He fell in love with her,

and is better expressed thus.

permanence, permanency Some distinction of meaning still exists between these two words. Both have the sense of 'the condition of being permanent', but *permanency*, the less common word, also refers to something which is permanent, such as a position or a job.

permissible, permissive *Permissible* means 'allowable or not prohibited':

It is permissible to leave your belongings in the cloakroom.

Permissive means 'granting permission to do something' without actual compulsion. In a broader sense it means 'sexually or morally tolerant':

We live in a permissive society.

permit, allow These verbs are often interchangeable but *permit* is a more positive word, suggesting formal assent or authorization:

The police will not permit you to park here.

Allow usually implies that there is no attempt to hinder or prohibit in any way:

They allow you to do what you like here.

permit to/of There is sometimes confusion about the use of the prepositions *to* and *of* after *permit*. Normally *permit* is followed by *to*. It can be followed by *of* only when it means 'to make possible' or 'to leave room for':

The problem permits of no other solution.

per proc., per pro., p.p. These are all abbreviations of the Latin phrase *per procurationem*, which means 'by the agency of'. They are used when one person signs a letter or form in the absence of the person who wrote it. The abbreviation, now usually *p.p.*, generally precedes the signature of the agent thus:

p.p. Jane Brown, John Smithson.

person In grammar distinction is made between the speaker (*first person*: I), the one addressed (*second person*: you) and anyone or anything else (*third person*: he, she, it). In the plural *we* is the first person, *you* the second person and *they* the third person. In English the verb changes only in the third person singular of the present tense: *he* or *she sings*, but *we sing*. [See also *pronoun*, *verb*]

personage, personality Both words are applied to people who are in some way different from the rest of us. A *personage* is someone of distinction or importance, as a high official or a member of the royal family. *Personality*, which is now the more common word, means a celebrity, particularly one who has achieved fame in the world of entertainment.

persona grata This Latin term means 'an acceptable person', particularly a diplomat who is acceptable to the government to which he is accredited:

He is persona grata with the new revolutionary regime.

personification This is a kind of metaphor in which the qualities or character of a person are attributed to inanimate objects or abstract notions:

Fortune smiles upon the brave.

perspicacious, perspicuous *Perspicacious* means 'having keen mental perception, shrewd or discerning' and is usually applied to people:

His perspicacious conduct of affairs was appreciated by all.

Perspicuous means 'clear to the understanding or clearly expressed' and usually refers to something written or spoken:

A perspicuous description of the situation.

The noun from *perspicacious* is *perspicacity* and that from *perspicuous* is *perspicuity.*

perturb, disturb Both verbs convey the idea of creating disorder or confusion and to some extent overlap. *Perturb* is now exclusively reserved for mental agitation or disquiet:

He was greatly perturbed by the news of his friend's illness.

Disturb usually refers to physical disorder, but it can also be used to express mental anguish.

phonograph, gramophone A *phonograph* is the U.S. term for a *gramophone,* which has now been more or less completely displaced by *record player.*

phrasal verb This is the term applied to the formation of new verbs by adding adverbial particles to a simple verb. This is a process which has enriched and continues to enrich the English language to a remarkable degree. Using verbs like *get, go, put* in combination with the adverbial particles (adverbs or prepositions) *in, out, up, down, out* and *over,* many new verbs can be formed.

phrase This means a sequence of two or more words in a sentence arranged in a grammatical construction and acting as a unit in the sentence. A *phrase* cannot stand alone since it does not have a verb, but must be seen in relation to the sentence as a whole.

pick, choose *Pick* is a more informal word than *choose* and suggests a rather more casual selection:

Pick any two cards.

Choose usually implies a deliberate decision made after weighing a number of possibilities:

We must choose our course of action very carefully.

picket, piquet A *picket* is 'a stake for driving into the ground', 'a group of people stationed by a trade union before a place of work' or 'a detached body of soldiers'. The spelling *piquet* should be reserved exclusively for the card game.

picnic see **panic**

pidgin, pigeon *Pidgin* is the usual form of this word in such phrases as *pidgin English*, although *pigeon* is also used.

piteous, pitiable, pitiful All three adjectives are applied to that which excites pity and provokes feelings of sympathy or contempt.

Pitiful means 'exciting pity' or 'contemptible':

A pitiful crippled child, a pitiful show of incompetence.

Pitiable means 'lamentable' or 'deplorable':

She was in a pitiable condition.

Piteous, now a less common word, means 'exciting or deserving pity' or 'appealing for pity':

A piteous state of misery.

plaid, tartan These two words are quite often confused. A *plaid* is a rectangular piece of cloth worn about the shoulders. A *tartan* is the name given to the distinctively patterned cloth out of which plaids and kilts are made.

pleonasm This is the use of more words than are necessary to express an idea. It is usually to be avoided but can be justified when used for the sake of emphasis. *Pleonasm* occurs in phrases like:

Continue to remain, the reason is because, an attempt to try and stop, the cause of the obstruction is due to.

plural forms As a general rule nouns in English add *-s* to the singular in order to form the plural. Those which already end in *-s* or *-ss* in the singular and those ending in *x*, *-z*, *-sh* or *-ch* make the plural by adding *-es*:

masses, bosses, foxes, bushes, wishes, coaches.

Some nouns, which have *-s* in the singular, do not change in the plural:

corps, mumps.

Others are used only in the plural:

forceps, alms, dregs.

Nouns ending in *-y* preceded by a consonant form their plurals by changing *-y* to *i* and adding *es*:

duty, duties; lady, ladies.

Nouns ending in *-y* preceded by a vowel form their plurals by adding *-s*:

donkey, donkeys; play, plays.

Nouns ending in *-o* may form their plurals in either *-os* or *-oes*:

cargo, cargoes; banjo, banjoes; potato, potatoes; photo, photos; folio, folios.

Generally, the more common words end in *-oes*, but see the entry *-o(e)s*. Nouns ending in *-f* or *-fe* usually form their plural by changing the *f* to *v* and adding *-es*:

leaf, leaves; thief, thieves; life, lives.

However, there are many such nouns which simply add an *-s*:

proof, proofs; cliff, cliffs; relief, reliefs.

Compound words normally form their plurals by adding *-s* to the most important part of the compound:

commander-in-chief, commanders-in-chief; brother-in-law, brothers-in-law; go-between, go-betweens; court-martial, courts-martial.

When the compound is considered as one word and normally written without a hyphen the *-s* is added at the end:

mouthful, mouthfuls; stepson, stepsons; sergeant-major, sergeant-majors.

The plural of proper nouns ending in *-s* is *-es*:

the Joneses, the Sallises, the Davises.

And names ending in *-y* do not change to *-ies* in the plural:

the four Henrys, the Barrys, the two Marys.

For plurals of foreign nouns, *i.e.*, those ending in *-a*, *-um*, *-ex* and *-is*, see *Latin and French plurals.*

poetess There are only a few words in which the ending *-ess* as a feminine designation is not considered derogatory, e.g. *actress* and *baroness*. The word *poet* should be used for either sex, or else *woman poet* if it is necessary to make a distinction.

poetic, poetical It is now very difficult to differentiate these two words and they are usually employed interchangeably. *Poetical* is perhaps a more neutral word and may simply mean 'of or pertaining to poetry':

Wordsworth's poetical works.

Poetic suggests the charm or qualities characteristic of poetry:

Poetic feeling, poetic licence, poetic justice.

point of view This is another phrase which has suffered severely from excess of popularity, and is often used as a rather clumsy roundabout way of saying something:

From the point of view of literary merit this book is worth reading.

This sentence would be better recast as:

This book is worth reading for its literary merit.

Do not use *point of view* where *view* or *views* alone would be sufficient:

They asked us for our point of view on the subject.

This would be better as:

They asked us for our views on the subject.

politics This may take either a singular or plural verb. When it is used to mean the 'science or art of political government' it generally takes the singular:

Politics is an attractive career for ambitious young men.

When *politics* is thought of as political beliefs, principles or opinions it takes a plural:

His politics are nothing to do with me.

port see **harbour**

portion, part Both words refer to something that is less than the whole. *Part* is the more general word:

Part of the building is to be let.

A *portion* is a part which has been allotted to a person:

Each received a portion of the cake.

possessive case The *possessive case* (also called the *genitive case*) is used to show ownership, origin, connection, authorship, association and duration:

John's book, the prime minister's speech, man's task, Shakespeare's works, a week's delay.

For use of the apostrophe *s* to express the possessive see *apostrophe.*

post- This Latin prefix, meaning 'behind', originally occurred only in words from Latin, but is now used freely to form words in English. It is usually written without a hyphen, except where it would produce an unsightly appearance:

postscript, postdate *but* post-Elizabethan, post-impressionism.

potent, potential These two words are occasionally used in error, the one for the other. *Potent* means 'powerful' or 'possessing great power or authority':

A potent drug, a potent ruler.

Potential means 'possible as opposed to actual', 'capable of becoming' or 'latent':

A potential prime minister, a potential source of trouble.

practicable, practical These adjectives are very close in some of their senses and an obvious source of confusion. *Practicable* means 'able to be done', 'capable of being put into practice or carried out in action':

> This is a practicable way of carrying large quantities of goods.

Practical, when applied to people, means 'sensible or businesslike':

> A practical man.

When applied to things it means 'efficient and workable' (as opposed to theoretical):

> He put forward practical suggestions for ending the dispute.

practically It is not perhaps too late to regret the fact that *practically* is in danger of losing its other meanings and of becoming a mere synonym of *nearly* or *almost*. It is reasonable to say:

> The work is practically completed,

since this means 'in practice completed'. But to say:

> The team practically lost the match

is ambiguous since it can mean they did in fact lose it, although what is probably meant is that they *nearly* lost it.

practice, practise In English usage the noun is spelt with a *c* and the verb with an *s*. In American usage *practice* is used for both noun and verb.

pre- This prefix meaning 'before' or 'prior to' is normally written without a hyphen, except before another *e*:

> prewar *but* pre-empt, pre-election.

precede, proceed *Precede* means 'to go before in place, order, rank or time':

> There was some dispute over who should precede the archbishop in the ceremony.

Proceed means 'to go or move forwards, especially after stopping':

> After the interruption at the entrance the party was allowed to proceed.

precipitate, precipitous These two adjectives are sometimes confused although their meanings are quite distinct. *Precipitate* means 'moving with great haste', 'sudden' or 'abrupt':

The soldiers made a precipitate retreat across the bridge.

Precipitous means 'like a precipice', 'extremely steep':

They followed a precipitous path down the hillside.

predicate In grammar the *predicate* is that part of a sentence or clause which expresses the action or state of the subject. It consists of the verb together with all the words it governs and those which modify it. In the sentences:

The children are here,
The girl cried bitterly,

the predicate is *are here* and *cried bitterly*. [See also *subject*]

predicate, predict These two verbs are occasionally confused. *Predicate*, a much rarer word, means 'to proclaim, affirm or assert'. *Predict* means 'to foretell or prophesy'.

preface, prefix When used as verbs *preface* and *prefix* are sometimes mistaken for each other. *Preface* is followed by *with* or *by*:

He prefaced his speech with a short reference to the financial situation.

His speech was prefaced by a short reference to the financial situation.

Prefix is followed by *to*:

He prefixed a title to his name.

Unlike *preface*, *prefix* cannot take as an object the thing to which something is added:

He prefixed his remarks with a few words of thanks.

This is not correct, and *prefaced* must be substituted for *prefixed*.

prefer This verb sometimes causes trouble because of doubt over which prepositions should follow it. It is usually followed by *to*:

I prefer beer to cider. She preferred flying to travelling by train.

The problem arises when *prefer* is followed by an infinitive. We cannot say:

They prefer to write to to read.

In this case *rather than* must be substituted:

They prefer to write rather than to read.

preferable This adjective is followed by *to* in comparisons:

I think my plan is preferable to yours.

Remember than *preferable* is already comparative and cannot be preceded by *more* or *most*.

prefix A prefix consists of one or more syllables attached to the beginning of a word which qualify or alter its meaning in some way. Common prefixes include *anti-*, *co-*, *ex-*, *in-*, *pre-* and *un-* and examples of their use are listed below:

aircraft, anti-aircraft; edition, coedition; president, ex-president; expensive, inexpensive; war, prewar; attractive, unattractive.

[See also *hyphens*]

preposition A preposition shows the relationship between a noun or pronoun and some other word in a sentence, clause or phrase, usually of time or place but also of means, manner and purpose:

Two minutes before noon, the dog jumped over the gate, through understanding, with great force, for future use.

In these examples *before*, *over*, *through*, *with* and *for* are all prepositions. Pronouns used as the object of prepositions are in the accusative or objective case:

After us, before him, by whom, with her, about them.

Prepositions generally come before their object but often follow and may even be placed at the end of a sentence (despite the protests of some authorities):

What is he talking about? It's the woman we are looking for.

prescribe, proscribe These two verbs are sometimes confused. *Prescribe* means 'to designate or order for use as a remedy' or 'to advise the use of':

She followed the course of treatment prescribed by the doctor.

Proscribe means 'to condemn as dangerous, to prohibit, banish or outlaw':

The terrorists were proscribed by the government.

present participle see **participles**

preserve see **reserve**

pretence, pretension Although there is some overlapping, the meanings of these two nouns are generally quite distinct. *Pretence* means 'make-believe' or 'a false show of something':

He made a pretence of friendship in order to deceive them.

Pretension means 'laying claim to something':

Her pretensions to superior merit were without foundation.

prevent The two correct constructions with *prevent* are:

We will prevent him from coming *or* we will prevent his coming.

We will prevent him coming is colloquial and best avoided in writing.

preventive, preventative There is no distinction in meaning between these two words. *Preventive* is, however, the preferred form, *preventative* being only rarely found.

prima facie This Latin phrase means 'at first appearance' or 'on a first impression' and is sometimes mistaken for *a priori* (*q.v.*).

principal, principle These two words are a rich source of confusion. Whether used as an adjective or a noun *principal* means 'chief':

The principal feature of the house, the principal of an educational institute.

Principle is a noun meaning 'a rule of conduct or action' or 'a fundamental doctrine':

The principles of government, a man of principle.

proceed see **precede**

programme, program *Programme* is the usual English form, *program* the American. The spelling *program* is however used in Britain in computer technology.

prohibit This verb can take a noun as its direct object:

They voted to prohibit the export of cattle.

But it can also be followed by *from* and a present participle:

They were prohibited from entering the building.

The use of *prohibit* and an infinitive is now archaic and an expression like *we prohibited them to come* is not correct.

pronoun A *pronoun* is a word which is used in place of a noun. There are several classes of pronoun including *personal* (I, you, him, her), *demonstrative* (this, that, these, those), *indefinite* (anybody, somebody, nobody, no one, each, both), and *relative* and *interrogative* (who, which, whose, whom, what, that). Care must be taken to ensure consistency in the use of pronouns, *i.e.* number and person must remain the same. Avoid sentences like:

We were frightened, for everywhere one saw evidence of violence.

We instead of *one* should be used in the second half of the sentence.

prophecy, prophesy These words are frequently mistaken for each other. *Prophecy* is the noun and *prophesy* the verb.

proportion This is another word whose meaning has been greatly enlarged, but not to the benefit of the English language. *Proportion* should be used to express the relationship of one size, quantity, number, etc. to another:

A man with a weekly salary of £100 who spends £60 on food may be rightly said to spend a large proportion of his income on food.

However, *proportion* is frequently used to mean a part or portion in relation to the whole without any idea of comparison:

A proportion of the work force failed to appear.

When it is preceded by *large* or *small*, this use of *proportion* is acceptable. It should not, however, be employed simply as a substitute for *a few* or *some* as in:

A proportion of the children were absent through sickness.

proportional, proportionate Both adjectives mean 'in due proportion'. The distinction between them is that *proportional* usually precedes its noun, *i.e.* is used attributively, and that *proportionate* usually follows its noun, *i.e.* is used predicatively:

A proportional share, proportional representation.

Each was given an amount which was considered proportionate to his needs.

proposition This is another word that has suffered excessive popularity. It is often confused with *proposal* in business matters and should only be used in preference to this word when terms are clearly stated and their advantages emphasized:

His proposition involved a 10% mark-up on all goods.

Proposition is also employed where words like *task*, *plan*, *job*, or *project*, would be far more suitable, and constant care should be exercised to see that it does not suffer from excessive abuse.

proscribe see **prescribe**

protagonist see **antagonist**

provided (that), providing *Provided (that)* is usually better than *providing*. It should be used only when there is a prior condition to be fulfilled:

She said she would go to church provided (that) I came with her.

Otherwise *if* is generally preferable.

punctuation see **brackets, colon, comma, dash, full stop, quotation marks, semicolon**

pundit see **pandit**

purport This is both a verb and a noun. As a verb it means 'to profess or claim' and is restricted in use. It cannot be used in the passive and it does not take a personal subject unless it is followed by the verb *to be*:

She purports to be an actress

is acceptable, but:

She purports to have acted in many plays

is not.

purposely, purposefully *Purposely* means 'intentionally' 'expressly':

He purposely tried to provoke her to anger.

Purposefully means 'resolutely', 'in a determined manner':

His mind made up, he walked purposefully into the room.

Q

quadroon A *quadroon* is the offspring of a white and a mulatto and is therefore one-fourth Negro. [See also *mulatto*]

qualitative, quantitative These words are quite frequently misspelt as *qualitive* and *quantitive.*

quantity This means 'a particular, indefinite or considerable amount of anything':

A small quantity of liquid.

It is better not to use it when referring to individuals or items, in which case *number* is to be preferred:

A large number (not *quantity*) of boxes.

question as to This rather ugly phrase has achieved a certain popularity, but good English requires that it should be avoided wherever possible. The *as to* can be omitted as redundant in such phrases as:

The question as to whether he would be elected president.

Alternatively, expressions like:

The question as to who would pay

can be changed *to the question of payment.*

question, beg the This means to assume without justification the very point raised in a question or to argue from an assumption which itself needs to be proved. Thus, in a discussion someone might say that prisons are necessary in order to avoid an increase in the crime rate, although it has not been proved that the provision of prisons does in fact keep down the rate of crime. *To beg the question* is also used colloquially to mean to evade the point at issue or to avoid giving a straight answer to a question.

question mark This is used at the end of a direct sentence:

Why didn't you come back last night?

It is not used at the end of an indirect or reported question:

He asked me why I didn't come back last night.

In instances where the question is in fact a request, although it has the form of a question, the tendency is to omit the question mark:

Will you please leave your hats and coats here.

quicker This is the comparative form of the adjective *quick* but it is frequently used as adverb instead of *more quickly*:

You can get there quicker by car.

In this instance *quicker* is really an equivalent to *sooner* rather than *faster*, and refers to the length of time taken.

quiet, quietness The main distinction between these two nouns is as follows. *Quiet* means 'freedom from disturbance' or 'a peaceful condition of affairs':

An atmosphere of quiet prevailed.

Quietness refers to a characteristic quality shown by a person or thing:

The quietness of the car's engine was surprising.

quite This is a word which tends to be used to excess. Unfortunately, its various senses are in some ways contradictory, since it can mean 'completely' or 'entirely' and also 'to a considerable extent':

The work is quite finished

but:

The house was quite attractive.

quotation marks The chief use of quotation marks or inverted commas is to set off spoken words from the rest of the text. They are used to enclose a direct quotation or direct speech:

'I must finish this report.'

Modern practice prefers single quotes (' ') to double ones (" "), but there are no absolute rules. When one set of quotes occurs within another set, as, for example, a quotation within a speech, use single quotes for the outer set and double quotes for the inner set:

> She asked, 'Have you any idea what the expression "begging the question" really means?'

Quotation marks should be placed before and after the paragraph, sentence, phrase, or word quoted. If a quotation consists of more than one paragraph, a single opening quotation mark should be placed at the beginning of each new paragraph, but the closing quotation mark should be placed only at the end of the final paragraph.

The use of other punctuation marks with quotation marks needs some careful study. A comma should be placed at the end of quoted matter before the quotation mark, since a punctuation mark usually refers to the group of words which precedes it:

> 'I must finish this report,' he said.

If a verb of saying is inserted in the middle of a sentence of direct speech, the insertion is preceded and followed by a comma:

> 'Before I go,' he declared, 'you must give me an answer.'

However, if the verb of saying is inserted in a continuous quotation which has no natural break, the first comma should fall outside the quotation marks:

> 'I will not', he declared, 'tolerate this.'

When the quoted matter forms a complete sentence which ends at the same point as the main sentence logic would require two full stops, one inside and one outside the quotation mark. In these instances it is usually better to place the full point inside the quotation mark:

> He said abruptly, 'I want that report to be ready by ten o'clock tomorrow morning.'

All punctuation used with quotation marks must be placed as far as possible according to sense. If a quotation ends with a question mark this must be placed before the closing quotation mark. If the question mark belongs to the whole sentence and not just to the quoted passage it should be placed after the closing quotation mark:

He asked, 'What are you doing here?'
What do you mean by 'I don't like it'?

Titles of articles within periodicals, chapters in books, single short poems, essays, etc. are usually placed within quotation marks:

He read Keats' poem 'Ode to a Nightingale'.

Quotation marks may be placed round letters, words, or phrases to which special attention is to be drawn. These are not separated off by a comma unless the sense demands it:

'A bunch of misfits' was his description of his colleagues.

Quotation marks should be placed around English translations of foreign words and phrases:

Qu'ils mangent de la brioche ('let them eat cake') is a saying attributed to Queen Marie Antoinette.

R

-r-, -rr- Single-syllable words ending in *r* double it before suffixes beginning with a vowel if the *r* is preceded by a single vowel:

tarring, furred, blurring, barred.

If it is preceded by two vowels the *r* is not doubled:

cheering, feared, soaring.

In words of more than one syllable the same rule applies as for single-syllable words if the last syllable is stressed:

deferring, preferred.

Otherwise they do not double the *r*:

conquering, entered.

Exceptions to the rule are words like *confer*, *prefer* and *refer* which, although stressed on the final syllable, shift the stress to a preceding syllable when suffixes other than verb endings are added:

conferring *but* conference, preferring *but* preferable, preference.

However, confer gives *conferrable*, which is, unfortunately, an exception to the exceptions noted above.

racket, racquet The spelling *racket* is now the generally accepted one both in the sense of 'disturbance' or 'noise' and in the sense of 'a bat for striking a ball.'

railroad, railway *Railroad* is the usual word in the United States and *railway* in Britain. *Railway*, however, is still used to some extent in the United States.

raise, rise Care is needed in the use of these words. *Raise* is a transitive verb and must therefore take a direct object:

He raised the stone above his head.

Rise is intransitive, that is, the verb is complete in itself without an object:

Prices are rising.

The noun *rise* is used in British English to mean an increase in salary, although the American version *raise* is edging its way into our vocabulary. *Raise* is also used in the United States to mean 'bring up' or 'rear'.

rapt, wrapped Identical pronunciation has led to some confusion in meaning. *Rapt* means 'deeply engrossed' or 'enraptured' as in *rapt in thought*. *Wrapped* means 'enclosed or enveloped in something', but it can be used figuratively as *wrapped up in* in the sense of 'engrossed or absorbed by'.

rare, scarce Both adjectives are used to describe what occurs only very occasionally or is found only in small amounts. *Rare* is applied to things which are seldom found, have scarcity value and may possess superior qualities:

A rare twelfth-century manuscript.

Scarce is applied to things which are in short supply, usually only temporarily:

Apples are scarce this year.

rase, raze *Rase* is the older form of this word, but it has now been generally supplanted by *raze*.

-re, -er There are many words ending in *-re* in British English which have *-er* in American usage:

centre, center; theatre, theater; sombre, somber.

However, British English has adopted such spellings as *diameter* and *filter* and shows a certain lack of consistency. [See also *American usage and spelling*]

re- This prefix has the meanings 'repetition' and 'backward motion' or 'withdrawal'. It is not usually hyphenated except when followed by an *e* as in *re-emerge*, *re-entry*, etc. However, it is also used with a hyphen to distinguish words with different meanings such as *recount* and *re-count* ('count again'), *recover* and *re-cover* ('cover again'), *reform* and *re-form* ('form again').

reaction This is another word whose increase in popularity has led to many unwarranted extensions of meaning. Its basic sense is, apart from its technical definitions, an action in response to some event, and it is properly used as follows:

The prime minister's hostile speech met with a strong reaction from his opponents.

However, it is constantly employed as a substitute for such words as *view*, *opinion*, *effect*, *response*, and sentences like:

What is your reaction?

would be better expressed as:

What is your view/opinion?

or simply:

What do you think?

readable, legible Both words may be used to mean 'capable of being read' or 'clear enough to be read', but this sense is usually confined to *legible*. *Readable* normally means 'interesting enough to be read'.

realistic Like the noun *reaction* this adjective has been over-exposed. It is now tending to displace such words as *sensible*, *reasonable*, *practical* and even *big* or *large*:

Quote me a realistic figure.

reason see **cause**

recall see **remember**

reciprocal, mutual These two words are to a certain extent synonymous: they both imply the idea of an exchange or balance between two or more people or groups of people. *Mutual* indicates an exchange of feeling or obligation:

Mutual esteem, mutual agreement.

Reciprocal can be used in the same way:

Reciprocal affection.

But it also indicates a relationship in which one service is given in return for another:

In view of the support they had given him they confidently expected reciprocal favours.

Whereas *mutual* involves the relationship of both parties *reciprocal* can be used to show the action of only one party with regard to the other. [See also *mutual*]

recollect see **remember**

recourse, resort, resource There is some overlapping of meaning between all three words. Both *recourse* and *resort* can be used for action undertaken for a certain purpose but the constructions are different:

To have recourse to desperate measures

is acceptable, and so is:

To resort to desperate measures,

but not:

To have resort to desperate measures.

The basic meaning of *resource* is 'a source of supply, support or aid'. It is occasionally wrongly substituted for *recourse* in *to have recourse to*, but it is also muddled with *resort* in the expression *in the last resort*. This frequently appears as *in the last resource* but the correct phrase with *resource* is *as a last resource*. Note that *recourse* and *resource* can be used only as nouns, but that *resort* is also a verb.

recrudescence This is another word which has suffered from excess of popularity. It is frequently used for any renewal of activity, although it is more properly applied to the outbreak or return of something disagreeable:

A recrudescence of violence.

redundant The basic meaning of *redundant* is 'excessive' or 'superfluous', but it has undergone various extensions of meaning for which it is wholly unsuited. It has been used as a synonym for *unnecessary*, *inappropriate*, *unsuitable* or *discontinued*, even by writers who ought to know better.

reference, testimonial *Reference* has had its meaning extended to include not only the person to whom one applies for testimony as to character or abilities, but also the written testimonial itself. The word *testimonial* is generally applied to a more formal document, but it does not differ essentially from *reference* in this respect.

reflection, reflexion It is very difficult to make a distinction between these two words. *Reflection* is now the much commoner spelling. *Reflexion* has the same senses as *reflection*, but it is also used in anatomy to mean 'the bending or folding back of a thing upon itself'.

reflective, reflexive *Reflective* is used as the adjective from *reflection*. *Reflexive* is now applied exclusively to grammar.

reflexive verbs and pronouns In grammar a *reflexive verb* is one which has an identical subject and object, as the verb *cut* in *he cut himself*. A *reflexive pronoun* is one that serves as the object of a *reflexive verb*, indicating identity of subject and object, as *himself* in *he cut himself*.

refute, deny These verbs are sometimes used as though they were synonyms, but there is an important difference between them. To *deny* something is to assert that it is not true:

He denied their allegations of corruption.

To *refute* something is to supply evidence that it is not true:

He refuted their allegations with documentary proof.

regard The prepositional phrases *with regard to*, *in regard to* and *as* regards are frequently used where a simpler construction with *in* or *about* would have been preferable. Note also the distinction between the two phrases *have regard to* ('to take into account or consideration') and *have regard for* ('to show respect or concern for'). Unlike verbs such as *consider* and *count*, *regard* cannot take two direct objects:

I consider it an insult

but:

I regard it as an insult.

regretful, regrettable *Regretful* means 'full of regret', 'sorrowful':

She was regretful for her lost youth.

Regrettable means 'causing regret':

Her hasty action was regrettable.

rehabilitate This means 'to restore to a healthy condition or a condition of respectability'. It should not be used simply as a synonym for *restore* or *repair* when referring to a building which has been damaged.

relation, relationship *Relation* and *relationship* both refer to the connection between people or things, but whereas *relation* has a number of different senses, most of them abstract, *relationship* is restricted to one or two meanings. Both can mean connection by blood or marriage but *relationship* has the additional sense of 'a particular connection' or 'a degree of similarity':

His relationship to the ruling family.
The relationship between art and sculpture.

relation, relative In the sense of 'one who is connected to another by marriage' *relation* and *relative* are virtually interchangeable. *Relation* is the more common word and tends to be used to refer to those with whom we are closely connected, but very often personal choice is the deciding factor in the selection of these words.

remember, recall, recollect All three verbs have the meaning of recalling to consciousness what exists in the memory. There are distinctions between them, which are worth noting, although they are often ignored in practice. *Remember*, the most common word, implies that a thing is present in the memory and can be brought to mind with only a slight effort:

I remember the days of my youth.

Recall implies a voluntary effort, possibly assisted by an association of ideas:

He recalled the words of the poem.

Recollect implies a conscious effort to remember something in particular:

I can't recollect the precise details of the car crash.

repairable, reparable Both adjectives mean 'capable of being repaired', but *repairable* is normally used only of material things:

Shoes which are still repairable.

Reparable is generally used of abstract things to be remedied or put right, such as a loss, a mistake or harm. The negative form, *irreparable* is far more common as in *an irreparable loss*. The negative of *repairable* is *unrepairable*.

repellant, repulsive Both words mean 'causing distaste or aversion' to an extent that drives one away, but *repulsive* implies a much stronger feeling and suggests violent reaction against what causes the repulsion.

repent, regret These two verbs are sometimes confused. *Repent* means 'to feel self-reproach or contrition for past action':

He repented his crimes.

Regret can mean the same as *repent*:

He regretted his misdeeds.

It does however, suggest, a far lesser degree of guilt than *repent* and is a much more general word.

repertoire, repertory Both words have the meaning of a list of dramas or musical pieces that a theatrical company or a musician can perform. *Repertoire* is the more usual word for this and *repertory* has the additional meanings of 'a type of theatrical company' and 'a stock or store of things of any kind':

His repertory of dirty jokes.

repetitious, repetitive Both adjectives mean 'characterized by repetition'. The main difference is that *repetitious* refers to undue or tedious repetition, whereas *repetitive* is a more neutral word.

replace This very useful word has frequently had to yield to *substitute*, which has often proved a less than satisfactory alternative. Care must be taken with the prepositions that follow *replace*:

We have replaced the old desks with new ones.
The old desks have been replaced by new ones.
The old desks have been replaced by the company with new ones.

[See also *substitute*]

require This verb is transitive, i.e. it takes a direct object, but it is often wrongly used as though it were an intransitive verb:

You require to have a letter from the manager

instead of the correct:

You require a letter from the manager.

requirement, requisite Both *requirement* and *requisite* refer to something that is necessary. A *requirement* is some quality which is needed in order to comply with certain conditions:

Requirements for admission to a university.

A *requisite* is something required by the nature of things or the circumstances of a particular case and is generally more specific:

The two requisites for this job are energy and initiative.

Requisite is also used for a concrete object:

Toilet requisites.

reserve, preserve Two of the various senses of these nouns are sometimes confused. A *reserve* is a tract of public land set aside for a special purpose, as a *a nature reserve.* A *preserve* is a place set apart for the protection and propagation of game or fish for sport.

resign This verb may be used with a direct object or alternatively followed by *from* when it means to give up an office or position:

He resigned the directorship.
He resigned from the company.

Note also:

To be resigned to one's fate.

resolution, motion Both words are used to refer to something to be debated and voted upon by a deliberative assembly. The difference is that a *resolution* may not be anything more than a formal determination or an expression of opinion:

The assembly passed a resolution deploring the recent outbreak of violence.

However, a *motion* leads to action:

The assembly passed a motion to adjourn.

resort, resource see **recourse**

respective, respectively These are words which are so often used incorrectly that it is probably better to avoid them altogether. The adverb *respectively* is properly employed when it shows the correct relationship between two groups of people or things. In:

Jane and Susan were given a book and a record respectively

it is made clear that Jane received a book and Susan a record. *Respectively* is often used superfluously, as in:

Peter, James and Charles respectively made successful appearances in the school concert.

The adjective *respective* is used correctly in:

The four teachers gave an account of how the new method was being used in their respective classes.

i.e., each in his own class. It is quite unnecessary, for example, in:

Each pupil gave his respective opinion,

since *respective* can add nothing to *each*.

restive, restless These adjectives are sometimes confused. *Restive* means 'impatient of control' or 'refractory', and *a restive horse* is one that offers resistance. *Restless* means 'unable to remain at rest', 'unquiet' or 'uneasy'. Thus, a *restive* horse may also be a *restless* one, but not necessarily.

restrictive and non-restrictive clauses A *restrictive clause* is one which limits or defines or makes specific:

Girls who laugh all the time are not very popular.

The relative clause, *who laugh all the time*, is essential to complete the meaning of the sentence. A *non-restrictive clause* is one which is not essential to the meaning but merely supplies additional information:

Jane, who laughs all the time, is not very popular.

The essential information, *Jane is not very popular*, has already been conveyed. *Non-restrictive clauses* are always set off by commas.

retrograde, retrogression, *Retrograde* is now the usual adjective accompanying the noun *retrogression*. The adjective *retrogressive* is not very commonly employed.

revenge see **avenge**

reverend, reverent It is important not to confuse these words. *Reverend* means 'worthy to be revered' or 'entitled to reverence'. *Reverent* means 'feeling or showing reverence', 'deeply respectful'.

reversal, reversion *Reversion* is occasionally used by mistake instead of *reversal*. *Reversal* is the noun which corresponds to the verb *reverse. Reversion* is linked with the verb *revert* and is mainly used in legal or scientific terminology.

reward see **award**

rhetorical question This is a question designed to produce a dramatic effect and not to elicit an answer. It is a favourite device of public speakers:

Who says we are not capable of defending ourselves?

rhyme, rime *Rhyme* is the established spelling, with *rime* as an alternative but now rarely used form.

right, rightly *Right* as an adverb has a number of other meanings, but both words are used in the sense of 'correctly, accurately or properly', although *rightly* tends to occur more frequently. *Right* can be used only after the verb but in some expressions both words are possible:

If I remember right *or* rightly.

Right should be used in preference to *rightly* when the meaning is 'so as to produce a correct or satisfactory result':

He guessed right. She was unable to do it right. Hold the pencil right.

Rightly must be used when the adverb is placed before the verb or when it modifies a whole sentence:

He rightly refused to answer.
She rightly guessed that he would not come.
They had not been rightly informed.

rise see **arise; raise**

rotary, rotatory Both words are used to mean 'turning round as on an axis', but *rotary* is the more common, especially when referring to machines.

round see **around**

rouse see **arouse**

rural, rustic Both adjectives refer to the country as opposed to the town. *Rural* is the usual term and may have a favourable sense:

Rural economy, the pleasures of rural life.

Rustic may be used with either a favourable or a pejorative meaning. It may suggest homeliness or lack of sophistication (*rustic simplicity*), or else something boorish, crude or uncouth (*rustic manners*). *Rustic* is also used to mean 'made of roughly dressed wood':

A rustic seat.

Russia, Russian *Russia*, strictly speaking, means either the Russian Empire overthrown in 1917 or else the largest of the constituent republics of the U.S.S.R., the corresponding adjective for each being *Russian*. However, both words are used loosely to refer to both the pre- and the post- revolutionary state. *Russian* as a noun can be applied to any inhabitant of the U.S.S.R., past or present, but it also has the narrower sense of a member of the Russian Soviet Republic. In speaking of the present-day country it is better to say either the *U.S.S.R.* or the *Soviet Union* rather than *Russia*.

S

-s-, -ss- There are so few single-syllable words ending in *-s* that the rules about doubling or not doubling the final consonant before a suffix beginning with a vowel can scarcely be applied. *Gas* has the plural *gases*, but the verb has *gassed*, *gassing*. In words of more than one syllable if the last syllable is not stressed the final *-s* is not usually doubled:

biased, canvases, bonuses, atlases.

However it should be noted that *focused* and *focusing* have the alternative forms *focussed* and *focussing*.

sabotage The first definition given in dictionaries is 'malicious damage to work, tools, machinery, etc.'. The word has now become so popular that both as a noun and a verb it is used to describe any kind of action which undermines or wrecks an agreement or scheme.

saccharin, saccharine The spelling *saccharin* is usually reserved for the noun and *saccharine* for the adjective meaning 'sweet', although the noun can also be spelt with an *'e'*.

sake This occurs in phrases like:

For heaven's sake, for mercy's sake.

When the noun preceding *sake* already ends in an *s* sound, the apostrophe *s* is not added:

For goodness sake.

salubrious, salutary *Salubrious* means 'favourable to health', especially of air or climate:

A salubrious resort.

Salutary also means 'conducive to health', but is more often used to imply moral benefit:

A salutary lesson in manners.

same The use of *same* or *the same* as a pronoun, which is still found in commercial English, is to be avoided. In a sentence like:

We have inspected the samples and are returning same

them should be substituted for *same*.

The use of *as* or *that* after *same* presents some difficulty. When the expression is intended to point out a resemblance *as* should be used:

She has the same hair style as her daughter.

However, *that* can be used when identification rather than resemblance is intended:

He was carrying the same book that he had with him last week.

same, similar Both words indicate a resemblance between things. *Same* means identical in every respect:

She wears the same clothes every day.

Similar means resembling in certain respects or in a general way, or having certain qualities in common:

Your views on the subject are similar to mine.

sanatory, sanitary These words may be occasionally confused because of the similarity in their spelling. *Sanatory*, which is a fairly uncommon word, means 'favourable to health', 'curative'. *Sanitary* means 'pertaining to health, especially with reference to cleanliness and precautions against disease'.

sanatorium, sanitarium *Sanatorium* is the usual English spelling. In American usage both *sanatorium* and *sanitarium* are found, although the latter is more common.

sanction This is a popular word whose various senses are in some ways contradictory. As a noun it means 'authoritative support given to an action' and, as a verb, 'to authorize or approve':

Their actions have been sanctioned by long usage.

In law a *sanction* is 'a provision enacting a penalty for disobedience':

They threatened to impose economic sanctions.

sarcasm This is a form of irony which takes the form of harsh or bitter derision and is intended to hurt the feelings of others. It is often expressed as the apparent opposite of what is intended:

A fine friend you turned out to be!

sardonic This means 'bitterly ironical' or 'sneering'. It can also mean 'sarcastic', but expresses a much milder form of sarcasm and may be directed against oneself as much as against anyone else:

The prisoner heard the jury's verdict with a sardonic smile.

satire This is the use of irony, sarcasm or ridicule in exposing, denouncing or deriding the shortcomings of society and of individuals. It often takes the form of a literary composition.

satiric, satirical Both adjectives mean exactly the same, but *satirical* is tending to oust *satiric* almost completely:

A satirical poet. Satirical remarks.

satisfy This verb has two quite distinct meanings: 'to fulfil desires, needs, etc.' and 'to give assurance to or convince'. The second meaning of *satisfy* is tending to displace *convince* and may lead to unfortunate ambiguity:

They were satisfied that no one could have escaped alive from the burning building.

save This is a preposition meaning 'except' or 'but', which is occasionally employed as an alternative to these words. It is, however, no longer in common use and adds an air of artificiality to any sentence in which it appears.

saw The usual past participle of *saw* is *sawn* but *sawed* is occasionally found.

scarce, scarcely *Scarce* as an adverb is now obsolete and *scarcely* should be used. *Scarcely*, like *hardly*, is followed by *when* and not *than*:

We had scarcely started when the front tyre went flat.

[See also *rare*]

sceptic, septic Similarity in spelling can lead to confusion between these two words, although their meanings are entirely different. *Sceptic* is a noun and means 'one who maintains a doubting or distrustful attitude towards people, ideas, etc.'. *Septic* is an adjective meaning 'affected by a microbe or bacteria'.

Scots, Scottish, Scotch *Scottish* is the usual adjective for 'belonging or pertaining to Scotland', but *Scots* can also be used in this sense and the two words apply to both people and things:

Scottish blood, Scots soldiers.

Scotch should be used only with reference to food, drink, animals, flowers and objects generally:

Scotch tweed, Scotch terrier, Scotch whisky.

scream, screech, shriek All three verbs refer to crying out in a loud, piercing way. *Scream* is often associated with pain or fear:

He screamed with anguish as he caught his finger in the door.

Screech refers to a harsh, disagreeable sound and may be used of birds or old women:

The screeching of crows in the night sky.

Shriek is usually associated with a shorter, sharper sound than *scream* and is frequently used of fear or pain of a more acute kind than is implied by *scream*:

She shrieked with terror at the sight.

scull, skull The similarity of these words may lead to confusion in spelling. A *scull* is an oar worked from side to side over the stern of boat as a means of propulsion. The *skull* is the bony framework of the head enclosing the brain.

seasonable, seasonal *Seasonable* means 'suitable to the season of the year':

We had some fine seasonable weather in August.

Seasonal means 'pertaining to or dependent on the seasons or some particular season':

To obtain seasonal work in the building trade.

seem Care must be taken in negative sentences to ensure that the negation applies to the main verb and not to *seem* when this is used as an auxiliary verb. This misplacement is frequent in colloquial speech but should not appear in the written language:

She can't seem to understand.

This is better expressed as:

She seems unable to understand.

seldom This is an adverb and should not be used as a predicative adjective, as in:

His trips abroad were seldom.

It can, however, be employed as a predicative adverb as follows:

It is seldom that we get the chance of a trip to London.

Seldom can also qualify a phrase:

When he stayed more than five minutes, which was seldom, we were all delighted.

self This should not be used as a substitute for *I* or *me* in such phrases as: *my friend and self* or *self and wife*. Likewise, *myself* should not appear instead of *I* or *me*. *My wife and myself* is better as *My wife and I*.

-self, -selves These endings are added to the personal pronouns to form either reflexive or intensive (emphatic) pronouns. The reflexive pronoun is used as an object which refers to the same person as the subject:

He cut himself.

The intensive pronoun is used to add emphasis:

They themselves persisted in denying everything.

semantics This is a branch of linguistics which is concerned with the study of the meaning of words and other linguistic forms.

semi(-) Most modern dictionaries tend not to hyphenate *semi* to the word with which it is compounded except to avoid an awkward combination of vowel sounds as in *semi-intoxicated*.

semicolon The semicolon indicates a longer pause or a more definite separation than the comma. It should be employed sparingly. It is used to separate main clauses in a sentence when these are not linked by a conjunction:

The man looked pleased when she arrived; the woman seemed indifferent.

It is used to separate main clauses linked by certain so-called conjunctive adverbs such as *indeed*, *nevertheless*, *moreover*, *hence*, *yet*, and *however*:

The plan has not worked; nevertheless, it was worth trying.

It is used to separate items in a series where the items themselves are already subdivided into a smaller series and thus helps to avoid ambiguity:

This book contains information about distribution and habitat; form, dimensions and colouring; life-cycle; and economic significance.

sensibility, sensitiveness, sensitivity All mean responsiveness or susceptibility. *Sensibility* denotes rather the capacity to respond to aesthetic stimuli:

The sensibility of a sculptor.

Sensitiveness is the quality of being sensitive or of responding to stimulation from outside:

Sensitiveness to light.

Sensitivity is used especially of capacity to respond in a physiological sense:

The sensitivity of a nerve.

sensible, sensitive The most common meaning of *sensible* is 'having or showing good sense or sound judgement'. It can, however, have the meaning of 'keenly aware', when it is usually followed by *of*:

Sensible of his errors.

In this instance it is close to one of the meanings of *sensitive*, 'readily affected by':

Sensitive to criticism.

sensual, sensuous Both words refer to what is experienced through the senses. *Sensual* is concerned with gratification derived from physical sensations, particularly sexual ones, and is usually pejorative:

A sensual delight in food. A man of crude sensual passions.

Sensuous is applied, with a favourable connotation, to what is perceived by or affects the senses:

The sensuous pleasure of good music.

sentence A sentence is a group of words that express a complete meaning. There are various types of sentences, expressing a statement, asking a question, issuing a command or making an exclamation, as in the following examples.

A sentence expressing a statement:

The Second World War ended in 1945.

A sentence asking a question:

What are we having for dinner?

A sentence expressing a command:

Get that window repaired at once.

A sentence expressing an exclamation:

Help! Fire! What a shame!

Sentences can also be divided up according to their structure. A simple sentence contains one subject and one predicate:

People are odd.

A compound sentence contains two or more independent clauses:

The door opened and a man stepped out.

A complex statement contains one or more dependent clauses in addition to the main clause:

When the concert finished (dependent clause) the audience clapped wildly.

sentinel, sentry Both words mean 'someone who stands guard' but *sentinel* is the more general word. *Sentry* is almost exclusively used in a military context.

sequence of tenses This means that the tense of verbs in subordinate clauses must be adjusted to suit the tense of the verb in the main clause. This does not usually present any great difficulty in English but it should be remembered that a main clause in a past tense can have a subordinate clause in the present tense if this expresses something which is true (or believed to be true) at all times:

They were taught that God is love.

sergeant, serjeant The form *sergeant* is used for the rank in the army and in the police force. *Serjeant* was a title formerly given to a member of a superior order of barristers. The spelling is preserved in *serjeant-at-arms*, an official of the Houses of Parliament.

service This is a comparatively recent verb meaning 'to make fit for service' and is useful in an age when motor vehicles are in regular need of attention. However, care should be taken to ensure that it does not usurp any of the various meanings of *serve*.

sestet, sextet These two words have the same origin. *Sestet* is now usually confined to poetry and means the last six lines of a sonnet. A *sextet* is a group of six, especially singers or players, or a musical composition for six voices or instruments.

sew, sow To *sew* meaning 'to attach with a needle or thread' has the past tense *sewed* and the past participle *sewn* or, rarely, *sewed.* To *sow* meaning 'to plant seeds' has the past tense *sowed* and the past participle *sown* or, rarely, *sowed.*

sewage, sewerage These words are sometimes confused. *Sewage* is the waste matter which passes through sewers. *Sewerage* is the removal of waste by means of sewers or a system of sewers, but it can be used to mean simply *sewage.*

shade, shadow Both words are used to describe an area of comparative darkness in relation to its surroundings. *Shade* indicates the diminished heat and brightness of a spot from which the sun's rays are cut off:

The tree provided sufficient shade.

Shade has no particular form or shape but *shadow* is often used to describe an object which intercepts the light:

He saw the shadow of a woman on the pavement.

Shakespeare, Shakespearian These are now the generally accepted spellings, the alternative forms being *Shakspeare, Shakespearean* and *Shaksperian.*

shall, will, should, would The correct use of these auxiliary verbs has always been a subject of controversy, but most authorities are agreed upon the following points. When a simple future is being expressed the forms are as follows:

I shall come	We shall come
You will come	You will come
He, she, it will come	They will come

I shall come to tea on Sunday. Mother will stay at home.

However, when the verb is used to express determination, obligation or permission the forms are changed:

I will come	We will come
You shall come	You shall come
He, she, it shall come	They shall come

I will come on Sunday no matter what she says.
You shall stay at home whether you like it or not.

The use of *should* and *would* is more complicated. When they express simple futurity from the point of past time (i.e. *he said he would come*) the pattern is the same as for *shall* and *will*.

I should come	We should come
You would come	You would come
He, she, it would come	They would come

However, *would* is frequently substituted for *should*, since *should* is not now generally used to represent past time.

Should is used with all three persons, singular and plural, to imply condition, obligation, doubt or supposition:

If I should be late. You should get up earlier than you do. He should arrive on time. If they should get here before me.

Would is used with all three persons, singular and plural, to represent determination, habitual action, or condition:

He said he would come despite their protests. She would go to bed regularly at nine o'clock. If they had the choice, they would come.

shambles The original meaning of *shambles* was a slaughter-house. It was extended to describe a scene of carnage or bloodshed. Such is its popularity that it is now used of any kind of chaos or disorder, much to the regret of some authorities.

shanty, chanty A *shanty* is a sailor's song. The original spelling was *chanty*, but *shanty* has now almost entirely displaced it.

sharp, sharply *Sharp* is still employed as an adverb when reference is made to abruptness or suddenness, punctuality and vigilance. It is also used in music:

He pulled the horse up sharp. Turn sharp right. Be here at six o'clock sharp. Look sharp! She was singing sharp.

Sharply is the adverb of the adjective *sharp* on all other occasions.

shear This verb has the past tense *sheared* and the past participle *sheared* or *shorn*. When the past participle is used as an adjective *shorn* is the usual form:

A shorn lamb.

shew, show The spelling *shew* was formerly quite common, but *show* is now the generally acceptable form. *Shew* is, however, still used in legal documents.

should see **shall**

shrink This verb has the past tense *shrank* or *shrunk* and the past participle *shrunk* or *shrunken*. When the past participle is used as an adjective the form *shrunken* is preferred:

A shrunken hand.

sic This is a Latin word meaning 'so', which is inserted after a word or phrase to show that it has been copied exactly from an original. It usually means that the writer knows he is quoting from something which is inaccurate and does not accept responsibility for it:

Brown wrote 'the author Graham Green (*sic*) is much overrated'.

The (*sic*) means that the writer is aware that *Green* should be spelt *Greene* but is quoting exactly.

sick see **ill**

significant This is a word which has achieved much popularity in recent years and unfortunately has undergone an unwarranted extension of meaning. It should not be used as a variant of *important* or *considerable* in such phrases as *a significant improvement* or *a significant change*.

simile This is a figure of speech which expresses a direct resemblance, in one or more particulars, of one thing to another:

He had a face like that of a frightened sheep.

simplistic, simplified Both adjectives mean 'made simpler' or 'made less complicated'. *Simplistic* is a new word which has currently become fashionable and tends to mean 'greatly simplified' or 'excessively simplified':

He is always proposing simplistic solutions to complex problems.

simulate see **dissimulate**

since When used as a conjunction *since* is normally followed by a verb in the past tense:

We have not heard from him since he joined the army. It is two hours since he left.

It is followed by a verb in the perfect tense when it refers to an action that is still continuing:

Since he has been here we have had no peace.

When *since* is used as an adverb it is usually preceded by a verb in the perfect tense and followed by an expression of time:

They have been here since six o'clock.

[See also *ago*]

sink This verb has the past tense *sank* (or rarely) *sunk*, and the past participle *sunk* or *sunken*. When the past participle is used as an adjective *sunken* is the usual form:

Sunken eyes.

slang It is not easy to offer a precise definition of slang but basically it is a language which differs from standard speech both in its choice of vocabulary and in its turns of phrase. Slang invents new words and gives established ones new meanings. It can be both imaginative and colourful, but if used excessively it becomes stale. It is considered by many to be inferior to standard speech, although numerous slang words do eventually win acceptance and respectability.

sled, sledge, sleigh All three words are used to describe a vehicle mounted on runners which moves over snow or ice. *Sled* is usually applied to a small *sledge*. *Sleigh* is often used for a horse-drawn vehicle. *Sledge* is the word most commonly employed for a vehicle which carries loads.

slovenly This is an adjective and for obvious reasons cannot take the ending *-ly* to form the adverb. Expressions such as 'in a slovenly manner' or 'in a slovenly way' must be used instead:

She dressed in a slovenly manner.

slow, slowly The adjective *slow* is used as an adverb in *go slow* and *run slow*. In the comparative and superlative forms *slower* and *slowest* are generally used as adverbs instead of *more slowly* and *most slowly*.

sly The normal comparative and superlative forms of this adjective are *slyer* and *slyest*, although *slier* and *sliest* are possible. The adverbial forms are *slyly* or (more rarely) *slily*.

small see **little**

smell This verb has either *smelt* or *smelled* in the past tense and in the past participle. When it means 'to give out an odour' it is followed by an adjective, not an adverb:

The flowers smell sweet.

so When *so* is used to introduce a clause expressing purpose or result it cannot stand alone but must be followed by *that* or *as to*:

He joined the club so that he could see her more often.

She stopped the car so that she could see more clearly *or* so as to be able to see more clearly.

The expression *to do so* is used to avoid repeating a verb:

Since she wanted to read I told her to do so.

It cannot, however, be employed as a substitute for a verb in the passive and the following is incorrect:

This door is not to be left open: anyone doing so will be severely reprimanded.

sociable, social Both adjectives are concerned with the relationship of people in society. *Sociable* means 'fond of the company of others' or 'friendly in company':

He was a good mixer and sociable at parties.

Social is a more neutral word, relating to society in general or to particular societies:

Man is a social animal. We have joined a social club.

soliloquy see **monologue**

soluble, solvable *Soluble* is used of both substances and problems and means 'capable of being dissolved' or 'capable of being solved'. *Solvable* means 'capable of being solved' and is applied only to problems.

some time, sometime Written as either two words or one word *some time* means 'an indefinite time' or 'some time or other':

The two men met in New York some time last year.

Written as one word *sometime* is used as an adjective meaning 'former':

Sometime senior lecturer in history.

sort This is a singular noun but it is frequently encountered with demonstrative adjectives in the plural in phrases like *these sort of*, *those sort of*. It is acceptable in conversation but it is advisable to avoid it in written English.

southerly see **easterly**

Soviet see **Russia**

sow see **sew**

speciality, specialty In British English *speciality* is the usual word, *specialty* being confined to the legal sense of a 'special agreement'. In American usage *specialty* is far more common and has some of the meanings of *speciality* in British English, notably 'a particular line of work'.

specially see **especially**

specie, species *Specie* means 'coined money' and cannot be used in the plural. *Species* meaning 'a group of individuals sharing common characteristics' is both singular and plural.

spelling The correct spelling of English words presents many formidable problems, some of which this *Guide to English Usage* can help to solve. There are a number of entries dealing with spelling including in particular *American usage and spelling*, *Latin and French plurals* and *plural forms*. However, it is useful to be able to summarize under one heading some of the main points which the reader will find treated under individual entries elsewhere in this book.

Words ending in a single consonant preceded by a single vowel double the consonant before suffixes beginning with a vowel, provided they are single-syllable words or have the stress on the past syllable:

bedding, drummer, regrettable, stopped, upsetting.

Single-syllable words ending in a consonant preceded by two vowels or another consonant, or words of more than one syllable which are not stressed on the last syllable do not double the final consonant:

roamed, limiting, heaped, peeping, seated.

For exceptions to the above rule see *-l-*, *-ll-* and *-p-*, *-pp-*.

Words ending in *y* and preceded by a consonant change *y* to *i* when a suffix is added:

easy, easily; party, parties; rely, reliable; mercy, merciful.

However, if the *y* is followed by *i* it is retained:

bury, burying; carry, carried; try, trying; occupy, occupied.

If *y* is preceded by a vowel it is usually retained:

employ, employable; play, plays; monkey, monkeys.

There are, however, some well-known exceptions to this rule:

pay, paid; say, said; gay, gaily.

In some cases final *y* is retained before suffixes although it is preceded by a consonant:

shy, shyness; sly, slyly; enjoy, enjoyment.

With words like *dry* and *fly* either *y* or *i* is permissible:

flier *or* flyer, drily *or* dryly.

Final *-ie* becomes *y* before *-ing*:

tie, tying (*but* tied); die, dying.

Final silent *-e* is usually dropped before a suffix beginning with a vowel:

shine, shining; believe, believable; name, naming.

However, when final silent *-e* is preceded by soft *c* or *g* it is usually retained in order to preserve the sound:

peace, peaceable; change, changeable; manage, manageable.

Final silent *-e* is also usually retained before a suffix beginning with a consonant:

elope, elopement; grave, gravely; achieve, achievement.

Final silent *-e* is retained in some words before *-ing* to prevent confusion over pronunciation and meaning:

dye, dyeing; singe, singeing.

Verbs ending in *c* add *k* before suffixes beginning with *e*, *i* or *y* so that the hard *c* is preserved:

picnic, picnicked, picnicking; mimic, mimicked, mimicking.

spin The generally accepted form of the past tense and past participle is *spun*. *Span* is still occasionally found, although some authorities consider it archaic.

spirituous, spiritual These words are sometimes confused. *Spirituous* means 'containing alcohol, alcoholic'. *Spiritual* means 'pertaining to the spirit or soul, as opposed to the body'.

split infinitive This is a construction in which an adverb is placed between *to* and the verb it goes with. Formerly grammarians condemned it out of hand, but strict observance of the rule frequently leads to awkward or ambiguous phrases, and a more flexible attitude is now adopted. In the two following sentences the position of *completely* alters the meaning and the infinitive must be split if the sense requires it:

He failed completely to finish the course = complete failure.
He failed to completely finish the course = partial failure.

The split infinitive is perfectly acceptable in such phrases as *to readily understand*, *to fully intend*, but it is still best avoided except in cases similar to those outlined above.

sprain, strain Both words (either as nouns or verbs) have the sense of injury done to muscles. *Sprain* suggests a sudden wrenching of the muscles or tendons, especially those of the wrist and ankle. *Strain* suggests a deformation caused by action over a long period (*to strain one's eyes*) or by the exertion of a muscle beyond its capacity:

The effort strained his heart.

sprint, spurt Both words are used to describe a spell of physical activity. A *sprint* is the name given to a race run at full speed. A *spurt* is a sudden increase in effort as might be needed in running or some other athletic sport.

staff, stave *Staff* is rarely used now in its old sense of 'stick'. However, its original plural *staves* has, by a process of back-formation, produced a new singular, *stave*. This has more or less replaced *staff* in the musical sense and is also used to mean a narrow, shaped piece of wood forming the side of a barrel. *Staffs* is now the normal plural of *staff*.

stanch, staunch When used as verbs both words mean 'to stop the flow of', but *stanch* is the more common form. *Staunch* is the usual spelling of the adjective meaning 'loyal, firm or steadfast'.

start see **begin**

stationary, stationery These words are frequently confused because of their spelling. *Stationary* is an adjective meaning 'standing still'. *Stationery* is a noun meaning writing materials, including, pens, pencils and envelopes.

stay see **stop**

stimulant, stimulus Both nouns are used to refer to something which incites mental or physical activity. However, the meaning of *stimulant* is usually limited to the effects of medicine or alcohol, and implies only a temporary increase in activity:

She was given stimulants to counteract her depression.

Stimulus is a more general word and is often used in a figurative sense:

The thought of the approaching strike was a stimulus to action.

stoic, stoical As an adjective *stoic* is generally attributive, i.e. it is placed before the noun. Moreover, it tends to have the original meaning of 'pertaining to Zeno's school of philosophy'. *Stoical* is used both attributively and predicatively, i.e. after the verb, and usually has the wider sense of 'impassive' or 'showing an austere fortitude':

He remained stoical although suffering much pain.

stop see **full stop**

stop, stay Apart from its basic sense of 'to cease moving' *stop* is quite frequently used in the sense of *stay*, i.e. 'to remain in a place'. Some authorities object to this use of *stop*, and it is probably better restricted to the idea of a short period which breaks a journey:

We stopped in New York overnight,

but:

They stayed in the country for nearly a year.

storey, story British English usage distinguishes between these two words, but the form *storey* meaning 'a floor of a building' has only recently been firmly established. In the United States *story* is the usual spelling for both 'a floor of a building' and 'a narrative'.

strategy, tactics *Strategy* is 'the planning and directing of large-scale military operations'. *Tactics* is 'the art of manoeuvring forces before or during a battle'.

stratum The usual plural is *strata*, but *stratums* is also found. [See *Latin and French plurals*]

string, strung, stringed The usual form of the past participle is *strung*, *stringed* being only rarely found. It is, however, used adjectivally as in *stringed instrument*.

subconscious see **unconscious**

subject In grammar the *subject*, together with the *predicate*, is an essential part of a sentence. The *subject* is the word or group of words which refer to the person who performs the action expressed in the predicate. The subject also determines the number and person of the verb. In the sentences:

John has a book.
We saw the train.
Who is that boy?

John, *we* and *who* are the subjects.

subject see **topic**

subjunctive The subjunctive mood of the verb is used to express a wish, condition, a mood of doubt, or a command. It is identical with the indicative of verbs except in the third person singular of the present tense, which drops the final *s*. Only the verb 'to be' has subjunctive forms in both present indicative and simple past tenses. The subjunctive is not much employed in present-day English except in conditional clauses and in subordinate clauses after verbs of asking, ordering and suggesting. In conditional clauses the subjunctive is used only when the condition is an unreal one, i.e. will not be fulfilled:

If he were to come (*but he won't*), he would tell us everything.

An example of the use of the subjunctive with verbs of asking and ordering is as follows:

He moved that the debate be adjourned until the next session.

It occurs in main clauses in certain set expressions:

Come what may. Peace be with you.

In fact the subjunctive in English is dying out and is frequently replaced by auxiliary verbs like *should*, *may* and *might*.

subnormal see **abnormal**

substitute, replace Care must be taken in the use of these words. *Substitute* means 'to put something in place of another' and *replace* means 'to take the place of'. The difference between them is illustrated in the following sentence:

When an encyclopedia is removed from a shelf and a dictionary put in its place, the dictionary is substituted for the encyclopedia and the encyclopedia is replaced by the dictionary.

succinct see **concise**

succubus see **incubus**

such When the pronoun *such* is followed by *as* it means 'of the kind specified':

There were monstrous animals such as I had never seen before.

When it is followed by *that* it implies a result or a consequence:

The density of the fog was such that we could scarcely see.

sufficient see **enough**

suffix A *suffix* consists of one or more syllables placed after a word to form a new word. It does not change the meaning in the way that a prefix does, but it does alter the grammatical function of the original word: a noun becomes an adjective, an adjective a noun or an adverb, etc. The endings of verbs are also suffixes. Examples of common suffixes are listed below:

bad, badly; go, going; desire, desirable; happy, happiness.

[See also *hyphens*]

suit, suite Both words are in fact the same, *suite* being a variant spelling of *suit*. Confusion arises over which spelling goes with which meaning. *Suit* is used for a set of clothes, a lawsuit, a set of cards, the courting of a woman and a petition to a person of high rank. *Suite* is used for a company of attendants, a connected series of rooms, a set of furniture, and a series of movements in music.

summon, summons The usual verb is *summon*. *Summons* is used only in the special legal sense of 'to serve with a summons'.

superior This unusual comparative form is followed by *to* and not *than*. When used in ordinary comparisons it must not be preceded by *more*:

The quality of his work is superior to that of his friends.

It cannot be preceded by *most* to form a superlative, but is used colloquially with *most* in the sense of 'displaying a feeling of being better than others', when it is no longer considered to be a true comparative:

He proved to be a most superior kind of individual.

superlative see **adjectives, comparison of**

supplement see **complement**

suppose, supposing Both words have very similar meanings. *Suppose* is generally used in the sense of 'to assume something for the sake of argument, without reference to its truth or falsity':

Suppose the factory workers go on strike, what shall we do?

Supposing is used in more realistic situations, in which something will or will not happen:

Supposing he gets here on time, we can start the meeting.

surprise When *surprise* means 'taken unawares' it is followed by the preposition *by*:

He was surprised by a burglar.

When it means 'astonished' it is followed by *at*:

We were surprised at his peculiar conduct.

susceptible When *susceptible* means 'liable to' or 'readily impressed' or 'impressionable' it is followed by *to*:

He was very susceptible to lavish praise.

When it means 'capable of' or 'admitting' it is usually followed by *of*:

His statement is susceptible of only one interpretation.

sustain This is often used as a synonym for 'receive' or 'suffer':

He sustained severe injuries when he fell down the steps.

However, in this sense *sustain* is rather formal and is better reserved for its original meaning of 'to bear (a burden)', or 'endure without giving way'.

swap, swop Both words can be used to mean 'exchange or barter', but *swop* is the more usual spelling.

swell This has the past tense *swelled*, and the past participle *swollen* or *swelled*. When the meaning is 'increase in numbers or quantity', *swelled* is the preferred form:

Their numbers were swelled by the arrival of large numbers of schoolchildren.

Swollen is used when the increase is considered to be a harmful or dangerous one:

The crowds of starving people were swollen by large numbers of sick and wounded.

sympathy This is usually followed by *for* when it means compassion or commiseration for someone:

He felt sympathy for the suffering woman.

It is generally followed by *with* when it expresses identity of view or understanding:

We are in sympathy with these people in their present difficulties.

syndrome In medicine this means a group of symptoms which, taken together, suggest a particular disease. It does not in itself mean a disease.

synonym A *synonym* is a word having approximately the same meaning and use as another, such as *royal* or *regal*. However, words which are called synonyms can rarely be substituted for one another in all their senses. We may talk about *royal power* or *regal power*, but we cannot use *a regal warrant* as an alternative to *a royal warrant*.

syntax see **grammar**

T

-t-, -tt- Single-syllable words ending in *t* double it before suffixes beginning with a vowel if the *t* is preceded by a single short vowel:

ratty, cutting, fatter, potted.

If, however, it is preceded by two vowels together or an *r* it is not doubled:

neater, sorting, seated, rooting.

Words of more than one syllable behave in the same way as single-syllable words if their last syllable is stressed and preceded by a single vowel:

besetting, befitted, abetter, regrettable.

They do not double the *t* otherwise:

unseated, maggoty, cosseting, hermitage.

-t and -ed verb endings There are a number of verbs whose past tense and past participle can end in either *-t* or *-ed*, such as *burnt* or *burned*. Other verbs of this kind are *dream*, *kneel*, *leap*, *learn*, *smell*, *spill*. English usage prefers the *-t* to the *-ed* ending, but American usage tends to favour *-ed*: *dreamed* rather than *dreamt*.

tableau This word of French origin normally takes *x* in the plural (*tableaux*), but most dictionaries give *tableaus* as an alternative.

talent, genius Both words are used to describe natural ability or aptitude of a high order. However, whereas *talent* is a capacity for achievement or success *genius* implies an exceptional natural ability for creative imagination or original thought.

tall, high Both words are to some extent interchangeable. *High* generally refers to distance from the ground or floor level:

A high mountain, a high window, high heels.

Tall is used of anything which is higher than usual of its kind or high in proportion to its breadth:

A tall girl, a tall building, a tall spire.

target This falls into the category of popular metaphors and is much overworked on that account. It is sensible to try to remember the literal meaning and that, to be successful, one must hit a *target* or, if unsuccessful, miss it. It is just possible to fall short of it but not to reach it, achieve it, obtain it, or do anything else with it. There are a number of other equally suitable words which can be substituted for *target*, including *aim*, *goal* and *objective*.

tartan see **plaid**

tasteful, tasty *Tasteful* means 'showing good taste'. *Tasty* originally had this meaning too, but is now almost wholly confined to what is pleasing to the taste. It is, however, considered a vulgarism by some authorities, and tends to be replaced by words like *appetizing* or *savoury*.

tautology This means saying the same thing twice over, especially the needless repetition of an idea in a sentence without adding anything to what is already there:

Their behaviour on all occasions was not always what we would have expected.

In the above sentence *on all occasions* is superfluous and adds nothing to the meaning.

temporal, temporary *Temporal* means 'pertaining to time' or 'concerned with the matters of this world':

He was dealing with temporal rather than spiritual matters.

Temporary means 'lasting for a time only':

He found temporary accommodation with friends.

tend, attend Both verbs can be used in the sense of 'to look after' or 'take charge of', but *attend* is always followed by *to*, whereas *tend* takes a direct object:

He attended to the needs of the children. The nurse was tending the sick.

tenses of verbs The tense of a verb indicates the time when an action takes place, either past, present or future.

The simple *present* tense shows that an action takes place now:

She cuts the cake.

The simple *past* tense shows that the action took place sometime in the past:

He drank the water.

The simple *future* tense shows that the action will take place in time to come:

You will receive a present.

The *perfect* tenses show that an action is complete at the present time, was completed at some time in the past or will be completed at some time in the future:

He has read the book. She had stayed at home. We shall have finished this evening.

[See also *verb*]

terminate This slightly pompous word frequently makes an appearance in official correspondence. In almost all cases it is better to use simpler words like *end*, *finish*, *conclude*, or *bring to an end*.

terminus, terminal In speaking of railways *terminus* is the normal word and its plural may be either *termini* or *terminuses*. For air travel use *terminal*.

than As a conjunction this is normally used only after a comparative adjective or adverb:

She is prettier than her sister. He can run faster than most of us.

Care must be taken with the case of pronouns after *than*. The same idea can be expressed in three different ways:

She is older than I am. She is older than I. She is older than me.

In the first two sentences *than* is a conjunction, but the use of *than I* in the second sentence is now considered rather pedantic. In the third sentence *than* can be considered as a preposition followed by a pronoun in the accusative case, *me*, and this usage is now acceptable in English. However, caution must be observed so as to avoid ambiguity in such sentences as:

You criticize her more than me.

If *than* is treated as a conjunction it means:

You criticize her more than you criticize me.

If *than* is treated as a preposition it means:

You criticize her more than I criticize her.

The last sentence could be better and unambiguously expressed as:

You criticize her more than I do.

Another common error is to follow *than* with an unnecessary *what*, which should be omitted in the following example:

It was cheaper than what we expected.

that, which Both are used as relative pronouns. Generally it is better not to use *which* where *that* would be sufficient and not to use either if the sentence can do without them:

There are the flowers (that/which) I bought.

In a restrictive clause, i.e. a clause that is essential to complete the meaning of the main clause, either *that* or *which* may be used:

Organic chemistry is a subject which/that has only limited appeal.

In a non-restrictive clause, i.e. one that is not essential to complete the meaning of the main clause, *which* (or *who*) must be used:

He asked me to stay to lunch, which had already been prepared.

The soldier, who had stayed in the hall, was too ill to walk any further.

That is sometimes introduced unnecessarily after a comparison. It should be omitted from the following example:

The sooner that he gets here, the better for all of us.

the The main function of the definite article *the* is to specify a particular thing which is distinct from others of the same kind, as opposed to *a* or *an*:

The apples are on the table. The girl is wearing an apron.

It is used in a generalizing sense to denote a particular member of a species as representative of the whole:

The fox is a quadruped.

The is used with adverbial force in such comparative expressions as:

The harder they try the more difficult they find it.

their Although the habit is frowned on by some authorities, this is often used in colloquial speech and also in writing as an equivalent of *his* and *hers*, since there is no singular possessive adjective covering both these words together:

I spoke to both Peter and Ann and each defended their point of view.

It is also used when the sex is not specified:

Everyone was told to bring a sample of their work.

theirs It should be noted that *theirs* is spelt without an apostrophe.

theism see **deism**

think When *think* is followed by *to* it can be used to mean 'remember' or 'occur to'. The usage is colloquial and not accepted by all, but seems to have established itself in conversation at least:

Did you think to lock the door?

though, although These words are more or less interchangeable, with some slight differences. *Although* is both a more emphatic and more imposing word than *though*. It tends to be used at the beginning of sentences, whereas the position of *though* is more flexible. It may be placed last in a sentence, which *although* cannot be.

thrash, thresh *Thrash* is in fact a variant of *thresh*, although the two words are now differentiated in sense. *Thrash* means 'to beat, especially as a means of punishment' or 'to defeat thoroughly'. It is also used figuratively meaning to 'discuss (a problem) exhaustively'. *Thresh* is used exclusively in the sense of separating grain or seeds from wheat and other crops.

through Used in the sense of 'up to and including' *through* is an Americanism:

From Sunday through Thursday.

It is, however, encroaching to some extent on British English.

thus This adverb is frequently used rather loosely before a participle, and care must be taken to ensure that the participle is correctly related to what precedes it:

His flat was destroyed by fire, thus making him homeless.

In the above sentence *making* refers back to his flat, but *his flat* did not make him *homeless* and so the sentence must be recast thus:

His flat was destroyed by fire and he was thus made homeless.

tight, tightly *Tight* can be used as adverb as well as an adjective and differs from *tightly* in that it emphasizes the result of an action:

He slammed the door tight. She screwed the bottle top on tight.

Tightly, on the other hand, generally refers to the manner in which something is carried out:

She grasped me tightly round the waist.

It can, however, be argued that in the expression *hold tight*, *tight* refers to manner just as much as it does to result.

till, until There is virtually no difference between these two words. Both have the meaning 'up to the time of', 'before' (with a negative). *Until* is more commonly used at the beginning of a sentence.

tire see **tyre**

titbit, tidbit *Titbit* is now the usual spelling in British English, although *tidbit* is the older form and the normal one in American usage.

titillate, titivate These verbs are often confused. *Titillate* means to stimulate or excite in an agreeable manner:

To titillate someone's fancy with the thought of good food.

Titivate means to make oneself spruce or to dress smartly:

The women were titivating themselves in preparation for the dance.

toilet, toilette The usual spelling is *toilet* for all meanings of the word, including lavatory, the act of dressing and the articles used in dressing. Most dictionaries, however, give *toilette* as an alternative form.

ton, tun A *ton* is a unit of weight equivalent to 2240 lbs as a *long ton* and to 2000 lbs as a *short ton*. A *tun* is a large cask for holding liquids, especially wine or beer.

too This is used before a past participle which has lost its verbal force and is purely an adjective:

He was too bewildered to notice.

When the past participle retains its verbal force *too much* is often substituted:

They were too much occupied with their own affairs to notice anyone else's problems.

It is often difficult to make a clear distinction between the two, and many writers would not bother to insert *much* in the second example.

topic, subject Both are used to mean a theme to be discussed or written about. *Topic* is, however, generally restricted to a particular part of a more wide-ranging subject:

Many aspects of the subject of race relations will provide topics for discussion.

total This undoubtedly useful word has in recent years suffered from a wave of popularity, which apparently began in the United States. It is now frequently used in place of words which are more suitable, such as *entire* or *complete*. *Total war* or *total eclipse* may be quite acceptable but *total control* is better expressed as *complete control*.

toward, towards As a preposition *towards* is the most common form in British English, but Americans seem to prefer the shorter word.

trace, vestige Both words are used to indicate signs of the existence of something. *Trace* is applied to a mark or slight evidence of something either past or present:

There were traces of blood on the staircarpet.

Vestige is more restricted in meaning and refers to a very slight remnant of something which no longer exists:

They found vestiges of an ancient civilization.

traffic This verb has the present participle *trafficking* and the past tense and past participle *trafficked*.

transcendent, transcendental These adjectives are frequently confused, because some of their senses overlap. *Transcendent* is used to mean going beyond ordinary limits, superior or pre-eminent:

A statesman of transcendent virtues.

Transcendental means going outside ordinary experience, idealistic or visionary:

He spoke about the benefits of transcendental meditation.

tranship, transship Dictionaries appear to be divided about the merits of these two spellings, with a slight bias in favour of *tranship*. *Trans-ship* is also found.

transient, transitory Both words are used in the sense of not lasting, temporary or fleeting. The distinction lies in the fact that *transient* has a special meaning in philosophy and *transitory* in law:

A transitory action.

transitive verb see **intransitive and transitive verbs**

transparent, translucent Both refer to matter through which light can pass. *Transparent* is the general word and means allowing things to be seen clearly through it:

In the transparent water of the swimming pool he could see a wristwatch lying at the bottom.

Translucent means letting light pass through in a diffuse manner so that objects beyond are not distinct:

He saw two vague shapes through the translucent glass.

transpire Many authorities deplore the use of this word in the sense of 'occur' or 'happen' and advocate that it should be confined to its original meaning of 'to become known gradually'. However, the popular sense is now so well established that nothing seems likely to shift it.

transport, transportation In American English the various meanings of the noun *transport* in British English are found mainly in *transportation*. In British English *transportation* usually, although not always, denotes the banishment of convicts to a penal colony.

trauma, traumatic Both the noun *trauma* and its adjective *traumatic* have achieved a popularity far beyond their original domain, that of medicine. *Trauma* means a bodily injury and, by extension, the condition which this produces. In psychiatry it denotes a deeply disturbing emotional experience which has a lasting effect. In everyday use *trauma*, and particularly *traumatic*, are used to describe any upsetting event.

travel This doubles the *l* in the present participle and past tenses (*travelling*, *travelled*), thus disobeying the rules about final consonants in unstressed syllables. However, American usage has *traveling* and *traveled.*

treble, triple Both words can be used as adjectives, verbs or nouns and in a sense are interchangeable. In practice, however, *treble* is the more usual form for the noun and verb and *triple* for the adjective. Moreover, *triple* as an adjective has the additional meaning of 'consisting of three parts' or 'threefold'.

trend, tendency Both words refer to an inclination towards a particular direction. *Trend* suggests something both firm and continuous, although the direction may be rather vague:

There is evidence of a trend in inflation rates.

Tendency is often used of a natural disposition or inclination:

He has a tendency to fall asleep at all hours.

triumphal, triumphant *Triumphal* means pertaining to or celebrating a triumph and is more restricted in meaning:

The emperor ordered a triumphal procession.

Triumphant means victorious or rejoicing in success:

They emerged triumphant after their ordeal in the boardroom.

try and The use of *try and* as an alternative to *try to* is now well established in conversation and is considered by many to be more a forceful variant:

Try and get here as fast as possible.

Try and cannot, however, be used in negative sentences or in the past tense and *try to* is always to be preferred in writing.

tsar This is now the preferred spelling, since it corresponds most closely to the Russian pronunciation. The alternatives *czar* and *tzar* are, however, frequently found.

turf The usual plural form is *turfs*. *Turves* is considered by some authorities to be archaic, but is still used in the sense of peat which has been cut for burning.

tyre, tire For a band of rubber fitted round the rim of a wheel *tyre* is the usual spelling in British English, although the form *tire* prevails in the United States.

U

ult., inst., prox. *Ult.* (last month), *inst.* (this month) and *prox.* (next month) are all examples of commercialese (see *jargon*). It is much better actually to name the month in question, which conveys the meaning intended more rapidly and more accurately. Fortunately the use of all three abbreviations seems to be dying out.

ultimatum This has *ultimatums* as the preferred form of the plural, with *ultimata* as an alternative.

-um, -ums, -a see **Latin and French plurals**

umpire, referee Both words are used of someone to whom a dispute is referred for decision. In sport they describe a person selected as a judge in certain games, who has the power to enforce rules and settle disputes. There is no real difference in function, the term *umpire* being used in cricket, tennis and hockey, and *referee* in football and boxing.

un- see **in-**

unanimous The word *unanimous* can be applied to a vote on a motion only when all those present are in agreement. If there are some abstentions, and provided nobody votes against, the motion is said to be carried *nem. con.* ('with no one dissenting').

unattached participle This is a participle that is related grammatically to a word which it was not intended to qualify or that has no word to which it can logically relate. It is a common error to leave participles unattached:

> Disturbed at the recent turn of events, it seems clear to us that prompt action is required.

This sentence should be recast along the following lines:

Disturbed at the recent turn of events, we see clearly that prompt action is required.

It is an equally common error to attach participles to the wrong noun:

Crossing the road, a lorry knocked him down.

This means grammatically that it was the lorry which was crossing the road. The sentence should be rephrased thus:

Crossing the road, he was knocked down by a lorry.

There are some participles which may be used without being related to a particular noun or pronoun, such as *considering*, *owing to* and *concerning*:

Considering the strain he had undergone, his appearance was normal.

unaware, unawares It is important to remember that *unaware* is the adjective and *unawares* the adverb:

She was unaware that she had already missed the train.
Arriving unexpectedly after lunch, they caught me unawares.

unconscious, subconscious Both words are used in psychology, as nouns and adjectives, to denote those mental processes of which the individual is unaware but which influence his conscious behaviour and conduct. *Unconscious* as an adjective also means 'oblivious of one's surroundings' or 'temporarily deprived of consciousness'.

under see **below**

underlay, underlie *Underlay* is a transitive verb meaning 'to provide (something) with support with something laid underneath it'. *Underlie*, which is a more common verb, is intransitive and means 'to lie under' or 'to be situated underneath'.

under the circumstances see **circumstances**

undiscriminating, indiscriminate Both adjectives mean 'making no distinction', but *undiscriminating* is normally used only of people:

He was undiscriminating in his choice of clothes.

Indiscriminate, which has the additional meaning of 'confused', or 'promiscuous', generally refers to behaviour, method or purpose:

The indiscriminate use of valuable material.

undue, unduly Both the adjective *undue*, which means 'unwarranted' or 'excessive', and its adverb *unduly* are often used when they add nothing to the meaning of the sentence in which they appear:

To exert undue influence

is quite acceptable but in:

There is no cause for undue haste

the *undue* is superfluous.

uneatable, inedible The main distinction between these two is that *uneatable* means unpalatable and is generally applied to something which could in normal circumstances be eaten:

The cold stew was uneatable.

Inedible, on the other hand, usually refers to something which could not be eaten under any circumstances:

There are many inedible plants.

unexceptionable, unexceptional see **exceptionable, exceptional**

uninterested see **disinterested**

unique This means 'of which there is only one' and if something is *unique* it is the only one of its kind in existence. This means that it cannot be qualified, as most adjectives can, by *very*, *more*, *less* or *most*. It is, however, permissible to use it with *almost* or *nearly*.

United Kingdom This term embraces Great Britain (England, Scotland and Wales) and Northern Ireland. The abbreviation *U.K.* can be used as an adjective, but should not be used as a noun except to save space. The *U.K. Government* is, strictly speaking, more accurate than the *British Government*, but *British* in this context is quite acceptable.

United States, U.S. The abbreviation *U.S.* should be used only as an adjective (*the U.S. Government*). It should not be used as a noun except to save space. *American* is generally preferable as an adjective to *U.S.* (*an American writer*, *an American farming community*), although it is a vaguer word than *U.S.* and can be applied to the whole of the Western Hemisphere. [See also *America*]

unlawful see **illegal**

unlike see **like**

unorganized, disorganized Both words mean 'lacking order', but *unorganized* is used of something which has never been properly organized or formed into a systematic whole. *Disorganized*, on the other hand, refers to an order or system which has been disrupted or overturned.

unreadable see **illegible**

unstructured This is a popular word, beloved of sociologists, and means 'informal' or 'unorganized'. It should be used with great caution, if at all.

until see **till**

upward, upwards *Upward* is both an adjective and an adverb, and *upwards* is an adverb only. *Upwards* is the more usual form of the adverb.

urban, urbane *Urban* means 'belonging to or situated in cities or towns'. *Urbane* means 'having the refinement and manners supposedly characteristic of city-dwellers'.

-us see **Latin and French plurals**

usage, use *Usage* is often employed where *use* would be the correct word, as in the following example:

There has been excessive usage of fuel during the recent cold spell.

Usage means 'the way in which something is used' or 'the habitual or customary way of doing something':

This car has received some rough usage. English usage changes over the years.

use In sentences in which *use* is preceded by *no*, *of* is usually but not always dropped:

This book is (of) no use to me.

In sentences of the following type it is always omitted:

It's no use asking for the impossible.

Of is, however, generally retained when *use* is preceded by *any* or *some*, and is always retained when *use* is not preceded by an adjective at all:

Will this be (of) any use to you? It must be of use to somebody.

use to, used to When *used to* refers to habitual or customary action it is followed by the infinitive:

He used to go to London every day.

Questions are usually formed with *do*:

Did you use to come only on Fridays?

It is possible to say *Used you to come . . .* ? but this is now very rare.

In negative sentences *used not to* is the correct form:

She used not to mind about the appearance of the house.

In negative questions *didn't use to* is the accepted phrase:

Didn't you use to work in Glasgow?

When *used to* is used as an adjective meaning 'accustomed to' it is followed by a present participle, a noun or a pronoun:

We became used to arriving late every day. I am used to a better standard of service.

utilize This is not really a longer variation of *use*, since it means 'to put to profitable use' and it should be avoided except when the sense requires it, as in the following:

We must utilize the energy available for both heating and lighting.

V

vacation This is the period of the year when the law courts and universities are closed. In America it is the normal word for holiday and is increasingly used with that meaning in Britain.

valet As a verb this has as its past tense *valeted* and present participle *valeting*. It thus obeys the rule that an unstressed final consonant is not doubled when followed by a suffix.

valour, valorous The adjective drops the *u*. The American spellings are *valor* and *valorous*.

valuable, valued *Valuable* is used of something which is known to have great value because of its usefulness or rarity. *Valued* means 'highly regarded or esteemed', but what it refers to may not be intrinsically *valuable*.

value Value must always be preceded by *of* when used with the verb *to be*:

Of what value has it been? This book is of no value whatsoever.

vantage see **advantage**

vapour Some words formed from *vapour* drop the *u*: *vaporous*, *vaporization*, but *vapouring*, *vapourish*. The American spelling is *vapor* and the *-or* form is found in all words derived from it.

variance The expression *at variance* is always followed by *with* and never by *from*.

venal, venial These adjectives are sometimes confused although their senses are quite different. *Venal* means 'open to bribery or corruption' and *venial* 'pardonable' or 'trivial', with reference to faults or shortcomings.

venture see **adventure**

venturesome see **adventurous**

verb The verb is a part of speech which expresses an action, a state or a condition. In form verbs are either strong or weak. Strong verbs show differences in tense by an internal vowel change:

sing, sang, sung; ride, rode, ridden.

Weak verbs use suffixes to show differences in tense, keeping the same vowel as in the present tense of the verb:

talk, talked; believe, believed; fill, filled.

Verbs can be either transitive or intransitive. A transitive verb requires an object to make its meaning complete:

The man finds the book.

An intransitive verb is complete in itself without an object:

She is coming. He slept. We shall go.

Some verbs do not fall into the categories of transitive or intransitive. The verb *to be* joins subject to predicate:

He is a good man.

Others like *become*, *grow* and *seem* link the subject with an adjective describing it:

She seems uneasy. They have grown old.

Auxiliary verbs are used with other verbs to express action or condition. They include *can*, *do*, *have*, *may*, *must* and *shall*:

I can come. Did she go? You must try. We shall see.

The persons of the verb are the speaker (first person), the one addressed (second person) and anyone or anything else (third person). The persons, singular and plural, are shown as follows:

I come	we come
you come	you come
he, she, it comes	they come

The tenses of the verb show the time when an action takes place – in the present, past or future:

I went, she has come, we shall try.

Verbs may be either active or passive. When the verb is active the subject performs the action expressed by the verb:

He read a book.

When the verb is passive the subject undergoes the action expressed by the verb:

The book was read.

The verb has three moods – indicative, imperative and subjunctive. The indicative mood expresses a statement of fact:

We shall have lamb for dinner.

The imperative mood is used to express a command or request:

Finish this work at once.

The subjunctive mood expresses doubt, command, condition or desire:

He asks that we come at once.
If he came, he wouldn't find us here.

Reflexive verbs have the same subject and object:

He shaved himself. The girl hurt herself.

verbal The basic meaning of verbal is 'pertaining to or consisting of words', but it is increasingly used to mean 'expressed in spoken words'. However, *oral* has the same sense, and it is probably better to use *oral* rather than *verbal* when referring to the spoken language in order to avoid any possibility of ambiguity as in *an oral examination*. Unfortunately, *verbal* continues to encroach upon the territory previously occupied by *oral*.

verbiage, verbosity Both mean an abundance of unnecessary words. *Verbiage* may be used of writing or speech, but *verbosity* generally refers to speech only.

verify, corroborate These words are often confused but have quite distinct meanings. *Verify* means to 'ascertain the truth of something':

It is essential to verify the prisoner's story.

Corroborate means 'to confirm' or 'to supply further evidence of the truth of something':

The police were able to corroborate the evidence provided by the witness.

vernacular This was originally used to mean the mother tongue as opposed to any foreign language. It is now generally applied to the language spoken by the people of a particular region or district – the native language – sometimes contrasted with the literary or learned language.

verso, recto *Verso* is the left-hand page of a book or manuscript and *recto* the right-hand page.

very see **much**

vestige see **trace**

via This means 'by way of' and is applied to a route:

We went to Spain via Paris.

It must not, however, be used to refer to a means of transport and in the following sentence is not acceptable:

We sent the consignment via rail to London.

viable This denotes the capacity of a foetus, having reached a certain stage of development, to exist outside the womb. It has suffered the fate of many popular words and has undergone an extension of meaning. It is now used as a synonym for *effective*, *practicable*, *durable*, *workable* and others, all of which would be far more suitable in most contexts.

vicious circle This is a situation in which the solution of one problem creates another or in which one difficulty inevitably produces another and so on.

vide This is a Latin word meaning 'see' and is used especially when making a reference from one part of a text to another.

view There are two important idiomatic expressions with *view* and care should be taken not to get them confused. *In view of* means 'considering' or 'taking into account':

In view of the gravity of our position, I suggest we ask for help.

With a view to means 'with the aim of':

I am going to Paris with a view to studying art.

vigour, vigorous The *u* is dropped in the adjective *vigorous*. In American usage the noun, too, is spelt without a *u*: *vigor*.

villain, villein A *villain* is a wicked person and a *villein* a serf under the feudal system. Some confusion may be caused by the fact that *villein* may also be spelt *villain*.

visit, visitation *Visitation* is a much more formal word than *visit* and its uses are strictly limited. It can mean a visit for the purpose of making an official inspection. It is also used for an affliction or punishment, especially one sent by God.

viz. This is short for *videlicet* which means 'that is to say' or 'namely', and is used to introduce examples or lists, or to specify what has previously been described more vaguely:

I have seen only three women on my visit to London, *viz.* Mary, Anne and Elizabeth.

Let us now discuss the person on whom our peaceful existence so much depends, *viz.* the ordinary policeman.

vocation see **avocation**

vogue words *Vogue words* are words which become fashionable at a particular period. Very often they are words with a specialized sense which have acquired a sudden popularity and an extension of meaning far beyond what they originally possessed. Such words, a number of which are mentioned in this *Guide to English Usage*, tend to be used far too frequently and to be lacking in clarity and precision. No one can predict what their future will be. Some disappear and others settle down to a respectable status, once their immediate fame has faded away. The only advice that can be given is that they should be used with great circumspection and that other words having a similar meaning should not be neglected.

W

wage, wages Both *wage* and *wages* are used in the sense of 'what is paid in return for work or services rendered'. *Wages* is no longer considered a singular noun and must be followed by a plural verb.

wagon, waggon The spelling *wagon* is now the more common one in both British and American usage.

wait see **await**

waive, wave These two words are quite distinct in origin but are sometimes muddled. *Waive* means 'to relinquish or forgo':

He waived his rights to the inheritance.

It is sometimes wrongly followed by *aside* in mistake for *wave aside*, which can mean 'to dismiss with a gesture'.

wake see **awake**

want, need The chief distinction between these verbs is that *want* means 'desire' and *need* implies a necessity.

We need food and water. He wants a new car.

In usage the distinction is often lost by the excessive use of *want*.

-ward, -wards In British English, as a general rule, *-ward* is used as a suffix for adjectives and *-wards* for adverbs:

He was a backward child. The children ran backwards.

In American English the suffix *-ward* is frequently used for adverbs.

waste, wastage There is a distinction between these two words, although in practice it is frequently blurred. *Wastage* means 'loss by use, wear, leakage or decay':

There was a considerable wastage of oil caused by an inefficient machine.

Waste means 'useless consumption or expenditure':

It is a waste of money to buy such an expensive gadget.

way, weigh Confusion between these words is caused by the fact that a ship is said to be *under way*, i.e. 'moving along' when it has *weighed anchor*, i.e. 'lifted its anchor'. Some dictionaries in fact accept *under weigh* as an alternative to *under way*.

we Apart from its usual meaning as the plural of *I*, *we* is used by a speaker or writer to refer to people in general, by a sovereign when alluding to himself or herself in formal speech, and by a newspaper editor in what is known as 'collective anonymity'.

wed, marry *Marry* is the usual word. *Wed*, which has as past tense and past participle either *wedded* or *wed*, is used in literature or journalism:

Bishop weds sex-kitten.

Wedded can also mean devoted to:

He was wedded to the idea of free trade.

well The phrase *as well as* forms a conjunction and not a preposition and, strictly speaking, in a sentence such as:

He is coming as well as me.

I should be substituted for *me*. However, *I* sounds artificial in such a context and it can be argued that the second *as* is in fact a preposition and is thus followed by a pronoun in the object case, *me*.

When *as well as* is followed by a verb great care must be taken. If the verb preceding *as well as* is a finite one it must be followed by a gerund:

She played tennis as well as taking part in other sports.

If it is an infinitive the *as well as* must be followed by an infinitive:

He must work hard as well as lead an active social life.

well- When *well-* is used with a participle to form a compound adjective it is usually hyphenated:

a well-known story, a well-aimed blow.

However, when the adjective follows the verb *to be* the hyphen is usually omitted:

The story was well known. The blow was well aimed.

Welsh, Welch *Welsh* is the normal form of the adjective, *Welch* being used only as the name of certain regiments, such as *The Royal Welch Fusiliers.*

Welsh rabbit, Welsh rarebit The former is the original spelling of the name, but the fairly recent variant, *Welsh rarebit,* has made such inroads into the language that it is too late to do anything except to acknowledge the existence of both forms.

westerly see **easterly**

wet The past tense and past participle of this verb are either *wet* or *wetted. Wetted* tends to be used when the idea of a deliberate action is involved, but otherwise *wet* is the more common form:

He wetted his finger in the blood.

wharf The normal plural is *wharves* but *wharfs* is also found. [See also *plural forms*]

what When *what* is used as a relative pronoun there may be some difficulty in deciding whether it should be followed by a singular or a plural verb. If it means *that which* it takes a singular verb:

Don't ask for more work. What we have is enough to last all day.

If it means *those which* it takes a plural verb:

They had lots of tomatoes and what they couldn't eat were given to the neighbours.

As a relative pronoun *what* must never be substituted for *who, that* or *which. The book what I read* and *The man what I saw* are both substandard English.

whatever see **-ever, ever**

whether see **if**

which, what Both *which* and *what* may be used as interrogative adjectives, but there are differences between them. *Which* means a choice from a certain number either mentioned or implied:

Which hat did you buy? (of the half a dozen on display).

What implies a selection from an indefinite number:

What car are you going to buy? (It could be any one of a large variety of makes and models).

When *which* is used as an interrogative pronoun, choice from a select number is also implied:

Which of them belongs to you?

When *which* is used as a relative pronoun it can refer only to things or animals:

The cat which was sitting on the mat. The book which lay on the table.

As a relative pronoun *which* is normally linked with a specific antecedent, but it can refer back to a whole clause:

He announced that he was going to resign, which pleased everybody.

while It is probably wisest to use this conjunction only in the sense of 'throughout' or 'during the time that':

He laid the table while his wife prepared the lunch.

It is not wrong to use it to mean 'although':

While I do not agree with you, I am willing to accept your decision.

However, it can lead to ambiguity:

While he is lacking in experience he is doing the job well.

The use of *while* to mean 'on the other hand', 'but', or even 'and' should also be avoided:

At the impromptu concert the student played the organ while his friend recited a poem.

who, whom When *who* and *whom* are used as interrogative pronouns they can cause many difficulties. *Who* is the subject case and *whom* the object case:

Who was speaking just now? Whom did you see at the station?

Normally *whom* and not *who* should follow a preposition but when the preposition comes at the end of a sentence it is customary to use *who*:

Who is that letter addressed to?

Another problem arises when *who* and *whom* are employed as relative pronouns. *Whom* is often wrongly used because it is thought to be the object of a verb:

The boy whom we said would win came in last.

In fact *whom* is not the object of *said* but the subject of *would win* and should therefore be replaced by *who*.

Who and *whom* are generally used only with reference to people:

The boy who broke his leg.

The couple whom we met at the concert.

They can, however, be applied to animals:

The cat who was sitting on the window ledge.

whoever see **-ever, ever**

whose The old rule that *whose* should not be used of inanimate objects may now be safely ignored. It is the possessive case of both *who* and *which*:

The girl whose parents were killed in a car crash.

The house whose doors are painted green.

The latter is now considered preferable to:

The house the doors of which are painted green.

wide see **broad**

will see **shall**

-wise, -ways These suffixes are used with adverbs and both denote attitude or direction although *-wise* is the more common form. Some adverbs take only *-wise*, such as *clockwise* and others only *-ways*, such as *sideways*. Some can take both as *lengthwise* and *lengthways*. *-Wise* is in addition now used to mean 'with respect to' or 'concerning', being attached indiscriminately to all sorts of words: *jobwise*, *moneywise*, *weatherwise*. This new departure is generally deplored and not to be imitated, especially in writing.

wit, humour *Wit* is the ability to perceive and express in a prompt and skilful manner connections between ideas or unexpected analogies and relationships in such a way as to give pleasure and amusement:

His conversation was noted for its wit.

Humour is more the capacity of understanding and appreciating what is inherently amusing, comical, or absurd in a situation, in a person's character or in the foibles of human nature generally:

He was the first to see the humour of his ridiculous position.

without *Without* in the sense of 'outside' is now archaic. It is sometimes wrongly used with the meaning of *unless*:

She won't do it without you tell her first.

wont This is the past participle of a now obsolete verb. It is used as a predicative adjective meaning 'accustomed':

He was wont to spend his mornings in bed.

When the adjective precedes the noun the form is *wonted*:

She was at her wonted place by the fireside.

Wont is also used as a noun meaning 'custom' or 'habit'.

wool This has the adjective *woollen* and *woolly* in British English and *woolen* and *wooly* in American English. [See also *American usage and spelling*]

would see **shall**

wrapped see **rapt**

wrath, wroth, wrathful As a noun *wrath* means 'a fierce anger'. As an adjective it is the alternative and archaic form of *wroth* which means 'angry' and can only be used predicatively. *Wroth* is rarely found and *wrathful*, which is used as an attributive adjective with the same meaning, is not now very common:

A wrathful man.

wrong This can occasionally be used as an adverb alongside *wrongly* with the meaning of 'incorrectly' or 'in a wrong manner':

He got his answer wrong. She guessed wrong.

wrought This is an obsolete past tense and past participle of *work* and is used only with reference to some metals such as iron or silver:

wrought iron.

X

-x Some words taken from French form their plurals by adding *-x*. [See *Latin and French plurals*]

-x-, -ct- There are a number of nouns ending in *-ion* and adjectives in *-ive* which may be preceded by either *x* or *ct*. On the whole the *-ct-* spelling is preferred: *connection*, *connexion*; *deflection*, *deflexion*, although in one case (*reflection*, *reflexion*, *reflective*, *reflexive*) the different spellings have different meanings.

Y

-y and i The rule is that final *y* changes to *i* before a suffix if the *y* is preceded by a consonant:

duty, dutiful; happy, happiness; pretty, prettily.

Exceptions are certain single-syllable words including the following:

shy, shyness; dry, dryness; sly, slyness.

Before a suffix beginning with *i*, *y* does not change:

marry, marrying; bury, burying.

If the *y* is preceded by a vowel it is retained:

toy, toys; play, played; volley, volleying.

Exceptions are certain common single-syllable words:

day, daily; pay, paid; lay, laid.

Yankee The term was originally used to describe an inhabitant of New England and later an inhabitant of any of the northern states of the United States. During the American Civil War Federal soldiers were called Yankees. Only in Britain is it used indiscriminately to apply to any citizen of the United States.

ye This is an archaic spelling of the definite article *the*. The initial letter *y* is due to a misreading of a medieval letter which was subsequently replaced by *th*.

yet This is sometimes used with the archaic or dialectal sense of 'still' and care must be taken to avoid ambiguity. *Are they here yet?* may mean *Are they still here?* or, in standard English, *Have they arrived yet?*

Yiddish This is a language, basically German in content, with a vocabulary containing some Hebrew and Slavonic words, which was spoken by Jews in eastern Europe and by Jewish emigrants to other countries.

young, youthful Both adjectives refer to the early stage of life or development. *Young* is the general word for everything which is growing and is still immature:

A young girl, a young puppy, a young shoot.

Youthful, which is mainly applied to human beings, emphasizes the favourable aspects of youth, such as vigour and freshness:

Youthful high spirits, a youthful outlook on life.

yours Remember that this personal pronoun is always spelt without an apostrophe.

youth This noun has three distinct senses. It means the condition or period of being young:

In his youth he travelled widely.

It is also used to refer to young people generally:

The youth of the country is up in arms.

Finally, it can mean a young man and in this case takes an *s* in the plural:

Five youths ran across the road.

Z

-z-, -zz- All words ending in *z* have a double letter, with the exception of *quiz*. This follows the rules for single-syllable words with only one vowel and doubles the *z* when followed by a suffix:

quizzed, quizzing, quizzer.

zigzag This doubles the *g* in the present and past participles: *zigzagged*, *zigzagging*. The stress falls on the first syllable and it is thus an exception to the rule that words of more than one syllable do not double the final consonant before a suffix, unless the stress falls on the final syllable.

Some foreign words and phrases commonly used in English
(F = French, G = German, Gk = Greek, L = Latin, S = Spanish)

à bas	down with (F)
ab initio	from the beginning (L)
ad hoc	for a particular occasion or purpose (L)
ad infinitum	to infinity; endlessly (L)
ad interim	for the meanwhile; for the time being (L)
ad majorem Dei gloriam	to the greater glory of God (L)
ad nauseam	to the point of disgust (L)
ad valorem	according to its value (L)
à la carte	according to the menu (F)
amour propre	self-esteem (F)
ancien régime	the old form of government; the old order (F)
annus mirabilis	a year of wonders; a wonderful year (L)
arrière-pensée	a mental reservation; an ulterior motive (F)
au courant	well informed; up to date (F)
auf Wiedersehen	goodbye (G)
au revôir	goodbye (F)
autres temps, autres moeurs	other times, other customs (F)
beau monde	the fashionable world (F)
bête noire	something especially disliked (F)
bêtise	a foolish action or remark (F)
bon marché	cheaply (F)
bon voyage	pleasant trip (F)
carpe diem	enjoy the present (L)
carte blanche	unconditional authority (F)
cause célèbre	a celebrated legal case (F)
caveat emptor	let the buyer beware (L)
ceteris paribus	other things being equal (L)
chacun à son goût	everyone to his own taste (F)
chef d'oeuvre	a masterpiece (F)

ci-devant	former (F)
cogito ergo sum	I think therefore I exist (L)
compos mentis	of sound mind (L)
coup de grâce	a finishing stroke; a death blow (F)
coup d'état	a sudden and decisive political move (F)
cui bono	for whose benefit? (L)
de gustibus non est disputandum	there is no disputing about tastes (L)
Dei gratia	by the grace of God (L)
de mortuis nil nisi bonum	(speak) nothing but good of the dead (L)
Deo gratias	thanks be to God (L)
de rigueur	strictly required (F)
de trop	in the way; unwanted (F)
Deus vobiscum	God be with you (L)
Dieu et mon droit	God and my right (F)
embarras de richesse	too much of a good thing (F)
éminence grise	one who wields power behind the scenes (F)
enfant terrible	an irresponsible person (F)
en passant	in passing (F)
esprit de corps	team spirit (F)
ex nihilo nihil fit	nothing is created out of nothing (L)
fait accompli	an accomplished fact (F)
faute de mieux	for want of anything better (F)
faux pas	a false step; a breach of etiquette (F)
fiesta	a holiday (S)
fiat lux	let there be light (L)
flagrante delicto	in the very act; red-handed (L)
Gott mit uns	God is (be) with us (G)
hic jacet	here lies (L)
honi soit qui mal y pense	evil to him who evil thinks (F)
hors concours	not competing; not in the running (F)
idée fixe	a fixed idea; an obsession (F)
in extremis	in extremity; near death (L)

in loco parentis	in the place of a parent (L)
in statu quo	in the state in which (anything was or is) (L)
ipso facto	by that very fact (L)
joie de vivre	joy of living; high spirits (F)
Kyrie eleison	Lord have mercy (Gk)
magnum opus	one's chief work, especially a literary or artistic one (L)
mañana	tomorrow (S)
memento mori	remember you must die (L)
mot juste	the exact or appropriate word (F)
mutatis mutandis	with the necessary changes (L)
nil desperandum	never despair (L)
noblesse oblige	noble rank imposes obligations (F)
nulli secundus	second to none (L)
obiit	he (or she) died (L)
obiter dictum	a passing remark (L)
opere citato	in the work mentioned (L)
panem et circenses	bread and circuses (L)
par excellence	pre-eminently (F)
pax vobiscum	peace be with you (L)
quid pro quo	one thing in return for another (L)
requiescat in pace	may he (or she) rest in peace (L)
resurgam	I shall rise again (L)
sauve qui peut	a stampede for safety (F)
savoir faire	common sense; tact (F)
sic transit gloria mundi	thus worldly glory passes away (L)
sine qua non	an indispensable condition (L)
succès de scandale	success due to notoriety (F)
table d'hôte	a fixed price menu (F)
tempus fugit	time flies (L)
tour de force	a feat requiring exceptional skill (F)
vae victis	woe to the vanquished (L)
veni, vidi, vici	I came, I saw, I conquered (L)
Weltschmerz	world weariness (G)
Zeitgeist	the spirit of the age (G)